THE UNIVERSITY OF
WINCHESTER

Martial Rose Library
Tel: 0196...

Palgrave Studies in British Musical Theatre

Series Editors

Millie Taylor
Department of Performing Arts
University of Winchester
Winchester, UK

Dominic Symonds
Lincoln School of Performing Arts
University of Lincoln
Lincoln, UK

Aim of the Series

Britain's contribution to musical theatre in the late twentieth century is known and celebrated across the world. In historiographies of musical theatre, this assertion of British success concludes the twentieth century narrative that is otherwise reported as an American story. Yet the use of song and music in UK theatre is much more widespread than is often acknowledged. This series teases out the nuances and the richness of British musical theatre in three broad areas: British identity; Aesthetics and dramaturgies; Practices and politics.

More information about this series at
http://www.springer.com/series/15105

Michael Goron

Gilbert and Sullivan's 'Respectable Capers'

Class, Respectability and the Savoy Operas 1877–1909

palgrave
macmillan

Michael Goron
Southampton Solent University
Southampton, UK

University of Winchester
Winchester, UK

Palgrave Studies in British Musical Theatre
ISBN 978-1-137-59477-8   ISBN 978-1-137-59478-5   (eBook)
DOI 10.1057/978-1-137-59478-5

Library of Congress Control Number: 2016941777

Cover illustration: © The Art Archive / Alamy Stock Photo
Series design image: © Marc Freiherr Von Martial / Getty Images

Printed on acid-free paper

This Palgrave Macmillan imprint is published by Springer Nature
The registered company is Macmillan Publishers Ltd. London

FOREWORD

It's hard to think of a more significant or substantial contribution to British theatre than that made by William Schwenk Gilbert and Arthur Sullivan. Over an intensive 20-year period, the pair created more than a dozen works, establishing a paradigm of popular yet respectable entertainment for the musical stage. The characters they created live on in popular memory, from the Pirate King to the Three Little Maids from School; and their songs continue to be sung by new generations, from 'Dear Little Buttercup' to 'Poor Wand'ring One'. Indeed, across the length and breadth of Britain, amateur societies continue to perform their shows as staples of the repertoire, enjoying in particular the delights of several classic major works: *HMS Pinafore* (1878), *The Pirates of Penzance* (1879), *The Mikado* (1885) and *The Gondoliers* (1889).

It is true that Gilbert and Sullivan have not been without their detractors, and their work in some circles has been much maligned. The Savoy operas are commonly perceived (especially by younger audiences) as old-fashioned, dated set pieces calcifying British traditions in song and satire. Yet in their day, these works were cutting-edge, contemporary satires of the political and social landscape, with characters keenly sketched from the wit of two masters of their craft. Individually, both Gilbert and Sullivan produced an impressive oeuvre, but together, and aided by the impresario Richard D'Oyly Carte, they lifted comic opera into a different realm. Here was work accessible enough to appeal to popular audiences, yet also refined enough to cater to the requirements of the middle class. In equal measure a fond reflection of contemporary society and a satirical jibe at the status quo, the collected work offered a precursor not only to the musical theatre repertoire of later years, but also the satire of journalism, radio and TV. Indeed, some of the greatest characters of British comedy can undoubtedly be traced back to role models invented and established by Gilbert and Sullivan: from Leonard Rossiter's Mr Rigsby in *Rising Damp* to John Cleese's Basil Fawlty in *Fawlty Towers*, and from Nigel Hawthorne's Sir Humphrey Appleby in *Yes, Minister* to Patricia Routledge's Hyacinth Bucket in *Keeping Up Appearances*, British situation comedy and its consumption by the British public has, to a large degree, been enabled by the foundational work created by Gilbert and Sullivan.

Unsurprisingly, there has been plenty of scholarship on the Gilbert and Sullivan canon, and their place in history is undeniably assured; yet scholars continue to produce work focusing on this fascinating series of comic operas, and on the collaboration between Gilbert and Sullivan. So why the need for a further study?

As the title suggests, Michael Goron's *Gilbert and Sullivan's 'Respectable Capers': Class, Respectability and the Savoy Operas 1877–1909* interrogates issues of respectability and class, as well as considerations of ephemerality and entertainment. To Goron, the works remain important as an abiding snapshot of Victorian Britain, shining a light on the legacy that this period has left on British values of today. As we are guided metaphorically by Goron to accompany him to a night at the Savoy, we appreciate the social etiquette and behavioural customs expected at the time; and we relive an impression of the way the experiences of attending the theatre in the late nineteenth century might have impacted on our lives. In this, Goron elevates studies of Gilbert and Sullivan beyond the standard approach to considering the works as texts and really observes their impact as staged performances engaged with by real people.

Goron's description of the Gilbert and Sullivan works as 'respectable capers' characterises cleverly both the identity of the shows themselves and also the perspective with which his critical lens captures them. These are shows from a period in which respectability meant everything, both socially and culturally; a period which in many ways forged the complex amalgam of 'class' as a concept that has defined subsequent British identity. It is in trying to negotiate that complicated, contradictory notion that characters such as Fawlty, Rigsby, Appleby and Bucket fall down, to our great amusement. It's also through the prism of that amalgam that Gilbert and Sullivan present to us their peculiarly British characters. Only in Britain, perhaps, can the concept of class be used 'as both an economic categorisation, and as a means of encapsulating a set of cultural values, a "middle-class" ideology'.

If this concern is the glue that binds the Savoy operas together (not to mention the sticky mess in which their characters become unstuck), it is an influence that has had just as much significance in the lives and careers of Gilbert and Sullivan themselves. Caught between their own pretensions of respectability and the trade-off they made in capering with commercial success, the artists themselves become characters who are at the same time frustrating and endearing, pompous and charming. In humanising their concerns and exploring their oeuvre from his particular perspective, Goron brings a very contemporary picture to life of a world of entertainment that still infects us today, and of a pair of collaborators whose brilliance came from their dynamic tensions as much as their creative talent.

So why another book on Gilbert and Sullivan? Adopting a cultural materialist perspective and exploring the Savoy operas from a viewpoint that takes in their reception and consumption as much as their value as compositions, Goron's exploration provides an answer to that question, and serves as a fitting first publication for this new series in British Musical Theatre.

Lincoln, UK   Dominic Symonds

Winchester, UK   Millie Taylor

NOTE

The business syndicate, headed by Richard D'Oyly Carte, which presented *The Sorcerer* in 1877 and *HMS Pinafore* in 1879 was called 'The Comedy-Opera Company'. After Carte's legal separation from the syndicate in 1879, the name was changed to 'Mr. D'Oyly Carte's Opera Company'. The name 'The D'Oyly Carte Opera Company' was not professionally used before 1889. Touring companies prior to 1889 had various naming systems, involving letter or number prefixes/suffixes. For the purpose of this study, except when specific touring companies are mentioned, the term 'The D'Oyly Carte Company' is used to cover all Carte's theatrical activities related to the Gilbert and Sullivan/Savoy operas. For convenience, the Gilbert and Sullivan operas produced under the D'Oyly Carte management will be referred to as the 'Savoy operas'. This follows conventional practice and disregards the fact that the first four operas under Carte's management were premiered at the Opera Comique, rather than at the Savoy Theatre, which opened in 1881.

Following a late-nineteenth-century usage (deriving from press coverage of the D'Oyly Carte operation) which is retained in contemporary Gilbert and Sullivan studies, Gilbert, Sullivan and Carte are referred to collectively as the 'Triumvirate'. In annotations, William Schwenck Gilbert, Arthur Seymour Sullivan and Richard D'Oyly Carte are referred to as WSG, AS and RDC, respectively.

Pre-decimal British currency is conventionally expressed in pounds, shillings (s) and pence (d). Two shillings and sixpence would therefore be written as 2s 6d.

West End productions of the Gilbert and Sullivan operas under the management of Richard D'Oyly Carte and Helen Carte, 1875–1909. (The list does not include non-G&S 'curtain raisers')

Title (original productions in bold type)	Dates	Number of performances	Theatre
Trial By Jury	25 March–18 December 1875	131	Royalty
The Sorcerer	17 November 1877–24 May 1878	178	Opera Comique
Trial By Jury	23 March–24 May 1878	56	Opera Comique
HMS Pinafore	25 May 1878–20 February 1880	571	Opera Comique
HMS Pinafore (Child cast)	16 December 1879–20 March 1880 (Matinees)	78	Opera Comique
The Pirates of Penzance	3 April 1880–2 April 1881	363	Opera Comique
HMS Pinafore (Child cast)	2 December 1880–28 January 1881 (Matinees)	28	Opera Comique
Patience transferred	23 April–8 October 1881	170	Opera
	10 October 1881–22 November 1882	408	Comique Savoy
Iolanthe	25 November 1882–1 January 1884	398	Savoy
Princess Ida	5 January 1884–9 October 1884	246	Savoy
The Sorcerer, Trial By Jury (Double bill)	11 October 1884–12 March 1885	150	Savoy
The Pirates of Penzance (Child cast)	26 December 1884–14 February 1885	?	Savoy
The Mikado	14 March 1885–19 January 1887	672	Savoy
Ruddigore	22 January–5 November 1887	288	Savoy
HMS Pinafore	12 November 1887–10 March 1888	120	Savoy
The Pirates of Penzance	17 March–6 June 1888	80	Savoy
The Mikado	7 June–29 September 1888	116	Savoy
The Yeomen of the Guard	3 October 1888–30 November 1889	423	Savoy

Title (original productions in bold type)	Dates	Number of performances	Theatre
The Gondoliers	7 December 1889–20 June 1891	554	Savoy

Non-G&S full-length works presented by the D'Oyly Carte Company between June 1891 and October 1896 were *The Nautch Girl*, *The Vicar of Bray*, *Haddon Hall* and *Jane Annie*.

Utopia, Limited	7 October 1893–9 June 1894	245	Savoy

Non-G&S works presented by the D'Oyly Carte Company between July 1894 and March 1895 were *Mirette*, *The Chieftain* and *Cox and Box*.

The Mikado	6 November 1895–4 March 1896	127	Savoy
The Grand Duke	7 March 1896–10 July 1896	123	Savoy

Non-G&S works presented by the D'Oyly Carte Company between February 1897 and May 1903 were *His Majesty*, *The Grand Duchess*, *The Beauty Stone*, *The Lucky Star*, *The Rose of Persia*, *The Emerald Isle*, *Ib and Little Christina*, *Willow Pattern*, *Merrie England* and *A Princess of Kensington*. These were interspersed with further revivals of *The Mikado*, *The Yeomen of the Guard*, *The Gondoliers*, *The Sorcerer*, *Trial By Jury*, *HMS Pinafore*, *The Pirates of Penzance*, *Patience* and *Iolanthe*.

Repertory seasons at the Savoy Theatre 1906–1909—Produced under the supervision of W.S. Gilbert:

8 December 1906–24 August 1907: *Patience*, *Iolanthe*, *The Yeomen of the Guard*, *The Gondoliers*.

28 April 1908–27 March 1909: *HMS Pinafore*, *The Pirates of Penzance*, *Iolanthe*, *The Mikado*, *The Yeomen of the Guard*, *The Gondoliers*.

ACKNOWLEDGMENTS

Thanks are due firstly to my University of Winchester PhD supervisory team, who aided the progress of this project through seven years of research and writing. Thus I would like to thank Professor Millie Taylor for her guidance and abiding support through some challenging times, Dr Stevie Simkin for his focused criticism and attention to detail, and Professor Roger Richardson, who helped me pinpoint the direction of my research. Professor Richardson's guidance, particularly in the early stages of the project, helped to shape my development as an historian—I wasn't one beforehand! I would also like to thank Dr Dominic Symonds, who as joint series editor with Professor Taylor has encouraged the progress of this book and whose enthusiastic comments have helped to inspire its completion. Also thanks to Jen McCall and April James at Palgrave Macmillan.

I'd like to thank Professor Jackie Bratton and Professor Jim Davis for their observations and recommendations. They, along with a number of significant contemporary historians of Victorian theatre, have provided the methodological templates which underpin this study.

I am indebted to a number of Gilbert and Sullivan researchers, writers and enthusiasts who have provided me with information and specialist advice and assistance over the years. So thanks to Peter Parker, Tony Joseph and Andrew Crowther, and also to Professor Rafe MacPhail for his support and encouragement.

Savoynet, run by Marc Shepherd, is the electronic mailing list where 'G&S' and related matters are discussed online. As a long-time 'lurker' and very occasional contributor, I have often been inspired by comments and observations which have appeared there. Whether they are aware that they have helped me or not, I would like to thank, among others, Dorothy Kinkaid, Michael Walters, Chris Goddard and Anthony Baker.

Thanks especially to Dr Helen Grime and Dr Cecily O'Neill for their support and advice—and, in the case of the former, for suggesting I undertake the PhD (from which this book derives) in the first place.

Finally, thanks to Rachel, Alex and Ronan for patiently putting up with it all.

CONTENTS

LIST OF FIGURES

CHAPTER 1

Introduction

INTRODUCTION

Why produce a new study of the Gilbert and Sullivan operas which seeks primarily to re-assert their appeal to late-Victorian 'middle-England'? Received wisdom, together with much existing literature on the Gilbert/ Sullivan/Carte collaboration would indicate that the values of both the creators and the original audience of the Savoy operas were self-evidently bourgeois. Indeed, it is likely that the subsequent survival of the company through the twentieth century depended on the extent to which such 'respectable' values, or at least a nostalgic affection for these values, remained relevant to succeeding generations of spectators.[1] However, the originality of this exploration derives in part from a desire to examine the much-discussed Savoy phenomenon and its historical context *specifically* from the viewpoint of ideas of class, culture and ideology. Perhaps because of the popularity and ubiquity of the Gilbert and Sullivan operas, and the fact that, unlike much Victorian theatre, they are well known and still performed (and therefore cannot be 'rediscovered'), they have, until recently, been relatively neglected by serious academics. In consequence, the application of issues of ideology and class as they relate to historical theatre production have rarely been employed to examine either the internal functioning of the original D'Oyly Carte Opera Company or its output and reception. This book is an attempt to redress the imbalance.

© The Author(s) 2016
M. Goron, *Gilbert and Sullivan's 'Respectable Capers'*, Palgrave Studies in British Musical Theatre, DOI 10.1057/978-1-137-59478-5_1

The *general* (non-specifically academic) literature on Gilbert and Sullivan is, to quote D'Oyly Carte historian Tony Joseph, 'colossal'. Dillard's Gilbert and Sullivan bibliography (1991) runs to 208 pages and contains 1056 separate items. As a bibliography, it omits press coverage, excludes unpublished archival material, and naturally predates information made available on modern electronic databases and in publications from the last 20 or so years. This superabundance provides a wealth of primary source material and secondary re-evaluation for the modern scholar, as well as much enjoyment for the interested general reader. However, while containing a great deal of biographical information and some criticism of musical and literary style, the overriding emphasis within the literature is on celebration and commemoration of a much-loved oeuvre and its creators. It does not provide much analysis or critical appraisal of the cultural forces which brought the operas into being and which underpinned their popularity.

Part of my task, therefore, is to locate a discussion of the company within the framework of contemporary academic trends towards reassessing the development of British theatre practice, and specifically that of the West End, during the nineteenth century. The bedrock of this recent reconsideration is formed by prominent studies such as Jacky Bratton's work on the increased divergence of high and low theatrical forms through the nineteenth century (2004), Davis and Emeljanow's study of audience demographics (2001) and Tracey C. Davis's examinations of the economics of production and women in the theatrical workplace during this period (2000, 1991). The results of such scholarship have cast new light on the social and cultural factors underpinning Victorian theatre performance and spectatorship, and have been correspondingly influential in the stimulation and explication of my ideas.

Gratifyingly, there has, very recently, been a small but significant increase in studies using modern academic methods to specifically reassess the Gilbert and Sullivan collaboration (Lee 2010; Williams 2011). Most closely related to my approach is Regina Oost's *Gilbert and Sullivan— Class and the Savoy Tradition* (2009). Oost's extensive and meticulous research concentrates on charting the development of the D'Oyly Carte theatre brand within a consumer culture. Her method is to establish relationships between the consumerist tendencies of the late-Victorian bourgeoisie and cultural values contained within the libretti. Oost's conception of the importance of social class is limited as, for her purposes, class identity is defined almost exclusively by consumption and brand loyalty. She bypasses discussion of the place of D'Oyly Carte personnel within the social structure of their time, and the effects of class-related attitudes on their working lives.

Instead, I examine potential fissures and disparities in what Oost takes to be a comfortably middle-class entertainment experience. Her coverage concludes with a return to the texts of the operas as a vindication of her ideas concerning consumption. In contrast with Oost's study and with most of the available literature, my argument uses the texts as one of several starting points for examining the *mentalité* of the late-Victorian bourgeoisie. Dramatic texts, while an essential component of this investigation, are not its focus. Consequently, my approach to the libretti is largely based on the function they fulfil in representing and reinforcing contemporary attitudes.

The operas are, and were, capable of being received and read polysemically by critics and audiences. They can be seen, for example, as genuine critiques of social practices and values (Hayter 1987), as reflecting 'the levelling absurdities of the human condition' (Crowther 2000, p. 121) or, as previously mentioned, as a celebration of conspicuous consumption, and veneration of social status (Oost 2009, pp. 1, p.107–16). For the purposes of the argument presented here, it will be presupposed that the satirical intent of the operas was intended primarily as a means of safely exploring and removing contemporary social and cultural anxieties through laughter, while tacitly reaffirming the values which instigated those anxieties in the first place.[2] Hence their popularity with an affluent audience base, whose social position and financial standing required the maintenance of a stable, hierarchical and essentially deferential society. The Savoy audience was presented with a satirical critique of itself which avoided any kind of true radicalism, and which implicitly celebrated the very values which were being mocked. Occasionally a hint of an earlier, more radical Gilbert appears. Take for example the song 'Fold Your Flapping Wings' from Act Two of *Iolanthe*. In its original incarnation, Gilbert's House of Lords satire contained a moment in which Strephon, newly elected to Parliament, reflects on the detrimental effects of social inequality on the disadvantaged:

Take a tipsy lout
Gathered from the gutter –
Hustle him about –

Strap him to a shutter:
What am I but he,
Washed at hours stated –
Fed on filigree –
Clothed and educated?

The social criticism is unambiguous. However, Gilbert was perfectly willing to cut the number following negative press reviews which commented on the inappropriateness of such sentiments in a comic opera (Bradley 2001, p. 436). Clearly he had gone too far.

In common with *Iolanthe*, the other Savoy operas are permeated by both a criticism and implied reassertion of the culture and values of the Victorian 'middle class'. Relocating the operas firmly within the customs of this culturally dominant group, and seeing the D'Oyly Carte Opera Company and its work as being specific to a particular time and place, can enable an examination of the relationship between 'historical forms of theatrical expression and the dominant ideology of a historical period' (McConachie 2007, p. 92). It can also rescue the operas from being regarded as the pieces of vague, culturally ubiquitous 'Victoriana' imagined by later (twentieth- and twenty-first-century) audiences when viewing the works through the nostalgic prism of 'heritage' culture.

So the fundamental intention of this book is to examine ways in which late-Victorian attitudes influenced the development and work of the D'Oyly Carte Company, and the early production and performance of this organisation's most important cultural product, the Gilbert and Sullivan operas. A basic premise of the argument is that a sector of West End theatre in the mid nineteenth century was remade in the image of the respectable 'middle classes',[3] and reflected the lifestyle, convictions and prejudices of this sector. Two interconnecting themes will be explored. First, that the presence of this organisation as a popular, financially successful and influential theatrical brand can be understood as a particularly important artistic manifestation of a specifically 'middle-class' nineteenth-century British cultural ideology. Second, that issues specific to the Victorian theatre, such as the drive towards social acceptability, and the recognition of theatre work as a valid professional pursuit (particularly for female practitioners) are particularly evident in the working lives of the D'Oyly Carte founders and employees.

Another central question is the extent to which the company and its output can be seen to represent a high point of 'middle-class' cultural dominance in the latter part of the century. 'Middle-class' culture can be so described because it was adopted and propounded by those who were members of the wide social grouping designated as middle class by the financial classifications of contemporary economists. But the term 'middle class' can be seen as a cultural, as well as an economic, designation. While the aristocracy retained much of the nation's wealth and ultimate political power, and the working classes were far more numerous,[4] the dominance of the middle classes as employers, and as the major creators and disseminators of cultural products, placed them in a position of cultural authority. Their values and practices were typically propounded in the wider culture by opinion formers who were themselves predominantly economically and occupationally bourgeois. Many of those who held positions of power as employers, professionals, administrators and educators were 'middle class' both occupationally and culturally.

Those who wished to improve their living circumstances might do so through processes of acculturation—adopting modes of thought, behaviour and consumption which enabled them to raise their social standing or affiliate themselves advantageously with the economically superior and higher-status 'middle classes'. People desirous of raising their economic and social conditions by pursuing non-manual occupations were inevitably doing so within the expanding middle-class sphere and were, to some extent, absorbing its values. This kind of acquisition has been explained by Pierre Bourdieu as a desire for 'cultural capital'—the 'form of value associated with culturally authorised tastes, consumption patterns, attributes, skills, and awards' (as described by Webb et al. 2002, p. x). Underlying the attributes of the types of 'cultural capital' available in mid- to late-nineteenth-century Britain can be seen a variety of modes of thought and behaviour which, in various combinations, were the manifestation of a late-Victorian 'middle-class' ideology. For the sake of conciseness, I propose to refer to this collection of values as 'respectable' or pertaining to 'respectability'.[5]

'Respectability' was, at least in the first half of the century, underpinned by the moral strictures of evangelical Christianity. It encompassed the acceptance and public demonstration of cleanliness, sobriety, thrift, sexual probity, appropriateness of dress and personal presentation, correct speech, and the importance of 'manners' and etiquette as indicators of individual status. To these may be added wider social concerns such as the general acceptance of existing social divisions and hierarchies to secure societal cohesion, and a consciousness of the importance of hard work to achieve financial and personal success. Domesticity was idealised, promoting a notional division between a comfortable, morally dependable family life and the distasteful problems of greed, exploitation and ambition associated with the workplace. Desirable bourgeois housing distanced the 'middle-class' family from the reminders of urban working life by being located as far away from the workplace as was financially practicable.

The foundations of this ideological outlook are marvellously lampooned by Gilbert and Sullivan in *Ruddigore*, which is set 'early in the nineteenth century'. Two theatrical stock characters, the villain of Victorian melodrama and the mad heroine of romantic opera, are introduced in Act One. By a twist of plot, they reappear in the second act transformed into starched, black-suited, evangelical do-gooders. They explain their transformation from reprobacy to respectability in song, while executing a comically stiff dance to Sullivan's intentionally portentous accompanying woodwind melody:

> *MARGARET*: I was once an exceedingly odd young lady
> *DESPARD*:   Suffering much from spleen and vapours.
> *MARGARET*: Clergymen thought my conduct shady
> *DESPARD*:   She didn't spend much upon linen-drapers.
> *MARGARET*: It certainly entertained the gapers.
> My ways were strange
> Beyond all range
> *DESPARD*:   Paragraphs got into all the papers.
> *(Dance)*
> *DESPARD*:   We only cut respectable capers.

As is sometimes the case in Savoy opera, Gilbert is satirising tendencies within Victorian society which, by the latter part of the century, had begun to seem old-fashioned and comically *déclassé*. Presumably, sophisticated West End audiences in the 1880s could be expected to raise a smile at the caricatured attitudes of their grandparents. However, from a twenty-first-century viewpoint, the 'respectable capers' of Despard and Margaret raise some crucial issues regarding cultural attitudes in the late-Victorian period. The comically abrupt change from the social undesirability of Despard's criminality to propriety and conformity carries several possible meanings. First, it reflects awareness among Victorians that, however absurd their manifestation, these traits were the bedrock of social acceptability and societal coherence. Even the possibility of pre-Victorian depravity is cosily diluted for spectators of the 1880s by Despard's innate 'goodness':

> SIR D: Poor children, how they loathe me—me whose hands are certainly steeped in infamy, but whose heart is as the heart of a little child! ... I get my crime over the first thing in the morning and then, ha! ha! for the rest of the day I do good—I do good—I do good! (melodramatically) Two days since, I stole a child and built an orphan asylum. Yesterday I robbed a bank and endowed a bishopric. To-day I carry off Rose Maybud and atone with a cathedral!
>
> (*Ruddigore*, Act Two)

Second, the dramatic rapidity of the moral 'makeover' in Act Two of *Ruddigore* indicates an awareness of the dramatic alteration in British attitudes which had occurred in the preceding century. The eminent social historian Harold Perkin notes that

> between 1780 and 1850 the English ceased to be one of the most aggressive, brutal, rowdy, outspoken, riotous, cruel and bloodthirsty nations in the world, and became one of the most inhibited, polite, orderly, tender-minded, prudish, and hypocritical.
>
> (Perkin 1969, p. 280)

This phenomenon is sent up in the opera through the apparent rapidity, in terms of stage time, of Sir Despard's moral regeneration. In performance he passes from Regency rake to Victorian prude in about half an hour, give or take an interval break. Connected to Despard's reformation is the suggestion that respectability is something which can be assumed as necessity dictates. It can be 'performed' both on the stage and off by a simple change of costume and a calculated alteration in demeanour. While an essential conformity to a set of dominant values underpinned the self-censoring nature of Victorian propriety, there remains the notion that the outward show of decorum was just as important as the moral rectitude which lay beneath. Indeed, Margaret's 'madness', which is really an 'unladylike' propensity to emotional outbursts, is shown to be in the process of being tamed through the use of a 'safe word'—'Basingstoke'—the

Fig. 1.1 The newly reformed Sir Despard (Rutland Barrington) and Mad Margaret (Jessie Bond) relax after their 'respectable capers'. *Ruddigore*, Act Two. Public Domain

name of a Hampshire town which ironically represents the apogee of suburban respectability. Personal characteristics which compromise a socially acceptable demeanour are seen to be improved through the application of accepted codes of conduct and behaviour which define respectability. Outward conformity to conventionally reputable conduct is a theme which, as later chapters will show, is fundamental to the ethos of both the Savoy operas and those who brought them into being (Fig. 1.1).

Thus, in order to investigate the extent to which the Savoy operas and the work of both their creators and the D'Oyly Carte Company were indeed 'respectable capers', a number of broad but interrelated areas of enquiry will be addressed. Chapter 2 will explore ways in which the ideological values of the 'middle classes' influenced the founding, organisation and internal operations of the D'Oyly Carte Company, and how this ideology was exemplified within the texts of the operas. Chapter 3 will investigate the growth of the West End in the latter part of the nineteenth century as a location for entertainment directed at affluent, socially respectable, middle-class audiences. Subsequent chapters will explore ways in which an evening at the Savoy can be seen to reflect and reinforce audience attitudes, the composition of those audiences, and the ethos of the working practices of the D'Oyly Carte Company. This will lead to an examination, in Chapter 7, of the extent to which production and performance practice demonstrated the existence of a distinctive company 'style' which exhibited and embodied the influences of social and cultural factors. Crucial to my argument is the concept of a dual process of cultural influence. If Victorian 'middle-class' ideology influenced the founding, organisation and style of the D'Oyly Carte Opera Company, then the company and its work became, in turn, an exemplification and disseminator of that ideology.

'Ideology' and 'Class' as concrete terms require some definition in order to explain their significance in this study. As the validity of a class-based approach to Victorian social history has been cast into doubt over the last 30 years, it is worthwhile nailing my colours to the mast from the outset by stating that, in my view, perceptions of class difference, and divisions within social classes, are major factors influencing the economic and cultural origins, and subsequent success, of the Gilbert and Sullivan operas. David Cannadine's comment that 'there is no such thing as *the* Late Victorian and Edwardian middle class: it was far too protean, varied and amorphous for that' (Cannadine 1998, p. 121) is a salutary reminder that such usages are often hard to define as tangible absolutes.[6] Nevertheless, if completely specific class definitions and affiliations are amorphous, and subject to interpretation by historians, it is impossible to deny that gross inequalities in distribution of wealth and standards of living were clearly observable in Victorian Britain and were clearly described by contemporaries in terms of 'class' difference (Hewitt 2008, p. 305). The triadic model of upper, middle and working classes, earning their livings from rent, from profit and from wages, proposed by Ricardo in the early part of the century, became a predominant (though not exclusive) method of describing social organisation in the nineteenth century. It formed the basis of Marxist class theory, which, in a developed form, underpinned the work of the influential post-war British school of Marxist social historians and cultural commentators (Borsay 2006, p. 75).[7]

The validity of these views as a determinant of the existence of actual social groupings, to which individuals claim specific and exclusive allegiance, has been eroded in the last 30 years by a number of historians, particularly Cannadine (1998), Joyce (1994) and Wahrman (1995). The concept of the 'rise of the middle classes' (popularised by Marxist historians), in which this group, as a 'new formation ... transformed Britain's economy, society and culture' (Kidd and Nicholls 1999, p. 2), was a major casualty of this revisionist analysis.[8] 'Class' became an 'imaginary or discursive construct' (Bailey 1998, p. 5) or 'rhetoric rather than reality' (Cannadine 1998, pp. 80–1), an inadequate descriptor of the way people thought, or communicated opinions about themselves. A distinct Victorian 'middle class' bounded by certain clearly definable economic, occupational or political parameters could, therefore, no longer be said to 'exist' as a historical phenomenon or even, according to Cannadine, as a realistic construct for the Victorians themselves (1998, p. 60).

But if it is no longer tenable to envision a view of society based on meta-narratives concerning 'class consciousness' and 'class antagonism', the use of class by historians of all kinds (including those who rejected Marxist usages) as a means of describing different types of social differentiation in Victorian Britain remains common among scholars of Victorian society and culture.[9] The 'mark of class sticks like a burr in nineteenth-century society and remains among the most potent vectors of difference' observes Peter Bailey. 'If class is largely an imagined or invented phenomenon then it must still be imagined or invented out of some thing or things which include material being or experience' (1998, p. 5). 'Material being and experience' are the factors which have been more recently employed to redefine the use of class by historians. For example, Simon Gunn (1999) uses the notion of identity as the means to explore and define the characteristics of the Victorian 'middle classes'. Factors such as perceived status, gender-based behavioural assumptions, leisure pursuits and modes of consumption are, for Gunn and a number of prominent cultural historians,[10] the identifiers of a social grouping which was subject to 'a constant process of forming and re-forming' and which resists categorisation via issues of politics or economics. Instead, cultural issues, which directly affected the everyday lives of individuals, can be seen as the factors through which social actors defined their 'class' or status position, or had it defined for them by contemporary commentators.

The proposition here is to use the concept of class as both an economic categorisation, and as a means of encapsulating a set of cultural values, a 'middle-class' ideology. By 'ideology' I follow Raymond Williams's definition. Ideology is 'the characteristic world view or general perspective of a class or other social group, which will include formal and conscious beliefs, but also less conscious, less formulated attitudes, habits and feelings, or even unconscious assumptions, bearings and feelings' (Williams 1980, pp. 26–7).[11] This position argues that commonly held values and preoccupations are fundamental to the way individuals perceive society and social relations. They are ubiquitous, are often accepted unquestioningly, and generally serve the interests and maintain the status of the dominant classes or social groups. The West End in which the Gilbert and Sullivan operas were first presented was characterised by concurrent attempts by managements to attract a particular type of audience which appears to have shared an identity based on broadly corresponding tastes and cultural preconceptions. I will argue that patterns of consumption and lifestyle became an indicator of 'middle-class' values and were reflected in the types of show, theatre architecture and performance ephemera which survive as material evidence for theatrical production and reception in this period.

To what degree did the performance of the Savoy operas actually recreate and augment 'middle-class' attitudes? Although the work of a theatre organisation in late-Victorian Britain could not be classed as constituting 'mass culture' in a twenty-first-century sense, reception of the D'Oyly Carte Opera Company was particularly widespread. Between 1880 and 1903 a D'Oyly Carte production could be seen in the West End, and on tour, in an average of four (and sometimes as many as six) different regional theatres from Penzance to Montrose and from Cork to Dover, six days a week, throughout the year (Rollins and Witts 1962, pp. 29–117). Its impact, though not as great as, say, print media at the time, might nevertheless be considered sufficient to be seen as integral to the ideological consensus of the 'middle classes'.

Central to this examination of the ways in which cultural production can exemplify and reinforce ideology will be an understanding that all *material* aspects of a theatre event, not just those pertaining to what performers do on stage ('embodied' performance), can be subject to critical reading as a 'text'. Informing this idea throughout several chapters is Rick Knowles's theory of 'materialist semiotics', as presented in *Reading the Material Theatre* (2004). Knowles's intention is to 'consider theatrical performances as cultural productions which serve specific cultural and theatrical communities at particular historical moments as sites for the negotiation [... and] transmission of cultural values' (2004, p. 10). To this end, I will, as Knowles does, 'read' the material evidence of theatre productions in order to understand the social and political significance of the 'theatre event'.[12] This evidence is not restricted to what happens on stage when an audience is present. Of equal importance to the theatre event are

> institutional and professional structures of theatrical organization, the structures of stage architecture, rehearsal and backstage space, and the

histories, mandates and programming of producing theatres [...] conditions of reception, such as the spatial geographies of theatrical location, neighbourhood, auditorium and audience amenities and the public discourses of producing theatres, including publicity materials, programs and posters, previews, reviews and the discourses of celebrity.

(2004, p. 11)

All these contribute to systems of signification, which when combined with an understanding of social, cultural and historical contexts can reveal the ideological position of a theatre event, and that of those who created it. Subsequent chapters consider how 'conditions of production' and 'conditions of reception' (2004, p. 19) can be seen to exemplify and maintain the ideology of the respectable late-Victorian bourgeoisie. So, 'production' (generally what happens before 'the curtain goes up') and 'reception' (which can happen prior to a witnessed performance in the form of publicity and reviews, as well as during and, indeed, after the show) can be discussed separately from 'embodied performance'—what the actors do on the stage. It is the 'effect of all these systems [...] working dynamically and relationally together' (2004, p. 19) which creates meaning. Thus, moments of *performance* are discussed in Chap. 7, which considers the style of D'Oyly Carte actors. The preceding chapters will provide the *contexts* of production and reception which inform the study of these performances.

A particular feature of the 'aftermath' of performance is the theatrical memoir, a form which often consists of engaging stories and theatrical anecdotes. I refer to such discourse throughout, and draw inspiration from methods advocated by Jacky Bratton in *New Readings in Theatre History* (2003). She remarks that an anecdote

occupies the same functional space as fiction, in that it is intended to entertain, but its instructive dimension is more overt. It purports to reveal the truth of the society, but not necessarily directly: its inner truth, its truth to some ineffable essence, rather than to proven facts, is what matters most.

(2003, p. 103)

The main purpose of the type of theatrical memoir written by leading D'Oyly Carte artistes such as George Grossmith (1888), Rutland

Barrington (1908) and Jessie Bond (1930) is to amuse and instruct the reader. Biographical detail is chosen selectively, and apparent 'facts' may be reorganised and reinvented to suit the narrative or dramatic purposes of the author. However, this apparent factual 'inaccuracy' does not deny the usefulness of such anecdotal sources, which remain valuable indicators of the shared opinions and preoccupations of the authors of these books and their intended audiences. Recurrent tropes in contemporary memoirs, such as backstage decorum at the Savoy, and the financial parsimony of the management, allow us to gain some insight into the responses of D'Oyly Carte actors to their pay and conditions, and to their attitudes and concerns. Read with care, and suitably contextualised, the evidence provided by memoir and anecdote can be used as a way of exploring the ideological assumptions of historical periods and moments.

Contextual coverage throughout will necessarily focus on the period of the inception of the Savoy collaboration (the late 1870s), as its early impact on audiences and critics marked an appreciable departure from existing forms of musical theatre entertainment and established the style of subsequent work. There is no attempt to provide a strictly chronological sequence in the following chapters. This differs from much previous writing on Gilbert, Sullivan and Carte, which starts with a biographical and contextual account of the protagonists before their association, followed by analysis of text and (sometimes) performance, interspersed with more biography (Cellier and Bridgeman 1914; Hibbert 1976; Wilson 1989). Here, contexts concerning class and culture which underpin cultural production are examined in Chap. 2. It is therefore appropriate to include an examination of these influences on the Gilbert and Sullivan texts (libretti and scores) in the second chapter rather than succeeding chapters in which issues of commerce, theatrical genres, space and place, theatre audiences, company morality and performance style are examined. Placing textual concerns in a chapter concerning class and culture is doubly appropriate, as the texts can reveal a degree of responsiveness to shifting social and cultural circumstances which form the background to the composition and production of the operas. However, the primary objective of Chapter 2 is to investigate the ideological background of the producers, practitioners and spectators of the early D'Oyly Carte performances—in other words, to explore what it meant to be, or to aspire to be, a member of the Victorian 'middle class'.

NOTES

1. The company folded in 1982 due to the removal of state funding by the British Arts Council. Rising production expenses had resulted in a reliance on this contribution to its running costs to keep the company on the road. See Bradley (2005, p. 41–52).

2. It could be argued that the comprehensive and sustained criticism of British institutions in *Utopia, Limited* (1893), which depicts, in one memorable moment, representatives of the British armed forces, the city, the law, the Lord Chamberlain's office and local government cavorting as performers in a minstrel show, presents a harsher view of society than any of the other operas. Contemporary reviews do not focus on any perceived increase in satirical intent, however. The next and final opera, *The Grand Duke* (1896), is noticeable for its absence of satire, and its similarities to the new genre, musical comedy, and to *fin de siècle* continental operetta, neither of which emphasised social satire. From a twenty-first-century perspective, *Utopia, Limited* may appear more uncompromising than it did in its own time.

3. For the purpose of this discussion, the term middle class—without inverted commas—will be used to denote a reading of class based on late-nineteenth-century classifications of occupation and income. 'Middle-class'—with the commas—will denote a looser definition, which combines the notion of a value-based ideology with economic considerations. The term 'bourgeois' will be used as an alternative to the latter designation, rather than in its strictly Marxist sense of those who own the means of production and exploit the proletariat.

4. They constituted around 75 per cent of total population (Perkin 1989, pp. 29–30).

5. A similar model is used by Asa Briggs in his chapter 'Victorian Values' (1988). Briggs identifies a set of key 'values' which typify the Victorian mentality. His topics include entrepreneurship, hard work, cleanliness, 'self help', duty, patriotism and the 'domestic sphere'.

6. I would argue that terms such as 'the late Victorian middle-class' *can* be used to facilitate an understanding of the way a particular society functions, if they are seen as 'models'—'intellectual construct(s) which simplify reality in order to emphasize the recurrent, the general and the typical which [... are presented] in the form of clusters, traits or attributes' (Burke 1992, p. 28). Associated dangers of generalisation and simplification can be countered by the argument that the purpose of models is to simplify in order to make the real world more comprehensible (Burke 1992, pp. 28–33).

7. Marxist explanations of the formation of modern British society focus on the interrelationships of mutually antagonistic classes, with specific

self-evident 'identities'. They use class formations and relationships—most significantly the notion of mutual class antagonism—to provide an overarching, explanatory account of British society from the industrial revolution onwards.

8. Newer accounts argued that the upper classes retained the real power. Rather than being dominated by a newly enfranchised bourgeois hegemony, the old order still held the upper hand, as more than half of Britain's wealth and a majority of cabinet posts remained in the possession of the aristocracy in the period covered by this study (Boyd and Macwilliam 2007, pp. 27–28; Hewitt 2008, p. 3).

9. For example, Thompson (1988) and Tosh (1999) afford the terms upper, middle and working class little definition, and use them as a commonly accepted shorthand method of describing Victorian society. Oost (2009) and Mason (1994) qualify their usage of class quite distinctly, but in different ways. For Mason, income and occupation are the important class delineators; for Oost, consumption and social behaviour.

10. See Bailey (1998), Davidoff and Hall (2002) and Rappaport (2000).

11. Raymond Williams's theory of cultural dominance provides the most useful model by which broad issues concerning the interaction between the material basis of society, its beliefs ('ideology') and its cultural production can be explained. Williams's basic position is that 'in any society, in any period, there is a central system of practices, meanings and values which we can call dominant and effective' (1980, p. 38). Such a system 'saturates society and even constitutes the substance and limit of common sense for most people under its sway [... so] that it corresponds to the reality of social experience.'

12. This is the 'materialism' in Knowles's 'materialist semiotics'. Cultural materialism, as expounded by Dollimore and Sinfield (1985) locates 'cultural production—including the production of theatre—within its historical, cultural and material contexts' (Knowles 2004, p. 11) in order to reveal the underlying ideological meanings, particularly those pertaining to issues of power and social dominance, present in any text.

CHAPTER 2

The Gilbert and Sullivan Operas and 'Middle-Class' Ideals

In general, those members of the D'Oyly Carte organisation who directly influenced audience reception—author, composer, management, designers, actors and musicians—could be thought of as earning the same kind of wages and embracing the same 'respectable' social and cultural standards as those which characterised the attitudes of the Victorian 'middle classes'. They were, in the broadest sense, the economic, demographic and cultural counterparts of most audience members attending the original West End performances of the Gilbert and Sullivan operas. Exceptions to this shared bourgeois status might be seen in the auditorium in the form of occasional visits by royalty and more frequent (and especially first night) attendance by the titled landed gentry and high-ranking state officials. At the other end of the social scale, located backstage and in the foyer, were the many stagehands, mechanics, cleaning staff, waiters and front of house operatives who kept the theatre and its services going.

How may we more clearly define the Victorian 'middle classes'? Obviously, as has been noted in Chapter 1, by a fundamental value system or 'ideology'. Part of this ideology consisted of status attributes. Commenting on the 'characteristics which distinguished [the middle classes] from those above and below', Martin Hewitt identifies 'property [...] the importance of appearances, which required the keeping of servants and the public commitment to certain codes of respectability; work, but "brain work" rather than manual work and [...] possession of the vote' (Class and Classes 2008, p. 308). To this value-based picture can be

© The Author(s) 2016
M. Goron, *Gilbert and Sullivan's 'Respectable Capers'*, Palgrave Studies in British Musical Theatre, DOI 10.1057/978-1-137-59478-5_2

added contemporary notions of class, based on income and occupation. Often cited (Best 1971; Mason 1994; Perkin 1969) are the social classifications derived from census data collected by Charles Booth in the 1880s,[1] which divide workers into specific categories according to their employment. There were eight for the middle classes: Law, Medicine, Education, Religion, Art and Amusement, Commerce (a catch-all title for a range of administrative, clerical and accountancy roles), Public Administration and Trade—wholesale and retail (cited in Best 1971, p. 105). Booth's findings record a rapid increase of middle-class employment in the second half of the nineteenth century. According to Perkin (1989, p. 79), 'as new and more varied businesses came into existence, the rise in the scale of business and government required more managers, administrators, office workers and supervisors, and the professions and would-be professions increased in size and numbers.' Perkin measures a rise in middle-class income receivers from 23 per cent of the population in 1867 to 30 per cent in 1900, and of male earners in this category from 166,700 in 1881 to 303,116 in 1900, a 'more than proportionate increase in the number of incomes of more or less middle-class people' (Banks 1954, cited in Best 1974, p. 83).

The established professions (such as law, medicine and religion) trebled in numbers between 1841 and 1881 (Stone and Stone 1984, p. 428). During the same period, those earning livings in the newer middle-class sectors of 'Art and Amusement' rose in England and Wales from 25,000 in 1851 to 47,000 in 1881, forming 0.3 per cent of the total working population in that year (Best 1971, p. 85). Middle-class wages could vary greatly. Upper division civil servants might earn between £200 and £1200 per year, while those in the lower division were paid between £70 and £350. Assistant clerks' salaries ranged between £80 and £150 per year, while boy clerks started on 14s per week (Perkin 1989, p. 91).

If D'Oyly Carte performers are regarded as forming part of Booth's 'Art and Amusement' category, wage comparisons show parity with the differentials within the middle-class sector as a whole. The basic rate for a chorister was £85 per year, a sum often increased by personal engagements or part-time work outside the company.[2] A small part player could earn between £160 and £260 (Bond 1930, pp. 34, 117) while by 1891 Jessie Bond brought home an annual income of around £1500 (1930, p. 92). George Grossmith could not be persuaded to return to the Savoy to perform in *His Majesty* in 1897 for less than £70 per week (Ainger 2002, p. 350). The increase in middle-class earners in general, and 'Art and Amusement' providers in particular, provides strong evidence for the growth and provision of 'middle-class' entertainment in the last third of the century. An expanded middle-class population, seeking leisure activities which accorded with their tastes, were catered for by an expanding employment group, who were (at least according to Booth) considered to belong to the same class.

Alongside its economic basis, any appreciation of Victorian society needs to derive from an examination of the way people thought about and described it at the time. Although such descriptions were by no means consistent, much nineteenth-century thinking about the social order was described in class terms (Hewitt 2008, p. 305). The 'middle-class' social attitudes which form the ideology of the time are fairly easy to locate. Those who wrote about them, either in novels which dealt with contemporary social mores, in magazines such as *Punch* (1841) and *Household Words* (1850), or within the more elevated monthlies such as *Cornhill Magazine* (1860) and *The Fortnightly Review* (1865) (both of which included in-depth social commentary as well as literary entertainment) invariably came from the ranks of the educated bourgeoisie.

These versions of self-definition can, in turn, help us to 'recover the ways in which Britons saw and understood the manifestly unequal society in which they lived' (Cannadine 1998, pp. 19–20). Although 'class was not conceived of in rigorously consistent ways' it nevertheless became the primary method of describing society. 'The inhabitants of the country, not just politicians and agitators, but social investigators, clergymen and novelists displayed a social vision dominated by class' (Hewitt 2004, p. 311). Chapter 1 posits the existence of a Victorian 'middle-class' identity, characterised by the pervasive 'respectable' ideology of the dominant social group. The way in which the social order was perceived in mid-nineteenth-century Britain broadly supports this definition, but also configures it in different ways.

Cannadine (1998, pp. 15–23) seeks to include the predominantly 'triadic' (upper, middle and lower or 'working' class) division of Victorian society with a paradigm in which this system provides only one of *three* class-based methods of depicting social structures. Alternative contemporary perspectives to this view are offered. First is the 'hierarchical view of society as a seamless web', a social structure extending from the highest to the lowest, lacking clearly defined 'horizontal' divisions. And second, the 'dichotomous' model of class, proposing a fundamental 'us and them' division, which 'emphasised the adversarial nature of the social order, by drawing one great divide on the basis of culture, style of life and politics' (1998, p. 19).

Cannadine argues that all three versions were adopted concurrently as ways of expressing differing perceptions of British society in the nineteenth century. Awareness of a variety of models permits diverse readings of social structure and can provide different, but mutually informative, perspectives from which to view such phenomena as a Savoy Theatre audience, and the constituency of the D'Oyly Carte company. This method can reveal some of the complexities within social groupings. It prevents an oversimplified response to social demography and encourages an exploratory approach towards the social make-up of audiences and institutions.

Addressing the first of these alternative models of class, the 'hierarchical' system was founded on an acceptance of the fundamental inequalities of society and one's place in it, and deference to one's social superiors. The Anglophile Henry James, examining British society as a semi-detached foreign observer, remarked that '[t]he essentially hierarchic plan of English society is the great and ever present fact to the mind of a stranger. There is hardly a detail of life which does not in some degree betray it' (James 1905, p. 99). It was upheld, not surprisingly, by politicians and by social commentators with an interest in promoting social cohesion and the maintenance of the established order (Best 1971, pp. 255–8). The influential political journalist Walter Bagehot, a voice of the professional middle class, encapsulated this viewpoint when he described England as representing

> The type of deferential countries [...] in which the numerous unwiser part wishes to be ruled by the less numerous wiser part. The numerical majority [...] abdicates in favour of its elite, and consents to obey whoever that elite may confide in.
>
> (Bagehot 1867, p. 50)

If we can accept Geoffrey Best's comment that 'Bagehot's generation was deferential through and through' (1971, p. 260) as meaning that, despite the presence of inevitable discontent and inequality, Britain was stabilised in the second half of the century by an essentially deferential compromise, then it is worth remembering that Gilbert, Sullivan and Carte, born around a decade after Bagehot, became part of that generation's prosperous middle-class elite. A representative example of acculturated class consciousness and acceptance of an essentialist understanding of British social hierarchies may be observed in the comments made by Sullivan during his first American trip. Uncomfortable with the egalitarianism of the United States during his 1879 stay, he wrote bitterly to his mother:

Eight weeks tomorrow since I left England, and I wish myself back already. Republicanism is the curse of the country. Everyone is not only equal to but better than his neighbour and the consequence is insolence and churlishness in all the lower orders.[3]

Originating from the lowest rank of the lower middle classes, this self-made professional gentleman was, in 1879, sufficiently confident in his own position to trumpet his allegiance to the conspicuous hierarchies of his native land.

HIERARCHICAL SOCIETIES: *THE SORCERER* AND *HMS PINAFORE*

Similar principles were reflected in the libretti of several of the Savoy operas. As a commercial dramatist writing to please his public, the 'conservative' satire which characterises Gilbert's libretti is partly founded on a concept of social order which accorded with that of the majority of his audience. Dramatic tension in the operas is partly created by challenges to 'natural' hierarchy. Characters who attempt to disrupt it, be they *parvenu* statesmen (Sir Joseph Porter—*HMS Pinafore*), would-be egalitarian aristocrats (Alexis Pointdextre—*The Sorcerer*) or misguided republicans (the eponymous *Gondoliers*), are to a greater or lesser extent mocked. Resolution and contentment occurs in most of the operas when the correct (hierarchical) social order is restored.

In *The Sorcerer*, for example, the aristocratic Alexis Pointdextre, inspired by the democratic notion that love should exist without social boundaries, hires the sorcerer John Wellington Wells to infuse the afternoon tea of the local villagers with a soporific love potion in order that they may fall in love with the first person they see upon waking. Wells is presented as a petit-bourgeois urban shopkeeper, an anomaly in a rural village whose social structure epitomises an age before the realities of late-Victorian industrial and urban change had complicated the simple hierarchies of earlier times. Such new-fangled social irritations are exorcised as Wells meets a comic death in order to save the village from the social disasters which result from the unequal pairings caused by the consumption of the love potion. Those bastions of hierarchical society, the church (Dr Daly), the law (the Notary) and the landed gentry—which here also includes the military elite—(the Pointdextre and Sangazure families) survive this challenge to the social order. Their position is secured by the working-class villagers, whose experience of the embarrassments of social equality leaves them content with their time-honoured lot.

The notion of egalitarianism is lampooned by comic irony arising from the gulf between the earnestness of Alexis's advocacy of equality and the ridiculousness of its effects when applied to the inhabitants of a 'traditional' English rural society (Hayter 1987, pp. 76–7). Alexis relates his notions enthusiastically to Aline, his aristocratic fiancée (who is, significantly, *not* included in the plans for societal reform):

ALEXIS: I have made some converts to the principle, that men and women should be coupled in matrimony without distinction of rank. I have lectured on the subject at Mechanics' Institutes, and the mechanics were unanimous in favour of my views. I have preached in workhouses, beershops, and Lunatic Asylums, and I have been received with enthusiasm. I have addressed navvies on the advantages that would accrue to them if they married wealthy ladies of rank, and not a navvy dissented.

ALINE: Noble fellows! And yet there are those who hold that the uneducated classes are not open to argument! And what do the countesses say?

ALEXIS: Why, at present, it can't be denied, the aristocracy hold aloof.

(*The Sorcerer*, Act One)

Gilbert presents texts which reveal inherent inadequacies within the status quo but which recognise that radical change would be impractical and, given the entrenched nature of social hierarchies, both unlikely and absurd.

Hierarchies, class fragmentations and 'them and us' dichotomies, along with an examination of class inequality and the hypocrisy of supposed egalitarianism, are investigated in *HMS Pinafore*. Here Gilbert parodies the popular, patriotic nautical melodrama of the early nineteenth century, epitomised by Douglas Jerrolds' *Black-Ey'd Susan* (1829). This genre, which emphasises shipboard authority and the heroism of the British sailor personified by the 'Jolly Jack Tar', is parodically inverted by Gilbert. The conventions of nautical melodrama were laughable dramatic clichés by 1879. Central to these were issues of class, manifested as the tribulations of the working man and woman exploited by those higher in the social hierarchy. William, the conscripted hero of *Black-Ey'd Susan*, is court-martialed for defending the honour of his wife against the advances of the corrupt Captain Crosstree. A happy ending is provided by an implausible coincidental exoneration—the revelation of a concealed document which proves that William had in fact been dismissed from the navy at the time of his assault on the ship's captain.

Working-class heroism is not Gilbert's concern. Instead he satirises the escapist egalitarianism of the melodrama and plays with the notions of power and oppression invested in stratified class-based systems. He achieves this by emphasising the stylistic implausibility of such clichés as the over-eloquent Tar and the improbable dénouement of the typical melodrama. *HMS Pinafore* provides a demonstration of the damaging effects on a smooth-running 'hierarchy' when social boundaries are breached and when the snobbery and egotism of its social actors begin to cause fragmentation within its structure.

Pinafore's plot concerns the prohibited love of the humble sailor hero, Ralph Rackstraw, and the captain's daughter, Josephine. Her father, Captain Corcoran, proclaims in Act One that he attaches 'little value to rank or wealth' and though 'related to a peer' proudly declares his ability to 'hand reef and steer' just like a common sailor. However, he hypocritically balks at the notion that his daughter might marry beneath her, while the prospect of Josephine's imminent socially advantageous match with Sir Joseph Porter, first lord of the Admiralty, exposes his innate snobbery: '[A]t last my fond hopes are to be crowned. My only daughter is to be the bride of a Cabinet Minister. The prospect is Elysian.' Such insincerity is echoed by Sir Joseph, the archetypal self-made man, who declares, when faced with the apparent amatory reluctance of the bourgeois Josephine to his 'upper-class' advances, that 'love is a platform upon which all ranks meet' (Act Two). When the final plot twist reveals that Josephine is actually of humble birth, Sir Joseph is horrified. The captain reminds him that 'love levels all ranks '. 'It does to a considerable extent,' replies Sir Joseph, 'but it does not level them as much as that' (Act Two).

Gilbert's satire of egalitarian attitude is made apparent by Sir Joseph's ambivalence towards equal opportunities. The removal of social inequalities is demonstrated not by a display of Sir Joseph's hard work and talent, but by his obsequious, mercenary and time-serving progress from 'office boy to an Attorney's firm' to 'Ruler of the Queens's Navee'. It allows Sir Joseph to insist that Captain Corcoran treat his crew with absurdly deferential civility. At the same time, and in a farcically contradictory way, Sir

Joseph continually reminds everyone of his *own* social superiority. Gilbert is surely demonstrating here that the prevailing notion of 'removable inequality', which declared that initial poverty can always be remedied by hard work, cannot and does not result in a more egalitarian society. This is especially true if its class barriers are enforced even more rigorously by those few who manage to surmount them.

The opera starts by presenting the audience with an essentially hierarchical view of British society as symbolically represented by the inhabitants of a British Man O' War. Captain and crew are aware of their social differences, but coexist in a cooperative and mutually affirming relationship, each respectful of each other's function in the smooth running of the vessel. However, the revelation of Ralph and Josephine's love engenders a social dichotomy, as those 'above'—the Corcorans, Sir Joseph and his family entourage—are set against those 'below'—Ralph, the *Pinafore* crew and Little Buttercup, the ex-baby farmer turned travelling saleswoman. During the course of the action we see internal class fragmentation, as the higher ranks divide, with Sir Joseph exercising his self-made status over the middle-class captain, and Josephine agonising over the possibility of the social degradation attendant on an inferior marriage.

At the other end of the social order, the egalitarian sentiments of the crew are challenged by one of their number, the deformed, cynical villain, Dick Deadeye. In Act One, he is given what is perhaps the most pragmatic description of naval society (and, by implication, Victorian society as a whole): 'When people have to obey other people's orders, equality is out of the question.' Here lies the real conservatism of Gilbert's satire, and the world view presented by this opera—that if society is to function effectively, its innate hierarchies need to be maintained, even if the result is often ineptitude and social rigidity. The possibility of radical action is present in the opera—but in the heavily satirised actions of Sir Joseph. It is he who insists that commanding officers should suffix all orders with the phrase 'if you please', and recommends that common sailors be instructed in 'independence of thought and action' by providing them a personally composed song, 'A British Tar is a Soaring Soul', which contains nothing but pseudo-patriotic nonsense.

Social conservatism is ultimately emphasised by the melodramatic device through which a conventionally happy ending is manufactured by means of a deliberately ridiculous and artificial dénouement. It transpires that Corcoran and Ralph were switched in infancy, so that Ralph is in fact the captain's social superior. Ralph is then free to marry Josephine, the captain is reduced to a common sailor who pairs up with Little Buttercup, and all ends happily. The chronological impossibilities of this exchange—the young hero is now revealed as being the same age as his erstwhile father-in-law—defy logic, suggesting that only in the surreal world of the stage is societal inequality surmountable.

Gilbert's notion of social hierarchy, at least in terms of the way it is presented in the operas,[4] is therefore essentially viewed from the standpoint of the confident, socially assertive 'middle classes'. Petit-bourgeois values are deemed potentially comic and dispensable in *The Sorcerer*, and egalitarianism is shown as untenable in that opera and in *HMS Pinafore*. Chapter 5 will consider the extent to which the treatment of class in the operas reflects changing attitudes on Gilbert's part towards audience expectations, but it is sufficient to note here that, while the working- and lower-middle classes are less frequently patronised as the series continues, the upper classes are consistently seen as satirical targets. The bourgeoisie could eagerly follow the activities of their fashionable patrician 'betters' in the press, and emulate their tastes and fashions. They could also regard them as feckless, unproductive and parasitical, particularly when contrasted with their own industry and contribution to national wealth. Although Gilbert's depictions of the gentry are invariably tempered with comic geniality—after all, his audience may have contained some of their members—he nevertheless presents us with an aristocracy who are self-consciously archaic (*The Sorcerer*), lacking in intelligence (Duke of Dunstable—*Patience*, Lord Tolloller—*Iolanthe*), incompetently militaristic (King Gama's sons—*Princess Ida*) or avowedly mercenary (Pooh-Bah—*The Mikado*).

This view of the social order presents society as a series of sometimes antagonistic, but certainly discrete, social groups. Cannadine's 'patricians' versus 'plebeians' model might be the obvious way of looking at society, and the D'Oyly Carte operation, in a 'dichotomous' way. Arguably the Savoy clientele constituted those who could be described as middle class from a monetary standpoint, and the pricing structure, in common with other West End theatres, effectively priced the mass of the working population out. Chapter 5 will further consider ways in which these demographic issues are reflected in the content of the operas. However, other kinds of 'dichotomies' can be observed in operation throughout the social order. Who was 'upper' and who 'lower' could depend on time, place and circumstance, and presumably the point of view of the describer, and was not restricted to 'triadic' class differences. Such division *within* classes was apparent both to Victorian observers, and to social historians. Harold Perkin remarks that

From top to bottom, the middle class was riddled with such divisions and petty snobberies, not only of income and geography, but of religion [...] of education [...] and of leisure [...] segregation at every level and in every occupation and pastime was the hallmark of the middle class.

(1989, pp. 82–3)[5]

More specifically, this model, which is better referred to as one of 'fragmentation' rather than 'dichotomy' when applied to divisions within a specific class, can be used to help explain how the internal spatial divisions of a typical West End auditorium could represent a variety of social boundaries, even within a predominantly bourgeois environment. The distance between 'us' and 'them' within such an audience could be manifested by exclusivity in dress, choice of restaurant facilities within the theatre or simply self-selection of those people with whom one wished to associate.

In her recent study of the ways in which the D'Oyly Carte organisation represented and influenced bourgeois material culture, Regina Oost (2009) presents what might be termed a 'hierarchical' Savoy audience. Here we see an audience not stratified by inter-class fragmentation but unified by its ability and desire, as part of the late-Victorian consumer culture, to indulge in a shared entertainment experience reflecting its material tastes. Alternative viewpoints are valuable. It is useful to be able to view the same audience (and the Savoy personnel) from several class-related standpoints. Following Oost's reading, the Savoy clientele can be seen as representing a 'hegemonic' or hierarchical entity who, despite differences of income and a tacit acceptance of their place within the pecking order, shared many cultural and social values. However, viewed from the perspective of class fragmentation, the same audience presents a different image. It becomes a disjointed group riven with petty distinctions of status and social importance, demonstrated by differences in dress, accent, means of transport, choice of social companion, and even levels of enthusiasm in responding to performance. These alternate viewpoints will contribute to the discussion of the social organisation of auditoria and audience make-up in Chapter 5.

After exploring the ways in which hierarchical, dichotomous and fragmented models can be used to examine the society which produced and received the Savoy operas, one may return to the more conventional expedient of adopting the 'triadic' usage of the term 'middle class'. This denotes a broad, central social group, who sometimes perceived themselves as antagonistic to the upper and working classes, and were unified by some basic common features. These might be economic, relating to jobs, salaries and the ability to employ servants; locational, in terms of various levels of suburban dwelling; and physical (at least by comparison with the poorly paid), in terms of health, stature, hygiene and appearance. Understanding of the similarities and differences in Savoy audiences and personnel can be obtained by an awareness of the shifting perspectives engendered by different models of class. But central to all three is a unifying 'middle-class' cultural identity based on a common ideology of *values*, endorsed and espoused by those Britons who considered themselves 'respectable '.

'RESPECTABLE' VALUES: *THE PIRATES OF PENZANCE, THE GONDOLIERS, PATIENCE, THE MIKADO, PRINCESS IDA* AND *UTOPIA, LIMITED*

The notion of 'respectability' was pervasive. In Victorian Britain it served the important purpose of distinguishing 'respectable' society from those sectors of the community who did not, apparently, share or exercise these values. Notions of respectability were disseminated through written 'narratives [...] popular fiction, religious tracts, political speeches, and newspaper reports' to demarcate an 'essential difference from members of the working-classes' (Oost 2009, p. 17). 'Respectability' can therefore be seen as a mark of superiority, and its pursuit could be seen as concomitant with a desire to rise economically and socially.

The origins of this kind of individualistic pursuit of ethical superiority lie in religiously motivated attempts to reform the morals of society. The fundamentalist evangelical movement, which exercised a powerful influence over middle-class society in the late eighteenth and early nineteenth centuries emphasised the achievement of salvation through proper conduct of one's earthly life: 'Every act, no matter how trivial, in earthly terms, would be of incalculable importance when the balance was struck at the gates of heaven' (Altick 1973, p. 166). The importance of ethical surveillance, combined with the 'traditional Puritanism of the English middle-ranks', created what Harold Perkin describes as a 'moral revolution' (1969, p. 281).

The puritanical rejection of pleasure and enjoyment of life, espoused by some early- to mid-nineteenth-century evangelicals, had abated by the

1860s (Altick 1973, p. 178; Thompson 1988, p. 270). However, its influence pervaded society as a means of social self-definition. Once again, the need to acquire and maintain a social status based on a consensual view of appropriate behaviour was achieved by defining oneself against a differentiated, inferior 'other '. Thus, 'the solid, industrious, and prudent middle classes' could achieve this through a 'conformity to a code of behaviour in public [...] which was clearly defined in the etiquette manuals which multiplied prodigiously in the early nineteenth century' and which could be contrasted with the conduct of society's 'idle, dissolute and thriftless' (Thompson 1988, p. 257).

These attitudes could be parodied in the Savoy operas for a metropolitan audience, who, by the late 1870s and 1880s, may have seen themselves as sufficiently sophisticated to be no longer in thrall to early Victorian rigidity. However, the very fact that such parody exists in the Gilbert and Sullivan works suggests that the difficult business of negotiating the implications of 'respectability' in social behaviour was still current. Charles Hayter (1987) makes a very persuasive case in arguing that the central theme of *The Pirates of Penzance* (subtitled *The Slave of Duty*) concerns the tensions caused by the twin pulls of respectable behaviour on the one hand and 'worldly interest' on the other. Hayter reminds us that *Pirates* premiered in 1880, the same year which saw the publication of Samuel Smiles' *Duty*. Like his earlier *Self Help* (1859), *Duty* was exhortation to self-improvement, this time focusing on 'obedience to duty at all costs and risks' as 'the very essence of the highest civilised life'. Smiles reminded his readers of the moral obligations of the 'strife between a higher and lower nature warring within us—of spirit warring against flesh—of good striving for the mastery over evil' (Smiles 1880, p. 26).

This kind of evangelical dogma is mocked in *Pirates* through the figure of Frederic, the 'heroic' tenor lead. His personal moral code is so strict that crises within the plot which require reconciliation based on logic or human feelings are dealt with instead through rigid obedience to an absurdly inappropriate ethical system. Because of the deafness of his nursemaid, who mistook the word 'pilot' for 'pirate', Frederic is apprenticed as a child to a gang of buccaneers. Having discovered the truth in Act One, he makes the moral decision to honour the arrangement, and remain a criminal until the end of the day in which the action takes place, which happens to be both his twenty-first birthday and the formal conclusion of his apprenticeship. Meanwhile, Frederic has fallen in love with Mabel, daughter of Major General Stanley, and plans to help the general apprehend his former comrades. A crisis is engendered when the Pirate King reveals to Frederic that, as he was born in a leap year, he will not reach legal adulthood until 1940. Frederic, dutiful to the last, decides to remain a pirate. When exhorted by Mabel to defend her and her family against the impending pirate attack, he can only sing ineffectually: 'Beautiful Mabel/ I would if I could, but I am not able' (*The Pirates of Penzance,* Act Two).

If unthinking moral obedience is ridiculed via Frederic's inflexibility, then the strict sexual puritanism of the Victorian evangelical is questioned by the reaction of the opera's heroine, Mabel, to the handsome stranger. Apparently, her first reaction to Frederic is to rescue him from the error of his ways. 'Her earnestness is reminiscent of the Women's Christian Temperance Union at its best' observes Hayter (1987, p.107). In terms of its text, her major first-act song, 'Poor Wandering One', is a quasi-religious parody, suggesting the New Testament parable of the lost sheep:

Poor wandering one!
Though thou hast surely strayed,
Take heart of grace,
Thy steps retrace,
Poor wandering one!
(*The Pirates of Penzance,* Act One)

But musically it is quite different. Sullivan sets it to 'the most sensuous of nineteenth century musical forms, a waltz' (Hayter 1987, p. 107), and in overall style it is reminiscent of (and successfully parodies) the type of display aria given to nineteenth-century operatic divas. It also presents a marked contrast with the biblical language of the text, and one which reminds us of Mabel's underlying passion for the dashing young pirate.

Pirates provoked laughter at what a 'sophisticated' West End audience might have considered to be an outdated, though still pervasive, ethical rigidity. In his study, Hayter does not mention that Smiles' *Duty* appeared seven months *after* the West End premiere of the opera, thereby indicating that the underlying issues, despite being the subject of satire, remained very current. To what extent was it necessary for the 'middle classes' to regard a more or less 'moral' view of life as a spiritual necessity? Or was 'respectability' merely a conventional facade to ensure social acceptance? Comedy arising from the extreme application of moral codes displayed in *Pirates* did not negate the fact that they remained central to the world view of the audience who laughed at them, and who had to reconcile the requirements of respectable behaviour with the disturbing impulses of human nature. The gratification of such urges (especially by married men with prostitutes) has led to accusations of hypocrisy levelled at Victorian 'middle-class' society (Altick 1973, pp. 302–3; Houghton 1957, pp. 394–430). Such criticisms derive from the notion that individual need to uphold a high level of *private* rectitude could matter less than the preservation of an unsullied *public* reputation. The disjunction between professed morality and hidden vice is a recurrent theme both in the popular imagination and in histories of the period (Best 1971, pp. 284–6; Thompson 1988, pp. 257–9; Himmelfarb 1995, pp. 21–36).

Such hypocritical behaviour can be seen, on one hand, as the unfortunate by-product of a society which wished to preserve its high ideals in spite of human nature, to 'maintain the appearance, the manners, of good conduct even while violating some moral principle, for in their demeanour they affirmed the legitimacy of the principle itself' (Himmelfarb 1995, p. 22). Alternatively, and more probably, along with other trappings of 'respectability', Victorian morality could be ascribed to a desire to publicly demonstrate personal standing, to belong to the 'status group' which purported to prize such values, irrespective of one's private activities. These extremes are not mutually exclusive and, for many, both attitudes may have been part of the same ideological outlook. Sir Arthur Sullivan led a well-respected professional life, and aspired to the fulfilment of his self-professed duty to an artistic calling. His sexual liaison with the married society beauty Fanny Ronald seems to have been politely ignored or accepted in the upper-middle-class and aristocratic circles in which he mixed. His promiscuity, energetic patronage of Parisian brothels and financially disastrous addiction to the gaming tables (Ainger 2002, pp. 66–7, 128–9, 209) were successfully concealed until revealed by the access to his diaries and letters, first published in 1983 (Jacobs 1992, p. xiii).

The operas do not completely ignore male sexual instincts, but they are generally parodied as the absurd desires of older, physically unprepossessing men for young, pretty women. As in most conventional comedy, the plans of the old lecher are frustrated, and the juvenile leads are reunited in the Act Two finale. This is certainly the case in *Pinafore*, as shown by Josephine's distaste for Sir Joseph's advances, and in *Iolanthe*, where the Lord Chancellor, who is 'highly susceptible' to the attractions of his young wards-in-chancery, is ultimately reunited with his estranged fairy bride. Ko-Ko, the 'cheap tailor' in *The Mikado*, and Jack Point, the down-at-heel jester in *The Yeomen of the Guard*, pursue (unsuccessfully) Yum-Yum and Elsie Maynard, both described as being in their late teens. The character of the elderly Grand Inquisitor, Don Alhambra Del Bolero, in *The Gondoliers* is somewhat different. He does not pursue a particular female character but continually reminds the audience that he has an eye for the ladies:

DON ALHAMBRA: So this is the little lady who is so unexpectedly called upon to assume the functions of Royalty! And a very nice little lady, too!
DUKE: Jimp,[6] isn't she?
DON ALHAMBRA: Distinctly jimp. Allow me! (*Offers his hand. She turns away scornfully*) Naughty temper!

(*The Gondoliers*, Act One)

There is an element of flirtatiousness and a focus on physical attractiveness in *The Gondoliers* (premiered in December 1889) which is absent in the earlier operas, and indicates a change in what was thought acceptable in 'respectable' entertainment. Twelve years after *The Sorcerer* opened, a new generation of theatregoers had to be lured away from George Edwardes' upmarket burlesque at the Gaiety, a fresh source of competition for the Savoy. Female costume in *The Gondoliers* reinforced these subtle changes in intent. A first-night review commented:

> The attractions of *The Gondoliers* are numerous. To begin with, the chorus wore comparatively short skirts for the first time, and the gratifying fact is revealed to a curious world that the Savoy chorus are a well-legged lot.[7]

Utopia, Limited, in 1893, again allows (slightly) salacious elements to appear in the dialogue, including several references to King Paramount's 'Royal goings on with our Royal Second Housemaid' (Act One), even if they are, in the action of the play, inventions rather than actual events. Although these changes of tone seem conspicuous when compared to the chasteness of the earlier pieces, they probably reflect no more than a subtle modification in moral acceptability by the consumers of what was, by the 1890s, a national entertainment brand which needed to move with public taste. However, such changes barely registered in the company's public relations strategy during its original incarnation as a West End producing organisation (1877–1903). Throughout this period, the need to maintain an outward show of (particularly female) propriety is clearly visible in the attitudes of the management.

The preservation of decorum through public defence of the reputation of the ladies of his company exhibits Gilbert as a visible personification of the typical Victorian 'gentleman'. In his rise from government clerk to would-be country squire and Justice of the Peace, Gilbert also typified the 'gentrification of the Victorian middle classes' (Wiener 1981, p. 13), which occurred as this expanding and increasingly affluent group 'eagerly sought to imitate [their social superiors...] aspiring to gentility by copying the education, manners and behaviour of the gentry' (Stone and Stone 1984, pp. 408–9). 'Gentlemanly' conduct outside the upper classes might be regarded as an appropriation of particular conventions of demeanour, rather than a wholesale emulation of upper-class practices, an idealised form of social interaction and *politesse* which defined the 'respectable' person.

A 'gentleman' was 'honest, truthful, upright, polite, temperate, courageous, self respecting and self helping' (Smiles 1859, p. 415). The French observer Hippolyte Taine, writing admiringly in 1860, regarded the English gentleman as the natural leader of his people:

> a real gentleman is a truly noble man, a man worthy to command, a disinterested man of integrity [...] to this must be added [...] complete self-mastery, constantly maintained *sang-froid*, perseverance in adversity, serious mindedness, dignity of manners and bearing, the avoidance of all affectation [...]. You will then have the model which [...] produces the man who commands obedience here.
>
> (Taine 1957, p. 145)

Gentlemanly status could be maintained and social mobility eased by the convincing adoption of external behavioural signifiers such as the observance of proper etiquette, correctness of speech, elegance of posture and restrained deportment. These traits were associated with respectable society (Picard 2005, pp. 122–3; Wilson 2003, p. 60) and were replicated by theatres which sought to represent 'middle-class' characters and subjects. Physical stylisation of performance gave way, in those theatres specialising in the 'cup and saucer' drama, to the restrained, 'gentlemanly' manner, emphasising 'an intimate and conversational performance style' (Schoch 2004, pp. 334–5; Davis 1991, p.77). Gilbert was a firm advocate of 'realistic' acting. Following the example of Tom Robertson, resident author at the 'gentrified' Prince of Wales theatre, with whom he worked early in his stage career, Gilbert encouraged the use of 'small understated gestures copied from reality', while exaggerated signalling of comic intentions was discouraged (Crowther 2000, pp. 90–1). Attempts by touring performers to introduce broader physical 'gags' were strongly discouraged by the D'Oyly Carte management, striving to preserve the decorous 'finish' of the West End productions (Crowther 2000, pp. 143–4). The relationship between 'gentle' behaviour and stage practice will be addressed in Chapter 7.

Polite behaviour can also be seen to have affected the conduct of some West End theatre audiences in the later nineteenth century. Clement Scott remarks on the 'orthodox and courteous assemblage to be found in the pit of an English theatre' (Scott 1875). At the Savoy, social decorum was apparent even in the gallery. François Cellier, resident conductor at the Savoy, commented that, 'If, perchance there were any *claqueurs* of the rowdy class they were never in evidence [...] every man and woman entering the sanctum of the Savoy [...] put on company manners' (Cellier and Bridgeman 1914, p. 131). The ready acquiescence of the usually disorderly crowds waiting for unreserved seats to the new queuing system, instituted for the first time in London by Carte at the Savoy in 1883, suggests that the clientele who inhabited even the cheapest seats were well mannered and relatively placid.

The kind of 'ladylike' behaviour advocated by Victorian etiquette handbooks was not in the public imagination necessarily associated with the figure of the actress. From a contextual viewpoint, successful middle-class female stage performers, such as the early D'Oyly Carte principals Jessie Bond, Leonora Braham and Rosina Brandram, who earned a living through nocturnal public display, pursued a lifestyle which challenged some essential Victorian ideals of bourgeois womanhood. Foremost among these was the role of women in the domestic sphere.

'Middle-class' Victorian society saw a clear divide between the comfortable haven of the home, in which the 'softer' virtues typified by the Victorian wife and mother as personal manifestation of modesty, purity and spirituality prevailed, and the commercial, competitive, self-aggrandising male world of work. Davidoff and Hall (2002, pp. 180–8) and Howarth (2000, pp. 164–8) argue that the moral reform of society propounded by the influential evangelical Christian movement in the late eighteenth century resulted in the idealisation of the woman, rather than men, as the natural reformers of manners and morals. Patriarchal ideals were strengthened with the acknowledgement of women as dependent on their husbands' support, while advice books and magazines promoted the ideals of female submissiveness, femininity and motherly dignity. Women did not work for financial gain. To do so would be to contravene what had become their accepted and prescribed social role, a function essential both to the family and to society as a whole.

Such attitudes were essentially those of the relatively affluent middle classes. They could be maintained in practice only by those households fortunate enough to possess sufficient income and domestic help to free a wife from the need to earn, or be engaged in continual household labour. 'Most middle-class women took a large share in looking after their children, mending clothes and nursing the sick' (Perkin 1993, p. 88) and could have their time filled with 'obligations to religion, philanthropy and public action' (D'Cruze 2004, p. 264). As the century progressed, increasing numbers of middle-class women were working in educational, administrative, service, and of course entertainment-related roles. 'In 1841, some 900 women made a living as artists, musicians and actresses; fifty years later there were over 17,000 in these occupations' (Howarth 2000, p. 173).

Nevertheless, the fact that reality did not always match domestic ideals does not mean that they were not pervasive. Conventional, educated male attitudes towards the role of their wives continued to affirm the non-sexualised, maternal persona (Picard 2005, p. 332) and, while the more excessive expressions of Victorian sexual prudery have been challenged as untypical extremes by modern writers (Mason 1994; Sweet 2001, pp. xii–xv, 209–19), outward shows of sexual moderation and prudery were nevertheless central Victorian preoccupations. This could be ascribed to Malthusian fears of overpopulation and the desire to ensure the financial prosperity of individual families (particularly those of the growing lower middle classes) by limiting family size, leading to the practice of abstinence within marriage, which, in turn, encouraged a generally prim attitude towards sexual matters (Daunton 2000, pp. 69–70; Howarth 2000, p. 166).

An additional explanation might be the status-driven need for the middle classes to define themselves against a working-class 'other'. This attitude is demonstrated to working-class female prostitutes, 'lower-class girls (who) might possess strong animal lusts natural to those of lesser intelligence'

(Thompson 1988, p. 257), who were contrasted with the purity of middle-class womanhood. The popular correlation between actress and prostitute retained its currency in this period, but actual prostitution among female performers seems to have been rare (Davis 1991, pp. 78–80). The Lord Chamberlain's office rarely concerned itself with matters of sexual impropriety in performance (Davis 2000, p. 117). However, there was, presumably, sufficient objection from some sectors of society to the types of operetta and burlesque performance in which female performance was characterised by scantiness of dress, and, in the case of some dance routines, sexual explicitness of posture and gesture, to warrant the popularity of 'respectable' entertainments, such as that provided by the German Reeds (see Chap. 3) and, of course, the D'Oyly Carte company.

Addressing the way in which Victorian ideologies concerning gender are reflected within the texts of the operas is problematic. Apart from the difficulty of dealing with (at least) 12 full-length texts within the restricted compass of this study—a corpus of work in which, according to Caroline Williams, gender is 'structurally fundamental' (2010, p. xiv)—there is the fact that *parody* of attitudes to gender roles and social decorum are often the stock-in-trade of these works. It is a complex matter to disentangle parodical criticism of Victorian attitudes from the notion that the caricature ultimately serves the purpose of *validating* such dominant beliefs. While it is possible from such in-depth research to conclude, as Williams does, that the operas can be understood as texts which often provide subversive readings of contemporary attitudes, the intention of the creators of these pieces was to provide commercially profitable entertainment which would appeal to their target audience through shared notions of what was socially and culturally acceptable. If, in the Savoy operas, Gilbert compromised the misanthropic view of social relations evident in some of his earlier works and presented an essentially conformist, bourgeois view of his world, it was because, from a pecuniary angle, he knew which side his bread was buttered. These caveats aside, I will attempt, in a necessarily limited fashion, to consider several instructive representations of gender relations and male and female behaviour in some of the operas.

Although one might expect to find a patriarchal world view underlying late-nineteenth-century popular entertainment aimed at the bourgeoisie, notions of conventional masculinity are sometimes held up to the same kind of mockery as unconventional female behaviour. Both aspects of Gilbert's parody are present in *Patience*. Masculine extremes are demonstrated by the bluff manliness of the Dragoon Guards as they emphasise their military prowess and boast about the 'pulling-power' of their uniform:

> When I first put this uniform on,
> I said, as I looked in the glass,
> 'It's one to a million
> That any civilian
> My figure and form will surpass' [...]
> I said, when I first put it on,
> 'It is plain to the veriest dunce,
> That every beauty
> Will feel it her duty
> To yield to its glamour at once.'
> (*Patience*, Act One)

Brash sexual self-assurance is contrasted with the ridiculousness of their subsequent attempts to emulate, in dress and posture, the posing of the artistically sensitive male. This figure, in the form of the aesthetic poet Reginald Bunthorne, is also rejected as an effeminate, hypocritical, self-serving outsider (Williams 2011, pp. 167–70). Existing as an independent female society, the 'lovesick maidens' in *Patience* free themselves from conventional dependence on men as providers or sexual partners by focusing their affection on the unattainable Bunthorne, and on emulating the trappings of the aesthetic movement. The pretentious absurdity of their conversational style and preoccupations conforms to 'the middlebrow appetite for ridicule of abnormal gender performance' also present in the popular, anti-aesthetic *Punch* cartoons of Gerald Du Maurier. Gilbert follows Du Maurier in presenting effeminate men and masculine women as preventing the 'normal' family relationships of the middle classes in their contravention of the conventional 'spheres' of domesticity and work.

Order is restored when Bunthorne's poetical rival, Archibald Grosvenor, reaffirms conformist masculinity by rejecting the pretentiousness of the 'Inner Brotherhood'. He reappears as a conformist city clerk—'a commonplace type/ with a stick and a pipe'—the kind of urban office worker who might have frequented the gallery or pit at the Opera Comique or Savoy theatres (*Patience*, Act Two). Similarly, the female chorus, who have rejected their former fiancés in order to become followers of the aesthetic movement, are shown to be happier enjoying a life of female consumerism, as, once their aesthetic idol has transformed, they revert to high-street fashions and conventional female behaviour: 'We're Swears and Wells young girls/ We're Madame Louise young girls/ We're prettily pattering, cheerily chattering, /Every-day young girls' (Act Two).

'Pattering' and 'chattering' choruses and songs are often used as a textual and musical method to characterise conventional youthful femininity, and are, according to Williams, 'ostentatiously feminine, for chatter [conveys] a gender-specific superficiality' (2011, p. 139). A typical example occurs in Act One of *The Pirates of Penzance*. When confronted with the socially embarrassing prospect of their sister Mabel engaged in a *tête-à-tête* with the handsome Frederic, the female chorus resort to the avoidance tactic of ignoring them completely and talking about the weather. The mechanical conventionality of this kind of feminine rectitude is demonstrated by the rhythm of Gilbert's deliberately inane lyric, and is perfectly underlined by Sullivan's metronomic musical setting:

How beautifully blue the sky,
The Glass is rising very high,
Continue fine I hope it may,
And yet it rained but yesterday.
Tomorrow it may rain again
(I hear the country wants some rain),
Yet people say, I know not why,
That we shall have a warm July.
(*The Pirates of Penzance*, Act One)

Gilbert actually calls this number the 'Chattering Chorus' in the libretto, and similar examples are to be found throughout the oeuvre, in *Patience* (as previously noted) and also in Act One of *The Mikado*. Here the chorus of schoolgirls also use 'chatter' to demonstrate an awareness of correct feminine conduct:

So please you, sir, we much regret.
If we have failed in etiquette
Towards a man of rank so high
We shall know better by and by.
But youth, of course, must have its fling,
So pardon us,
So pardon us,
And don't, in girlhood's happy spring,
Be hard on us,

Be hard on us,
If we're inclined to dance and sing.
Tra la la, etc. (*Dancing*.)
(*The Mikado*, Act One)

As in *Patience*, *Iolanthe* represents a female society which rejects male influence as socially unviable. Here, female 'chattering' is used to show that the
apparently independent females—in this case, a chorus of fairies—actually crave male company. While not possessing a rhythmically metronomic
lyric, the duet by the fairies Leila and Celia in Act Two of *Iolanthe*, in
which they simultaneously reject and desire the male aristocrats ('In Vain
to Us You Plead'), is underscored by a continuous, rapid, semi-quaver
violin accompaniment, which emulates the 'chattering' in musical form.

In vain to us you plead—
Don't go
Your prayers we do not heed—
Don't go!
It's true we sigh,
But don't suppose
A tearful eye
Forgiveness shows.
Oh, no!
We're very cross indeed—
Yes, very cross,
Don't go!
(*Iolanthe*, Act Two)

This number goes on to counterpoint, both textually and musically, an
entirely opposing set of sentiments, expressed by the male chorus:

Our disrespectful sneers,
Ha, ha!
Call forth indignant tears,
Ha, ha!
(*Iolanthe*, Act Two)

In doing so it provides an example of the most often employed method
used by the authors to present gender relations in the operas: the gender-
divided chorus (Williams 2011, pp. 17–23). Gilbert's desire to integrate
the chorus, which had previously been a musical necessity in grand opera,

and an opportunity for female display in burlesque, into the dramaturgical fabric of the operas resulted in a group who embody dramatic opposition. From the purely musical point of view, male and female voice types allowed for musical differentiation, and opportunities for vocalised counterpoint and conflict. There are many examples where melodically independent male and female vocal lines, expounding opposing opinions, are ingeniously combined by Sullivan to present a musical whole which nevertheless highlights opposition.[8]

These musical issues, together with the strong visual contrast of gender-specific costumes—often male uniforms of various types, contrasting with flowing gowns, or pretty daywear—and the dramatic techniques of introducing male and female choruses into the action separately, led to an existing gender divide being exploited as a device through which 'stereotypical masculine and feminine social positions, behaviours and points of view are structurally differentiated, opposed, related to one another and made available for critique' (Williams 2011, p. 19). It is in the earlier operas, which deal with specifically British issues, or at least those of contemporary topical interest, that this gender split is most pronounced. And while this divide is often the catalyst for dramatic conflict, it is always healed by the end of the opera. Just as social hierarchies are shown to be problematic but are finally accepted as inevitable in the Savoy operas, transgressive gender behaviour is explored, laughed at and replaced by the type of 'normality' most palatable to the target audience.[9]

Princess Ida demonstrates this pattern most effectively. Here the female community takes the form of a women's university, presided over by the eponymous princess, from which men are barred. The notion that women can benefit from higher education and should avoid their 'natural' function as wives and mothers is ridiculed. Admittedly, the deliberately remote fairytale setting somewhat mitigates the disdain for contravention of gender norms in late-Victorian society. But *Princess Ida* substantiates conformist gender as the demonstration of natural impulse, heterosexual desirability and the requirement for human procreation. This opera 'makes fun of the very idea that conventional gender norms could be changed or transcended [… it] justifies the reproduction of the status quo' (Williams 2011, p. 222). In Act Two the audience are presented with a female chorus who have deliberately shut themselves away from male intrusion. The use of conflicting gender groups and choruses is heightened by several male 'invasions' during the second and third acts, first by a group of young aristocrats who have come in search of Ida, then by the invading army of King Hildebrand.

In the end, Prince Hilarion obtains Ida (who was betrothed to him in childhood) by winning a duel. Ida voluntarily resigns her position to the ambitious, elderly Lady Blanche who can presumably no longer fulfil society's need for biological reproduction. Hilarion's final speech of persuasion to Ida manages to show her that mutually supportive female communities are doomed to fail, and returns her firmly to the domestic sphere. As a sort of chivalrous palliative, Hilarion reiterates the conventional notion of woman's (evangelically derived) moral and spiritual superiority to men:

> Madam, you placed your trust in Woman—well,
> Woman has failed you utterly—try Man,
> Give him one chance, it's only fair—besides,
> Women are far too precious, too divine,
> To try unproven theories upon.
> Experiments, the proverb says, are made
> On humble subjects—try our grosser clay,
> And mould it as you will!
> (*Princess Ida*, Act Three)

While conventional female social roles are endorsed within the operas, exaggerated examples of socially acceptable female behaviour are sometimes parodied. However, satire is not funny if its subject is irrelevant or passé. Although written at the latter end of the collaboration, when attitudes towards women's education and excessive social decorum were altering, Gilbert's send-up of 'proper' feminine behaviour in *Utopia, Limited* (1893) nevertheless indicates its cultural prevalence. Here, the archetypal English governess, Lady Sophy, a woman with 'Respectability enough for six' (Act One) is employed by the king of an exotic south-sea island to properly 'finish' his daughters in the decorous English manner. The princesses, Nekaya and Kalyba, sing:

> BOTH: Although of native maids the cream,
> We're brought up on the English scheme—
> The best of all
> For great and small
> Who modestly adore.
> NEKAYA: For English girls are good as gold,
> Extremely modest (so we're told),
> Demurely coy—divinely cold—
> And that we are—and more.
> (*Princess Ida*, Act One)

They subsequently provide a list of traits which typify polite English maidenhood. Carolyn Williams remarks how this behaviour is shown to be inculcated rather than instinctive, achieved through lessons which are self-consciously practised 'before the glass', and intended to disguise real feeling—'English Girls of well-bred notions/ shun all unrehearsed emotions' (*Utopia, Limited*, Act One). The artificiality of such polite female conduct is emphasised by the fact that it is only meaningful when performed to others (Williams 2011, pp. 339–40). This is exemplified on the island of Utopia, where decorous behaviour is turned into a conscious public display. The newly educated princesses declare that '[we] show ourselves to loud applause/from ten to four without a pause' (Act One).

If standardised behavioural codes are the subject of parody in *Utopia, Limited*, as they were in *The Pirates of Penzance* 14 years earlier, attitudes towards female education are no longer ridiculed to the extent they were in *Princess Ida*. In *Utopia*, the fact that Princess Zara has attended Girton College is not in itself the subject of satire. More worthy of comment is Zara's incarnation as the 'bright and beautiful English girl' who, in 1893, can hunt, swim and row, play cricket, tennis and golf. Female modesty, as exhibited by the injunctions of Lady Sophy, is challenged by this modern version of acceptable young womanhood. However, the fact that the 'hale and healthy' attributes of the prototypical 'new woman' are listed as attractive by a man, in the character of the financier Mr Goldbury, serves to quantify, objectivise and present them for an essentially male gaze. This young woman is presented as vigorously desirable, 'Her eyes a-dance, and her cheeks a-glowing—/ Down comes her hair, but what does she care?/ It's all her own and it's worth the showing' (*Utopia, Limited*, Act Two). By 1893, the trend towards sexual equality in terms of women's education, employment and independence had become a highly contentious issue. It is significant that young women in the operas generally display a non-threatening, pre-emancipation persona. When opposing traits are exhibited by the Aesthetic Maidens in *Patience* or by Princess Ida, normative roles are re-established at the end of the piece. In general, women who are powerful, or who aspire to power, are presented in the form of the contralto, 'older female' roles.

The archetypal example of objectified youthful femininity in the operas is Marco's song 'Take a Pair of Sparkling Eyes' from *The Gondoliers*. This supposed paean to female beauty describes desirable physical attributes in a style reminiscent of 'the manufacture and ownership of a man-made product' (Hayter 1987, p. 135).

> Take a pair of sparkling eyes,
> Hidden, ever and anon,
> In a merciful eclipse –
> Do not heed their mild surprise
> Having passed the Rubicon,
> Take a pair of rosy lips;
> Take a figure trimly planned –
> Such as admiration whets –
> (Be particular in this);
> Take a tender little hand,
> Fringed with dainty fingerettes,
> Press it—in parenthesis; –
> Ah! Take all these, you lucky man –
>
> (2001, pp. 925–6)

The eyes are sparkling, but demurely 'hidden', and surprised at the male gaze, rather than making full, overtly bold, contact. Lips and body are sexually desirable, while the 'tender, little' hand is fringed with 'dainty fingerettes', suggesting to Hayter 'a tablecloth in a linen shop [...] a gaudily decorated object'. As he goes on to remark, textually, musically and in terms of its placing within the action, this song is free from any hint of irony or parody (1987, p. 137). Examples like this and the previously mentioned *Utopia* song would indicate that the prevailing ideological stance encompassed in both the writing and the intended reception of the operas is essentially geared to the patriarchy. The assumption throughout is that while there is nothing in the operas to offend female sensibilities, while female characters are often afforded as much stage time as their male counterparts, and while overt display of lavish, colourful and fashionable costumes and decor are present to engage conventional female interest, the operas are emanations and reflections of a society in which the male viewpoint is *naturally* prioritised.

This is not to say that male characters are shown in a particularly complimentary light. Men are shown to be fallible and foolish throughout the Savoy operas. In *Princess Ida*, for example, King Gama is a grouchy misanthrope, King Hildebrand overbearing and bellicose. Cyril is a braggart, and Gama's three soldier sons typify the dim-witted, upper-class, military type:

We are warriors three,
Sons of Gama, Rex,
Like most sons are we,
Masculine in sex [...]

Politics we bar,
They are not our bent;
On the whole we are
Not intelligent [...]
(*Princess Ida*, Act One)

Satirical comedy in a male-run society allows the patriarchy to laugh convivially at its failings, while retaining its confidence in the continued existence of both its power and of the status quo in general. Women with conventional attitudes can rest assured that their world will not be turned upside down, or their fundamental values compromised. This is the tacit ideological stance of the Savoy works. It is not, however, necessarily that of their librettist.

Gilbert had previously dealt specifically with the 'Woman Question' in several 'Problem Plays', notably *Ought We to Visit Her?* and *Charity*, both of which premiered in 1874. *Charity* deals head on with the Victorian double standard of the 'ruined woman' who is vilified by society and the seducer who is let off. Here (in a storyline strangely reminiscent of Shaw's *Mrs Warren's Profession*), the ex-courtesan Mrs Van Brugh is transformed into an entirely sympathetic character, a worker for the rehabilitation of fallen women, who is blackmailed by the father of her future son-in-law (Stedman 1996, pp. 114–17), but who survives to start a new life. *Ought We to Visit Her?* attacks conventional 'respectable' attitudes towards the figure of the actress, showing its heroine, the 'bright, natural, spontaneous' actress Jane Theobald (Stedman 1996, p. 119) to be the victim of 'middle-class' hypocrisy. Neither play was well received by critics. Gilbert was criticised for letting Mrs Van Brugh go unpunished in *Charity*,[10] and *Ought We to Visit Her* was considered to be 'a little too strongly flavoured for English taste' and 'not very healthy'.[11]

I am presenting this short digression on two of Gilbert's non-musical texts to suggest that the ideological position of the Savoy operas, particularly regarding the depiction of women, was, in the light of Gilbert's earlier work, adapted to suit the type of piece he was writing. It was in turn therefore also suited to the preoccupations of the affluent middle-class patronage envisaged (and achieved) by the triumvirate. The 'Problem Play' was one kind of genre, the comic opera something very different; and in a profit-driven theatrical marketplace, Gilbert seems to have suited his ideological stance to the kind of audience he was writing for. Popular 'middle-class' theatre needed to cater for the attitudes of spectators who, at least when attending the Savoy, required an experience which verified, rather than challenged, their value system. The following chapters will discuss ways in which managements responded to the middle-class West End audience, but it is worth reiterating the fact that the D'Oyly Carte enterprise was entirely commercially based. Artistic standards in terms of writing, production and performance were of the highest—certainly in the field of the musical stage—but then, as Chapter 4 will demonstrate, so were the front of house facilities and the decoration of the foyer and auditorium. The ideology of the operas was therefore inextricably linked with their marketability. And commercial and public success was the motivating factor behind Victorian entrepreneurship in the theatre, and in the wider business world.

ENTREPRENEURSHIP AND PROFESSIONALISM

Contemporary comment demonstrates how the attainment of personal wealth and the visible trappings of social status were closely entwined in the Victorian 'middle-class' mentality to represent superiority—in terms not only of personal ability and achievement (attaining a remunerative position, supporting a family in comfort, pursuing a comfortable domestic life), but also as a demonstration of *moral* pre-eminence. In such an environment, the middle-class capitalist entrepreneur was seen as the 'lynchpin of society [...] the impresario, the creative force, the initiator of the economic cycle. He it was who conceived the end, found the means, bore the burden of risk and paid out the other factors of production' (Stone 2001, p. 222). His success in the struggle for survival in the competitive marketplace could receive approbation which assumed a quasi-religious significance:

> We have begun to think that men who make their way to the front, becoming rich or famous by the force of their personal characters, must, after all have something in them [...] To honour what has won success is worthy worship not to be condemned or restrained. It is veneration for that type of

manhood, which most nearly approaches the divine, by reason of its creative energy. [12]

In a society which considered reliance on charity as immoral unless circumstances made it absolutely essential, a dedication to hard work (and, by implication, the benefits it provided) could translate human acquisitiveness and the pursuit of status into a spiritual duty. By the latter part of the century, the increasingly influential 'Social Darwinist' view of a societal order in which only the strong succeed rendered those unable to support themselves as biologically, as well as morally, inferior (Stone and Stone 1984, p. 280). Those who, through innate ability and hard work, attained some degree of wealth and position were, in this view, inherently superior to those whose position remained static, or declined into financial dependence. 'Removable inequality', the notion that, in an evidently unequal social order, gifted and industrious individuals might surmount 'natural' disparities of birth, was essential to this outlook. The idea that it was possible to advance through the established social hierarchy, set forth as doctrine by Samuel Smiles in his best-seller *Self Help* (1859), meant that middle-class status was theoretically available to those who pursued it with enough energy. Ambition, or lack of it, became a marker of social worthiness. Hard work and respectable behaviour engendered financial and social advancement across the social spectrum, and generated a desire to disassociate oneself from those who did not, or could not do the same. The urge towards social and economic advancement can be observed in the working and public lives of theatre practitioners in this period, and their relationship to the work of the D'Oyly Carte organisation will inform the central arguments of Chaps. 4 and 5.

Most pertinent to the discussion of theatre makers and practitioners in this period is the increase in numbers and status of the professional segment of the bourgeoisie. Urbanisation, industrialisation and the rise in living standards caused an enlargement of the white-collar sector, and 'doctors, lawyers, writers and even the clergy found an enlarged demand for their services' (Perkin 1969, p. 254). The civil service expanded hugely in response to governmental reform and the extension of empire. Professional associations, such as the Law Society and the Royal College of Surgeons (founded in 1825 and 1800 respectively), enhanced the social respectability of professional occupations through increased regulation of entry and conduct.

In relation to the 'professionalisation' of the theatre, the passing of the Theatre Regulation Act of 1843 removed the originally 'royal' monopoly of the patent houses, Covent Garden and Drury Lane, in the provision of 'legitimate' drama. Jacky Bratton convincingly presents this event as a specifically middle-class attempt to 'gentrify' the theatre. She argues that a professed resuscitation of the supposed 'great tradition' of English theatre and a reversal of the perceived 'decline in the drama' in fact wrested power from controlling theatrical dynasties and replaced them with specifically 'middle class', and thereby professionalised, authors. Bratton draws a parallel here with the apparent rise in status of the middle classes following the passing of the Parliamentary Reform Act in 1832. She explains the attempts of the primary driving force in the agitation for the 1843 Act, the novelist Edward Bulwer Lytton and his followers, as the newly confident 'middle-classes' demonstrating their influence in the world of the arts as well as that of national politics (Bratton 2003, pp. 67–70, 88–91).

As the century wore on, this movement encompassed a desire by theatre practitioners to join the ranks of professional and entrepreneurial society, as managers and leading performers attempted to raise the public acceptability of their work. On a more mundane though socially advantageous level, it also encouraged them to participate in such status-affirming activities as membership of gentlemen's clubs and active involvement in the genteel sports—golf and cricket (Sanderson 1984, pp. 136–45).[13] By the end of the century, the West End was dominated by an elite coterie of socially aspirational male actor-managers, authors and entrepreneurs, some of whom had received knighthoods and most of whom adopted fashionable lifestyles (Pick 1983, p.103). In a society which valued affluence as a sign of importance, the achievement of social status could be seen as a valuable by-product of the fundamental impetus to increase revenue and personal wealth. On their retirement from performance and production at the Prince of Wales and Haymarket theatres in 1885, the Bancrofts had amassed a net personal profit of £180,000 (Pick 1983, p. 55). But only *after* Henry Irving's knighthood in 1895 had established the public respectability of the theatre practitioner could Squire Bancroft's high social credentials be similarly honoured, and his position in society ultimately validated with a knighthood.

Public honours exemplified the desire of theatre people to enhance their standing in a milieu in which the respectable professional individual was accorded high social status. They could now assume an equal position with the self-confidently professionalised 'lawyers, doctors, public officials, journalists, professors' who no doubt constituted a significant proportion of a typical

West End audience. 'Respectability was the conscious aim of the "gentleman practitioners"' (Stone and Stone 1984, p. 252). Both Gilbert's rise from civil service clerk to estate owner, and Sullivan's transition from Lambeth terrace to honoured guest of European royalty, exemplified the journey of those practitioners who managed to attain, through talent, industry and ambition, the high levels of wealth and status enjoyed by the more privileged members of their audiences. Although thoroughly middle class (both were university-educated), Gilbert and Carte had to work extremely hard to attain the level of wealth and fame both enjoyed at the end of their careers. Carte's eventual business empire, which included the proprietorship of hotels and restaurants, as well as entertainment venues, could not have been a foregone conclusion to the 33-year-old theatrical agent who, in 1877, struggled to set up a theatre company to present a Gilbert and Sullivan opera.[14]

While entrepreneurs and successful creative artistes could attain wealth and public honour, performers often had to be content with lower wages and less social recognition (Sanderson 1984, p. 80). Although a very few women could make as much money as men in the theatrical profession (Davis 1991, p. 24), the dubious status of the actress delayed the public appreciation and financial remuneration accorded their male counterparts. Nevertheless, upward mobility was always a possibility. The Savoy stars George Grossmith, Rutland Barrington and Jessie Bond rose to fame within the ranks of the company and, in the cases of Bond and Grossmith, achieved levels of personal wealth characteristic of the upper middle classes.

Avoidance of the stigma of poverty may well have been a strong motivational factor in the attitude to hard work, financial aggrandisement and self-betterment apparent in the working lives of Grossmith and Bond. It certainly explains the prodigious amount of outside performance and compositional work undertaken, particularly by Grossmith, to supplement his D'Oyly Carte earnings (Joseph 1982, pp. 117–19). The absence of a national old-age pension or sickness and unemployment insurance meant that 'the aged or unemployed actor whose earnings had been too low to permit adequate saving was often forced into destitution' (Sanderson 1984, p. 86).[15]

All three of the aforementioned Savoy artists recorded their experiences in autobiographical form and, despite the diverting and anecdotal nature of their respective memoirs, the pursuit of money and status is often implicit. Grossmith and Barrington criticise Carte's close dealing and apparent parsimony in matters of salary. Both were writing when future employment in the company remained possible, so criticism is tempered by affable jocularity. Barrington ironically describes how he 'made the initial success of [his] career in one of the most important parts in a comic opera for the stupendous stipend of £6 per week' (Barrington 1908, p. 13). Grossmith's account of how some fine dining '*a la* Carte' persuaded him to drop his initial fee by three guineas a week ends with the wry observation: 'I calculate that, irrespective of all accumulative interest, that lunch cost me, up till now, about £1800' (Grossmith 1888, p. 90). Jessie Bond, writing more candidly from a safe distance of 40 years, recounts every pay rise received during her Savoy tenure as a personal triumph of ambitious perspicacity against the odds (Bond 1930, pp. 91–2). She frequently asserts her devotion to 'hard work and ceaseless effort' (pp. 61, 79, 138) as a self-justifying mark of propriety in an age in which 'respectability' and 'actress' were often seen as contradictory terms.

SUMMARY

The need to appeal to 'respectable' values and to preserve social boundaries between those who were respectable and those who were not can be seen as motivating factors in the provision of certain types of 'middle-class' theatrical production in the West End in the mid to late nineteenth century. The middle classes were a broad grouping whose unity could be defined both in economic terms, and as a sector whose identity was created by a commonly held ideology. This ideology became integral to the texts of the Savoy operas, though not in a simplistically representational form. Though consisting of parody based on criticism of societal and cultural norms, the operas ultimately validate the standards which are being lampooned. They achieve this as performance texts, because they are, from the commercial point of view, as bound up with the prevailing need of their creators to achieve money and status (in itself a manifestation of the bourgeois ideology of the moral validity of entrepreneurship) as they are with not disturbing the ideological preconceptions of their relatively affluent target audience.

Chapter 3 will develop this argument by bringing its implications to bear more closely on the material aspects of the production and reception of popular West End musical theatre performance in the period leading up to, and including, the first Gilbert/Sullivan/Carte collaborations. How did Carte's company, its audience, and the kind of entertainment it offered, develop from a milieu inculcated with 'middle-class' values?

NOTES

1. Mason (1994) expresses some criticism of Booth's findings, but the questionable areas concern the unskilled and semi-skilled sectors, rather than the middle-class sectors, which are my focus here. Mason's comment that Booth's 'scheme has stood the test of time', as well as its use by Best (1971) and Perkin (1969) to inform their work on nineteenth-century social structure, would appear to validate its use.

2. WSG, interviewed 1889, mentions the Savoy chorus: 'Many of them have been with us for twelve years, getting salaries at the rate of £85 a year, and working for themselves in the day' (*Era*, 12 July 1889).

3. AS to Clementina Sullivan, 20 December 1897. Cited in Jacobs (1986, p. 135).

4. Gilbert's spiky early journalism for *Fun* (a more subversive alternative to *Punch*), the ironic social criticism implicit in plays such as *An Old Score* (1869), *Charity* (1874) and *Engaged* (1877), the pungent political satire which caused *The Happy Land* (1873) to be banned by the Lord Chamberlain's office, and the prescient social realism of his final short play, *The Hooligan* (1911), would suggest that the satirical content of the Savoy operas, though certainly true to some aspects of the author's world view, was constructed with the specific intention of satisfying conventional bourgeois sensibilities. The less comfortable depictions of human nature exhibited in the play texts named above received some critical censure, and were less remunerative than the Savoy works. For a discussion of these texts in relation to their reception and to WSG's creative personality, see Crowther (2011, pp. 78–108, 130–3, 231–2, and Chap. 4).

5. Perkin, using the triadic model of three classes, imagined as 'horizontal' strata, one on top of the other, envisages these antagonisms as 'vertical' social divisions, cutting through each class layer (1989, pp. 62–84).

6. 'A word of Scandinavian origin, meaning slender, slim, graceful or neat' (Bradley 2001, p. 888).

7. *Topical Times*, December 1889.

8. Opposing double choruses are often to be found when major dramatic conflicts come to a head. A striking example occurs at such a point in *Patience*, where the love-struck maidens lament Bunthorne's forthcoming marriage, while their former fiancés, the Dragoons, express their outrage at the turn of events. Both sing completely different but intersecting melodic lines. In Act Two of *Pirates*, the convention is used for comic effect when the heroic female melody, intended to inspire the unwilling policemen to confront the approaching pirates, contrasts ironically with the plodding reticence of the policemen themselves.

9. An exception to this might be *Iolanthe*, in which the male peers sprout wings, are turned into fairies and are whisked off to fairyland. However, crucially, it is the female fairies that in the end compromise the rules of their society and embrace supposedly 'natural' female inclinations by accepting male partners.

10. *Era*, 25 January 1874.

11. *Era*, 25 January 1874.

12. Kaye, W. (1860). *The Cornhill Magazine*, Vol. 2, pp. 7, 729.

13. WSG was a member of the Junior Carlton and Garrick Clubs (Stedman 1996, p. 365), as well as being a keen yachtsman. Rutland Barrington makes frequent mention of his sporting prowess playing for various 'theatrical' teams, and D'Oyly Carte touring companies regularly played teams from other organisations (Joseph 1994, pp. 99–100).

14. WSG's estate was worth £111,971 at his death. AS's, depleted by gambling losses and the continual support of his dead brother's family, was valued at £56,536. RDC, whose business interests were more extensive than those of his Savoy colleagues, left £240,817 (Ainger 2002, pp. 391–2, 443). AS and WSG received knighthoods, in 1883 and 1907 respectively.

15. Despite the existence of the Royal General Theatrical Fund, a private insurance scheme founded in 1839, many artists did not avoid the disgrace of penury (Sanderson 1984, pp. 87–90). Rutland Barrington was such a one. He suffered a paralytic stroke in 1919, and died penniless in Battersea Workhouse infirmary in 1922. His previously unmarked pauper's grave in Morden cemetery was provided with a headstone funded by private donations in 1997 (Walters 1998, p. 19).

CHAPTER 3

The West End: 'Middle-Class' Values and Commercialisation

Starting with *The Sorcerer* in 1877, Richard D'Oyly Carte's bold attempt to create a new form of mainstream entertainment which would appeal to an upscale, 'respectable' clientele was typical of the vibrant, expansionist theatrical environment which had emerged in the West End of London in the second half of the nineteenth century. It coincided with the mid-century economic upturn, from which the middle classes 'reaped most of the benefits of national affluence and bestowed their favours upon the West End' (Booth 1991, p. 3). An increase in potential audience figures resulting from the expansion of London's population from 1,949,000 to 2,808,000 between 1841 and 1861 (Best 1971, p. 7), combined with an apparent relaxation of anti-theatrical prejudice and restrictive attitudes towards the general enjoyment of leisure (Bailey 1998, pp. 13–15), encouraged the refashioning of the West End in the 1850s and 1860s. This period witnessed deliberate attempts by certain managements to attract a specifically 'middle-class' patronage by providing a particular type of theatre experience which accorded with bourgeois tastes and preoccupations.

The West End was transformed into a distinctively 'middle-class' commercialised entertainment area, and it is in this context that the financial viability and popularity of the Gilbert and Sullivan operas among the 'middle-classes' can be explained. The ideology of respectability underpinned this commercial and stylistic innovation. The realisation that, if presented with a theatre experience appropriate to their tastes, 'respectable' patrons could form a large and profitable audience sector inspired

© The Author(s) 2016
M. Goron, *Gilbert and Sullivan's 'Respectable Capers'*, Palgrave Studies in British Musical Theatre, DOI 10.1057/978-1-137-59478-5_3

managers, writers and composers to cater for such consumers. At the same time, a drive towards respectability, social acceptability and recognition, on the part of the theatre makers themselves, provided a concurrent stimulus for change in the West End. This can be seen as a dual response to the dominant cultural ideology, one which both reflected and reaffirmed it. This chapter will explore ways in which some aspirational theatre practitioners geared their musical theatre output, and their commercial thinking, towards a specifically 'respectable' market, and locate the work of the Savoy Triumvirate in this changing environment.

REMAKING THE WEST END

In the second half of the nineteenth century, London's West End was redeveloped as an 'enterprise zone' which successfully transformed itself in order to profit from alterations in audience habits which were themselves the result of social and economic change. Crucially, it became an entertainment area which specifically sought to attract its key audience from outside its immediate environs, becoming a location devoted to what is aptly described as 'theatrical tourism' (Davis and Emeljanow 2001, p. 170). The transition encompassed the change from a downturn, characterised by dwindling audiences and a resultant stultification in theatre-building in the 1840s (Booth 1991, p. 7), to the booming theatrical marketplace of the 1880s. Nine new theatres were built between 1866 and 1881, the year in which Carte's Savoy Theatre was opened, in an area which by 1874 could accommodate nearly 29,000 spectators nightly (Davis and Emeljanow 2001, p. 273). The West End notionally encompassed 'all the areas of London immediately to the west of Temple Bar and the City, bounded by the Thames to the south and Oxford Street to the north' (Davis and Emeljanow 2001, p. 167). But as John Pick remarks, the 'West End' was more 'an amalgam of fashionable London conventions [... than] a particular locality' (1983, p. 22), emphasising its function, by the 1870s, as locus for visiting pleasure seekers with money as well as time to spare. It became a bourgeois playground offering opportunities for personal display and conspicuous consumption, with theatrical entertainment as its defining feature. While acknowledging the materiality of the West End, Jacky Bratton rightly goes further by emphasising it as an imaginary construct: 'an idea about a space, the special and elusive place that is the goal of dreams and pleasure, of admission or exclusion' (Bratton 2011, p. 86). Certainly, part of the West End's allure was an imaginative amalgam of the multifarious entertainments, sights, sounds and smells, in the minds of its prospective visitors. But these visitors were primarily consumers, and the respectable middle classes were, in the middle of the century, a relatively untapped commercial source.

Davis and Emeljanow describe a deliberate and renewed commercialisation of the West End in the latter half of the century. They regard it as a response to the vast success of the Great Exhibition of 1851, which proved that a centralised collection of attractions could exert a pull on the newly suburbanised middle classes. The 1843 Theatre Regulations Act had removed the restrictions on performance of the spoken drama in the capital, attracting localised and socially diverse London audiences to local neighbourhood theatres. Consequently, West End managers realised that:

> the success of the West End might depend upon the recognition that perhaps the decrease in regular playgoers could be offset by turning the West End itself into an elaborate theme park, whose uniqueness might attract a body of visitors from other places.
>
> (Davis and Emeljanow 2001, p.173)

The existing infrastructure of restaurants and bars, together with the secure and convenient access provided by improved and redeveloped road and rail networks, established the West End as a destination which had unique appeal to a largely suburbanised 'middle-class' audience.

Re-evaluation of repertoire and refashioning of theatres into locations suited to upscale patronage is typified by the work of the actor-managers Sir Squire and Lady Marie Bancroft [nee Wilton] (Pick 1983, pp. 45–60; Rowell 1979, pp. 52–5), although this process was already underway when Marie Wilton became the lessee of the Queen's Theatre in 1865. It had been both preceded and accompanied by similar attempts at attracting a specifically affluent (but perhaps less 'respectable') audience by other managements, notably that of Madame Vestris at the Olympic in the 1830s (Bratton 2011, p. 205; Davis and Emeljanow 2001, p. 159). The commercial ambitions of the Bancrofts and other bourgeois theatrical entrepreneurs, rather than some kind of inevitable 'triumph' of the cultural values of the respectable classes, was the driving force in the shift of custom in the West End towards the affluent. Marie Wilton's business model, summarised by Tracy C. Davis as an attempt to enhance productivity by [...] increasing the up front investment while improving the cost ratio through longer runs [and] targeting a small but higher-paying audience during an economic boom time

(Davis 2000, p. 283)

became a method of working which characterised much West End theatre production during the last four decades of the century. The new phenomenon of the long run started with the staging of *Our American Cousin* at the Prince of Wales in 1861. It relied for its success on the kind of high production values offered by the Bancrofts and later by the Gilbert and Sullivan collaboration, enabling managements to recoup a far larger return for their original investment. A lavishness of staging and internal decor was necessary to provide an additional level of attraction to audiences by venues which no longer offered a high turnover of repertoire. The resultant increase in production expenses was easily offset by such practical savings as the removal of the storage of large stocks of scenery and, crucially, the exploitation of a single (or, in the case of Gilbert and Sullivan, a series of) highly successful show(s). Fewer scripts required less research and development expenditure, although the initial gamble on finding the most commercially viable creative input was potentially hazardous (Davis 2000, p. 213).

Carte was willing to accept just such a calculated risk with Gilbert and Sullivan as his collaborators. He had previously worked with them on the hugely popular one-act afterpiece *Trial by Jury*, while acting as theatre manager for Selina Delaro at the Royalty Theatre in 1875, and his initial speculation in their ability to provide the right product proved to be amply justified. A popular product combined with a business model derived from the successfully fashionable world of the Prince of Wales Theatre underpinned Carte's managerial policies. An organisation which followed such methods and aligned its repertoire with the tastes of a respectable, middle-class audience could achieve not only artistic acclaim but also substantial financial rewards. It could also help ensure the social advancement of its managers and creators, particularly if those individuals were publicly visible in creative, as well as administrative, capacities: for example, the Bancrofts as star performers, and Gilbert and Sullivan as a newsworthy creative team.

In order to achieve commercial and social advantage, certain West End managements began to direct both their output and facilities in terms of decor, dining and overall comfort, to a specifically well-heeled audience. Representative evidence is provided by the content of theatre programmes,

which by the 1870s had become a widely employed vehicle for mass advertising. The Savoy programmes of the 1880s feature a varied selection of
advertisements for Liberty fabrics, private banks and brokers, and expensive
couture, all of which attest to the expected purchasing ability of at least
some sections of the audience. Similar evidence predates the inception of
the Triumvirate at the Savoy. A Gaiety programme for the first Gilbert
and Sullivan collaboration, *Thespis*, in February 1872 contains a half-page
advertisement for the theatre's '[s]pacious dining and supper saloons'
offering 'English, French and German Cuisine' and 'choice wine of the
finest vintages' (Sands 2014).

The presence of consumers such as these can also be ascribed to
changes in middle-class leisure habits around the middle of the nineteenth
century. Anti-theatrical prejudice, which saw 'the social institution' of
theatre-going as 'a standing encouragement to the waste of scarce money
on frivolities, and to promiscuous socializing in bad company' (Barker
1985, p. 26), was undoubtedly present in the 'middle-class' consciousness. However, there does not appear to have been a wholesale rejection
of theatre-going by those who considered themselves respectable, even in
the more austere moral climate of provincial towns and cities. The annual
public denunciations of theatre-going by the Sheffield Anglican clergyman
Thomas Best, preached between 1817 and 1864 (Barker 1985, p. 26),
were presumably motivated by unwelcome levels of theatrical attendance
among his parishioners. Queen Victoria, the contemporary embodiment
of wholesome domesticity, was a regular theatre visitor in the 1850s, and
her attendance at the public playhouse, accompanied by husband and children, undoubtedly heightened the respectability of theatre-going (Schoch
2004, pp. 339–40).

The so-called 'fast'[1] 1860s saw the 'middle-classes', and in particular
the children of those who had prospered in the early part of the century,[2]
loosening the fetters of early-Victorian self-denial. They began to embrace
the pursuits which an overall upsurge in national prosperity, described
by Harold Perkin as 'a shift of income towards the wealthy' (Perkin
1969, p. 418), allowed them to enjoy. According to F.M.L. Thompson,
this phenomenon became increasingly marked in succeeding years. The
'middle classes in the age of Gilbert and Sullivan [...] had shed the husk
of earnestness and self righteousness and had embraced the notion of
fun, its pursuit constrained by strict adherence to the secular rules of
etiquette governing social relationships rather than by religious scruples'
(1988, p. 260).

The fact that newspapers and religious organisations were debating the proper use of recreational time for all classes is an indicator of its increased availability and, for the middle classes especially, demonstrates the emergence of leisure pursuits from the domestic sphere into the world of public entertainment (Bailey 1998, pp. 16–26). The early- and mid-Victorian cult of domesticity encouraged 'God fearing, middle class families [...] to internalize relaxation and pleasures and to regard permissible outside activities as matters of moral duty, not enjoyment' (Thompson 1988, p. 254). It appears to have been replaced by the 1870s by a notion of leisure which made its pursuit *outside* the home socially acceptable, if properly conducted in appropriate locations. The commercial development of an upmarket and relatively expensive West End during this period would have abetted the maintenance of a status-driven, middle-class exclusivity in terms of 'etiquette' and 'social relationships' in the leisure activity of theatre-going. It would also strongly indicate a direct entrepreneurial response to these growing consumer requirements.

The success of the West End was assisted by the development and expansion of both national railway systems and London's transport infrastructure, which allowed rapid and convenient rail travel from the suburbs into the centre, and provided a network of bus and cab services from railway termini to theatres (Booth 1991, p.14). The relative improvement in social conditions which in part rendered the West End attractive to suburbanites was part of an extensive 'social cleansing of inner London' involving massive slum clearances and street improvement which occurred from the middle to the end of the century (White 2008, pp. 59–9). Public safety was improved, and gas street lighting was universal by 1842. Performance licenses for venues offering 'sexualised, late night kind of entertainment', such as the Coal Hole in the Strand, were revoked (Bratton 2011, p. 59), and disreputable areas within the theatre-going district, such as the Haymarket, were subject to 'clean-up' operations in which public locations where the sex trade flourished were systematically removed (White 2008, pp. 22, 302–4).

Thus, by the time Gilbert and Sullivan began to collaborate under Carte's auspices, the West End offered a theatre-going experience which could appeal to a respectable public. This grouping became well catered for in terms of the accessibility and type of entertainment on offer. It was provided in venues situated in relatively secure surroundings, which reflected the degree of luxury and service which such patrons would expect to find in their own homes. This is not to say that all West End theatres were geared to a specific and fixed patronage, but an amount of product specialisation was essential to securing a share of available custom. In terms of the popular musical stage, burlesque at the Strand and the Gaiety, risqué *opéra bouffe* at the Globe, and the witty but chaste entertainments on offer at the Royal Gallery of Illustration, would appeal to different and overlapping sectors of the available audience. Internal improvements in these theatres, in terms of comfort and decor, newly available advance booking systems and the presence of well-mannered, formally attired front of house staff, indicate the extent to which a prosperous clientele was being sought.

John Pick provides convincing evidence to support the notion that, as part of this process, higher income custom was courted at the expense of the working classes, who were actively priced out of West End theatre through managerial desire to increase profits (Pick 1983, pp. 81–5). The disappearance of 'half price' theatre admittance after nine o'clock at night, which had accommodated the longer working hours of the 'lower orders', when an afterpiece would be played which could appeal to a broader, popular trade, again signifies a movement towards targeting more affluent audiences. A show (such as a typical Savoy programme of the 1880s) normally containing one, or at the most two pieces—generally a two-act entertainment, preceded by a short 'curtain raiser'—started at half past seven or eight and was down by ten-thirty or eleven. It would conform to the practical requirements of professional men and employees whose office hours terminated at five or six, but who needed to be back at their desks by ten the following morning.

Similarly, the increasing prevalence of advance booking discriminated against those working-class clients whose long working day prevented them from reaching booking offices open during office hours (Pick 1983, p. 81). A gradual reduction or eradication in some fashionable theatres (such as the Haymarket) of unreserved, low-priced seating available on the day of the performance further enhanced the social exclusivity of the West End. Daytime performances could only be attended by those not engaged in daytime employment. According to Gaiety manager John Hollingshead, the recently established provision of matinees attracted the 'decorous suburban [...] invalids of both sexes [...] parsons and players, severely devout spinsters, superior men, and strong minded women [...] the London lounger and the country cousin' (1877, p. 275). This group could include those free of work in the afternoon who could afford the travel and admission costs of a West End theatre trip. Hollingshead asserts the attractions of the matinee for those 'who never go to the theatre in principle, but [...] occasionally make an exception in favour of afternoon performances' (p. 275), a numerous group according to the author, and undoubtedly the 'respectable' patrons sought by Carte. Hollingshead's 'strong minded women' were most probably those unchaperoned, middle-class women revelling in the newly liberating experience of combining department-store shopping with an afternoon at the theatre—likely customers for the respectable and stylish Savoy entertainments.

REMARKETING THE MUSICAL STAGE: THE SAVOY OPERAS

In order to attract such patronage, the Savoy Triumvirate faced the task of reinventing and remarketing the musical stage, with its associations of low-art 'popular' entertainment and salaciousness, into something which accorded with the core values of the target audience. In 1877 the West End offered various forms of musical theatre entertainment which combined solo and ensemble musical numbers interspersed with spoken dialogue. Foremost among these was the burlesque, a popular form which provided comical parodies of literary works, legitimate drama and opera. Burlesque was a topical, boisterous and irreverent entertainment combining an 'up-front' performance style with opportunities for individual 'gagging' (Schoch 2003, pp. xxx–xxi). It was a heterogeneous mixture of 'singing, and dancing, and acting, and personal beauty, and puns and gauzy nymphs, and nigger [sic] melodies, and classic fables and apt allusions, and coloured fire all at once'[3] (cited in Booth 1991, p. 197). Its reputation for salaciousness was the result partly of cross-gender performance, with performers such as the Gaiety's Nellie Farren playing breeches roles in tight bodices and close-fitting tights, and partly the revealing costumes of the chorus dancers (Davis 1991, pp. 108–12). This kind of female display became a major attraction of the late-nineteenth-century burlesque, a 'debased' form in which parody and satire had given way to 'semi-obscene dances ... performed by jiggling hussies' (Schoch 2003, p. xxxix). However, such attractions appear to have been integral to the genre, albeit less prominently, from the early nineteenth century onwards (Schoch 2004, p. xxxvi). Female display would have provided an additional appeal to burlesque's predominantly masculine audience, drawn from the single young 'men about town' who had 'professional careers, disposable incomes, leisure time, and few domestic responsibilities' (Schoch 2003, p. xxxiv) and were sufficiently educated to appreciate burlesque's literary and theatrical allusions, and punning wordplay.

The raffishness and masculine appeal of these performances was emphasised by the positioning of the principal West End burlesque houses, the Olympic, Adelphi, Strand and Gaiety, towards the eastern end of the Strand, close to Holywell and Wych Streets, the primary location of the London pornographic book and print trade. This atmosphere no doubt contributed to the critical reception of burlesque, which was generally patronising, acknowledging its popularity, while lamenting its general vulgarity and lack of aesthetic taste:

> Let any one [...] ask himself if they are exhibitions which he can with propriety take any woman or child to witness. The sickening vulgarity of the jokes, the slang allusions ... the ridicule of associations which are all but sacred, the outrageous caricature of grave passions ... above all the way in which young actresses are made to say and do things which must destroy every shred of modesty and feminine grace in them make these burlesques pernicious alike to performers and audience.[4]

French operetta, imported during the 1860s and 1870s, was similarly popular, especially in the form of Offenbach's lively *opéra bouffe*, which debunked mythological or literary subjects with boulevard irreverence. Like burlesque, operetta drew criticism for its immorality of tone and daring dance routines (Oost 2009, p. 48). However, it is important to note that condemnation was not the universal reception of works of this sort. When Hortense Schneider danced the *cancan* in Offenbach's *Orphée aux enfers* in 1866, the *Daily Telegraph* reported that 'the delight of the audience knew no bounds, and the reviled dance was repeated amid frantic applause'.[5] There was clearly a public interest in this kind of show as both operetta and burlesque performance ran concurrently with the Savoy pieces until the end of the century.

But for the growing middle-class family audience, the underlying sexuality of such performance was unacceptable and Gilbert (and, by implication, his impresario, Carte) regarded their success as evidence of this trend. Gilbert noted in 1885 that 'we have enjoyed good fortune far above any achieved by *opéra bouffe* or burlesque without the adventitious aid of sprawling females in indecent costumes'. The concomitant embourgeoisement of the acting profession prompted Gilbert to continue in a similar vein. 'What has been the result of the semi-nude burlesque? No genuine comedy actress will appear in it [...]. Now, a comedy actress bars burlesque by the terms of her engagement.'[6] Astute performers and managements had, for some time, realised that there was also a market for a type of performance which contrasted markedly in content with burlesque and operetta, and which might appeal to a different and possibly unexploited audience. From the mid 1850s, solo 'entertainers' offered programmes specifically geared to respectable tastes. They contained comic songs, monologues and 'personations' in the semblance of gentlefolk entertaining their guests 'at home', rather than as 'that unacceptable creature, an actor' in a 'theatre' (Bratton 2011, p. 64).

In a similar vein, but on a larger, though still relatively intimate, scale, the German Reeds and the Howard Pauls presented 'entertainments' which offered some of the wit, musical verve and topicality of burlesque and operetta while eschewing the elements likely to deter an audience concerned with preserving a respectable image. The apparently cosy domesticity of these husband-and-wife pairings was justified by Reed's euphemistic camouflaging of the 'theatrical' nature of his establishment by calling it the 'Royal Gallery of Illustration' in which he presented 'illustration(s) of character from real life' rather than burlesques or operettas. This was more than an attempt to appeal to an audience whose morals might be affronted by the sight of scantily clad ballet girls. Reed's marketing strategy, based primarily on the language used to describe his venue in press advertisements, offered an exclusive type of entertainment, which, despite modest admission prices,[7] might actively *deter* a clientele not willing to conform to 'middle-class' standards. *Cruchley's London in 1865: A Handbook for Strangers* (Jackson 2001) described the Gallery as 'one of the most popular and fashionable places of recreation in the Metropolis'. Use of the terms 'fashionable' and 'recreation' are significant. The Prince of Wales Theatre is similarly described, in *Dickens's Dictionary of London, 1879* (Jackson 2001), as 'one of the most fashionable theatres in London [...] Evening dress is not *de rigueur* in the stalls, but it is usual here' (i.e. in the stalls). The Bancrofts presented their theatre as a destination for well-heeled, middle-class clientele, the same well-dressed, 'fashionable' audience who might have patronised Reed's Gallery. 'Recreation' implies a specifically 'middle-class' view of leisure which stressed its worth 'as an adjunct to work', enabling the conscientious worker to 're-create' himself in preparation for another day's worthwhile effort (Bailey 1998, p. 23).

Significantly, the general premise behind these shows was the pretence that the artists were essentially portraying *themselves*—respectably behaved and attired members of the bourgeoisie—in fictionalised comic situations. Audiences began to identify with the performers and returned often to see their favourites, creating a 'fan base' which was in turn fostered by a self-referential style within the dramatic writing of these pieces (Bratton 2011, p. 77). The influence of these 'entertainments' on the Savoy operas has often been stated (Hayter 1987, pp. 29–31; Wilson 1989, pp. 12–13). Working independently, Gilbert had provided six libretti, and Sullivan two scores, for the Reeds before 1877, and both were in a position to appreciate the kind of material which would appeal to a similar clientele in their later collaborations. Oost comments extensively on the calculated creation of 'tradition' at the Savoy, which implicated loyal customers ('Savoyards') in an entertainment experience in which they could 'revel collectively in attitudes and behaviours deemed appropriate and desirable for the urban bourgeoisie' (2009, p. 156). What has not been remarked upon is the analogy between the Reeds' development of a 'respectable' fan base and the way in which Carte fostered a relationship between performance 'brand' and a returning audience. This validation of the habits and attitudes shared by creators, performers and audience underpins both the success of the D'Oyly Carte enterprise and that of the Gallery of Illustration.

Carte as a manager and Gilbert and Sullivan as a creative team seem to have realised the value of providing a series of novel but essentially related entertainments, often featuring a permanent and recognisable company of actors, for a similarly respectable, fashionable, status-conscious audience. This type of brand loyalty, which originated in the necessarily 'respectable' content of both the 'entertainments' from the 1850s and the operas from the late 1870s onwards, was fostered by the same sense of belonging to a broad fellowship of like-minded consumers. It was also promoted by the sale of product-related ephemera. For example, sheet music bearing images of Priscilla Horton (Mrs German Reed) in various character guises was available for purchase for home use (Bratton 2011, pp. 74–5). By the 1880s, Savoy patrons could buy libretti and sheet music in the theatre. Illustrated souvenir programmes were provided free of charge, and various related items, such as visiting cards bearing pictures of Savoy actresses, trade cards used to advertise a wide variety of products, and decorated fans, became available as the popularity of the operas grew.

If the Savoy operas derived partly from the respectable 'entertainments' of the 1850s, it is surely no accident that some of Carte's leading practitioners were drawn from their ranks. Indeed, it would seem that a 'respectable' performing background was necessary for D'Oyly Carte personnel from the beginning of the collaboration. Personal conformity to the ethos of the Savoy Company was a likely by-product of such casting, as was, presumably, a decorous manner of performance, appropriate to the intended house style. The original production of *The Sorcerer* exemplifies this kind of attitude towards casting. George Grossmith, who made his first theatre appearance as John Wellington Wells, began his performing career giving 'penny readings'. These were originally intended as improving recitations from contemporary literature, conducted under the patronage of local clergy, but by the 1870s they consisted of humorous recitations and comic songs, often composed by the performer. Such artists were essentially amateur practitioners, and so theoretically dissociated from the theatrical profession with its dubious moral standing and profit-driven motives (Bratton 2011, p. 65).

By the time Grossmith was making a name in this field, the venues in which the 'readings' took place were a breeding ground for would-be professionals. Grossmith took this step in 1870, when he began touring with Mr and Mrs Howard Paul. His performance background clearly accorded with their style, and with what audiences expected from 'wholesome' entertainment. Grossmith continued his career with appearances at such worthy venues as the Royal Polytechnic Institution in Regent Street, and at various branches of the YMCA. He also obtained engagements as a paid entertainer at private parties for respectable middle-class households, and toured as part of a double act with Florence Marryat, which self-consciously based itself on the German Reed/Howard Paul model (Joseph 1982, pp. 47–65). When offered the role of Wells in *The Sorcerer*, Grossmith's first reaction was to refuse:

> I said to Carte: 'Look at the risk I am running. If I fail, I don't believe the Young Men's Christian Association will ever engage me again, because I have appeared on the stage, and my reputation as a comic singer to religious communities will be lost forever.'
>
> (Grossmith 1888, p. 90)

His doubts were assuaged when he learned that his former employer, Mrs Howard Paul, was also to play a principal role in the production, as was her young protégé, Rutland Barrington. Unlike Grossmith, Barrington started his career as a professional at the Olympic Theatre. However, he soon began to work exclusively with the Howard Pauls and was, by the time of his employment by Carte, clearly associated with their kind of material and performance style (Barrington 1908, pp. 5–11).[8] Similar backgrounds were shared by smaller-part principals. Fred Clifton, who played the small role of the Notary in *The Sorcerer*, had also performed at the Polytechnic Institution, and Frank Thornton, engaged as Grossmith's first understudy, began his career giving evening 'entertainments' (Stone 2001).

The connections between the world of the Victorian 'entertainment' and the concerns of the D'Oyly Carte management are clear. The respectability of the former, represented by the deliberate rejection of the features of burlesque and the adoption of the manners and culture of the 'entertainments', ensured the acceptability and profitability of the latter. The remaining principal cast members of *The Sorcerer* were drawn from the socially acceptable 'high art' world of the opera house or concert platform, which certified their repute. Performers varied through the first four years of the collaboration, but by the opening of *Patience* in 1881, a repertory company of principals had been assembled who would work as a team until 1888. Grossmith and Barrington, neither of them trained singers, played the more overtly comic roles. The remainder of the principals were opera or concert singers who could act.

While the D'Oyly Carte management were recruiting performers whose background and performance style were antithetical to the world of the burlesque, it is important to bear in mind that the desire for social acceptability on the part of theatre makers can be most clearly observed in those practitioners who self-consciously remodelled their own image in pursuit of such goals. Originally a writer of burlesque and pantomime, Gilbert distanced himself from such forms throughout the 1870s. Perhaps more tellingly, those doyennes of the 'respectable' entertainments of the 1870s, Mrs German Reed and Mrs Howard Paul, had, earlier in their careers, as Priscilla Horton and Isabella Featherstone, been successful and popular burlesque performers. Their deliberate transformation of image was calculated to appeal to the 'large class of the public which, while hankering after amusement, professes to abominate the theatre'[9] (cited in Bratton 2011, p. 71). Marie Wilton's career followed the same path, though it shifted to spoken drama rather than the musical stage. As Bratton and Davis (Davis 2000, pp. 287–90) point out, the apparent concealment of their previous personae behind the name of a husband and partner endowed their enterprises with an acceptably genteel facade. No longer single women on display, they were, at least on paper, the inhabitants of an implicit, if theatrically recreated, 'domestic sphere', which intentionally matched the idealised domesticity of their intended audience.

Another aspect of the change might have been the realisation, by male spectators in particular, that the well-mannered female entertainer, who provided decorous entertainment to himself and his family in the 1860s, was the same person whose legs he might have ogled as a young bachelor at the Haymarket 20 years earlier (Bratton 2011, p. 71). Perhaps we can observe, by these changes of appearance and emphasis, a tacit understanding that 'respectability' was often an identity choice. It was driven partly by maturity and responsibility, partly by the needs of performers to continue to work once youthful attractiveness was waning, but also by the desire to conform to the predominant ideology of respectability which was often demonstrated through outward show. Crucial to their success in a changing moral environment was the need for purveyors of respectable entertainment to be perceived as belonging to the same 'status group' as their customers. This trend is as observable in the ethos which accompanied the 'entertainments' predating the Savoy operas as with the performances, performers and public relations activities characterising the D'Oyly Carte enterprise. The connections between Wilton, Horton and Featherstone and the Savoy Triumvirate have already been alluded to in passing. It is worth remembering that Gilbert was a friend of Marie Bancroft and had learned the art of directing for the stage by watching rehearsals at the Prince of Wales (Crowther 2000, p. 90). Both Gilbert and Sullivan had worked for the Reeds (Goodman 1988, pp. 80–1); the Reeds and Mrs Howard Paul were clients of Carte's theatrical agency (Ainger 2002, p. 130); and Mrs Howard Paul appeared in the first production of *The Sorcerer*. Such links (as well as the secondary connections to performers such as Grossmith, Barrington and Thornton mentioned earlier) demonstrate the way in which the idea of the 'respectable' musical stage was formed, transmitted and realised in the West End at this time.

The image of the former burlesque performer who subsequently attires herself in the fashionable evening dress of the mannerly bourgeoisie could be applied as a metaphor for the hybrid texts of the Savoy operas themselves. Although stylistically derived from burlesque and operetta[10] (Hayter 1987, pp. 35–43)—Gilbert and Sullivan's first collaboration, *Thespis* (1871), was a Gaiety burlesque—the operas could, in terms of content and performance style, refute point by point the contemporary criticisms of that genre mentioned above. While requiring a similar level of educated 'competency' to the burlesque in order to fully appreciate their cultural and musical allusions and parodies, the Savoy products were tailored for a mixed audience of all ages, rather than a predominantly younger male clientele. In an interview given in 1888, Gilbert remarked on his deliberate rejection of 'the rows of ladies' tight-clothed legs, which are merely worn [...] to gratify the eyes of the young gentlemen in the stalls'. He goes on to remark that '[i]n the old days, when I wrote burlesques, I was glad enough to get my pieces produced; but, having no authority, I had no choice in the matter'.[11] Once in a position of power, Gilbert was able to tailor the older form for a refined audience. Significantly the operas were clearly subtitled as 'new' or 'original' in order to dissociate the pieces from their less wholesome theatrical antecedents and from any suggestion that they had been translated 'from the French'.[12]

Another promotional method was to elevate the status of the Savoy pieces through comparison with other less 'respectable' forms. The term 'operetta', with its risqué, foreign connotations, was never used in conjunction with the D'Oyly Carte productions. Appealing to national pride by asserting the 'Englishness' of the operas, Carte sought to distance them from 'adaptations of French pieces of more or less questionable character', which, despite 'having made a considerable stir here', apparently 'suited the tastes of a limited section of the public'. *HMS Pinafore* was recommended to potentially reticent provincial audiences in advance of a national tour 'on the strength of its genuine English fun and its graceful stirring music'.[13] Such patriotic sentiments also appear to have been absorbed by the acting company. Jessie Bond saw the operas in which she performed as 'an entirely new manifestation' insofar as 'they were thoroughly English' (Bond 1930, p. 56), while Rutland Barrington remarks on the 'patriotic glow' experienced within the 'home for English talent' established by the Triumvirate (Barrington 1908, pp. 15–16).[14]

Press releases and interviews were used to forestall preconceptions of vulgarity associated with both English burlesque and French *opéra bouffe*. A few days after the opening of *The Sorcerer* in 1877, Carte pronounced that it would succeed 'simply on its merits, and not on any meretricious displays of costume, or rather absence of costume—or any objectionable suggestiveness of motive or dialogue' (cited in Joseph 1994, p. 70). The avoidance of cross-dressing and emphasis on the modesty of female costume further demonstrates the need to distance the operas from existing types of musical theatre performance. Commenting retrospectively on the deliberate propriety which inculcated the 1877 venture, Gilbert remarked that

Their dialogue should be void of offence [...] on artistic principles no man should play a woman's part and no woman a man's [...] we agreed that no lady of the company should be required to wear a dress that she could not wear with absolute propriety at a private fancy-ball.[15]

(cited in Cellier and Bridgeman 1914, p. 291)

While suggestive language and scanty dress are clearly understandable signifiers of vulgarity, cross-dressing provided a particularly worrying prospect for Gilbert as a purveyor of contemporary comic entertainment. Its summary rejection could be seen as indicative of the way in which middle-class social conventions had developed by the time the Savoy operas came to be written. Such principles were closely related to the marketability of the brand. 'As a product in the market,' writes Caroline Williams, 'the Savoy operas did claim respectable gender norms as an identifying feature of their genre' (Williams 2011, p. 21).

Male cross-dressing, in the form of the Dame, was common in burlesque, and could provide a grotesque exaggeration of the appearance and behaviour of the older woman. The role of the Dame 'often focuses on her sexual desire, which is portrayed as particularly ridiculous' (Williams 2010, p. 206), and as such could not be permitted within a type of entertainment which eschewed sexual reference or innuendo. An example of male to female cross-dressing occurs in *Princess Ida*. But here it is used as a plot device—the men are seen to be disguising themselves in order to infiltrate the all-female university precincts—and there is no suggestion that they are anything but the male characters temporarily adopting female dress.

An important comic device in the Savoy operas is that recognisable social types find themselves caught up in absurd 'topsy-turvy' situations or locations. Comic incongruity often depends on the contrast between the normality of their reactions and the absurdity of their situation. This can be observed in the *Ida* reference above, for example. The Dame figure in burlesque was essentially grotesque to begin with (Stedman 1972, p. 22) and associated with the exaggerated 'low comedy' which Gilbert eschewed in order to present the understated performance style which was required if his comedy was to work. According to Stedman, 'their make-up was caricature, their actions slapstick' (1972, p. 23), and these features are rarely, if ever, to be found in Savoy production photographs, texts or prompt-books.[16] Stedman makes a convincing case for Gilbert's transmutation of the Dame into the often critically maligned, middle-aged contralto roles in the operas, describing this as a method of retaining some of the dramaturgical usefulness of such characters, while avoiding the excesses of burlesque.

Significantly, as a previous purveyor of burlesque, Gilbert was self-consciously distancing himself, and the image of the D'Oyly Carte organisation, from this kind of theatrical output, and in doing so was positioning the operas as modern departures from previous popular forms (Williams 2011, pp. 19–22). Bratton (2011) has demonstrated that the performances of artists for whom cross-dressing was a speciality (for example, Madam Vestris, Virginie Dejazet, Mrs Keeley and Madame Celeste), while popular in the first part of the century, could also be considered transgressive. This was not simply to do with the obvious sexual 'display of the actress in male dress [...] because it is close fitting and bifurcated, revealing the body and allowing her (dancing) legs to be seen and enjoyed' (Bratton 2011, p. 128). Gilbert seems to assert that cross-dressing infringes artistic taste on stage ('artistic principles'). This view is linked to Bratton's notion that women who played men, in melodrama as well as on the musical stage, who impersonated (often foreign) thieves and brigands, and who kissed other women on stage, were marking out the boundaries of what was becoming socially acceptable. Early- to mid-Victorian society was increasingly codifying and regulating its behaviour, forming 'a new substantiation of social role definition that touched every aspect of middle-class life' (Bratton 2011, p. 144). These portrayals, Bratton argues, were popular at this time with audiences coming to terms with developing aspects of bourgeois social acceptability, such as tighter definition of sexual roles, the domestication and desexualisation of women, the affirmation of masculine power, and the nationalistic assumption that foreignness could be quaint, or threatening, but was essentially representative of the 'other'. Cross-dressing epitomised exoticism and excitement and could therefore allow 'the law abiding, anxious general public to ... enjoy and rule out many kinds of aberrant behaviour and come to a safer grasp of its own place' (Bratton 2011, p. 144).

However, as 'respectable' conventions became entrenched in the latter part of the nineteenth century, such performances might be seen as serving no useful artistic purpose. Gilbert was not simply railing against sexual titillation when dismissing transvestism on stage. He was affirming a middle-class social outlook which, by the late 1870s, *no longer needed* to explore 'what was right, proper, responsible behaviour for the class in power' (Bratton 2011, p. 144). To Gilbert, a progressive writer and producer, who also possessed many attributes of the conventional Victorian middle-class male, cross-dressing could easily be rejected as pointless, vulgar and out-of-date.

Consequently, through a combination of Gilbert's artistic taste and the commercial lure of an increased potential audience, Carte's formula proved a 'respectable' success. Contemporary reviews express a sense of relief that attending West End musical theatre was at last a morally uncompromising pastime for the family. The *Era* critic was delighted that *The Sorcerer* was a work which could be discussed

> over the supper tables afterwards [...] does not cause us to hush our voices if there are young people in the room. Here is a work which does not shock the feelings of the delicate and cultured lady [...]. Here is a work which schoolgirls may laugh at.[17]

Relying on a literate, middle-class readership, the *Era*, in the same article, was presumably happy to advise 'those straightlaced persons who have "conscientious scruples about going to the theatre"' to pay a visit to the Opera Comique. 'They will be grateful for us ever after, and will go about making converts everywhere.' In a similarly evangelical vein, *The Graphic* commented on the debt owed to Gilbert and Sullivan by 'all those who look on the theatre as a purifying, rather than as a corrupting medium of public entertainment'. Their 'scrupulous regard to propriety' made the operas perfect family entertainment. They were 'impotent to raise a blush on the cheek of any boy or girl, yet not a bit less entertaining to any man or woman'.[18]

There is an element of crusading zeal regarding the public decency of theatre-going present in both critical reception and Carte's publicity material that emphasises the extent to which moral probity was a consideration for a specific sector of the Victorian public. Self-righteous moralising against the dangers of the wrong kind of theatrical experience could be a distinct selling point to the right clientele. In his publicity material, Carte took the moral high ground by implicitly blaming the immorality of other managements for deterring potential audiences:

> In these days when so much has been done at some theatres to keep many of the public away from them, and prejudice them against the stage [...] my theatre in London is visited [...] by the clergy, who have given to it a support which they withhold from others.[19]

This kind of public relations exercise was successful. The *Era*, reporting on *HMS Pinafore* a few months into its run, made a point of commenting that a 'comic opera' had been patronised by 'the highest persons in the land', signifying that this was not generally the case in West End entertainments of this kind. Also surprising is the observation that 'Solemn bishops have failed to keep their faces from grinning while listening to it. High church ladies have tittered behind their fans. Low Church curates have indulged in hearty guffaws'.[20] There was little acceptance of theatre-going among the Victorian clergy (Booth 1991, pp. 22–3). Their patronage would probably have been uncommon in a religious climate where any kind of approbation for theatre was frowned on. In 1878, the same year as the *Pinafore* premiere, the radical Anglican priest Stewart Headlam was sacked by the Bishop of London for presuming, in a public lecture, to give his support to theatre and music hall (Sanderson 1984, p. 146). However, notwithstanding the journalistic hyperbole of the *Era* report, it seems that Carte had indeed succeeded in attracting, at least to some extent, the most 'respectable' audience sector from among those formerly least likely to frequent theatre performance.

Part of this attraction might have been due to the way in which the Savoy 'operas' grafted some of the qualities and status associations of 'high art' onto popular musical theatre entertainment. In the latter part of the century, artistic creativity was elevated in some quarters into a force for social good, which could result in the improvement of the individual through its power to educate, enliven and spiritually uplift (Altick 1973, pp. 281–8; Pick 1983, p. 65). Art music (or, as it became known for the first time in the nineteenth century, 'classical' music), especially of a religious sort, could also fulfil this function. The patronage and shared enjoyment of classical music, including its theatrical manifestation, Grand Opera, had by the nineteenth century become a signifier of social status (Weber 1996, p. 20). Thus, the presence in the creative team of Arthur Sullivan, who was not only a conductor and first Principal of the National Training School for Music, but also an esteemed classical composer of religious and ceremonial works, provided a link with both high society and good taste.

> Sullivan was widely regarded as the greatest English musician since Purcell. He was a close friend of the Prince of Wales and the Duke of Edinburgh, his music was much admired by Queen Victoria [...]. That such a paragon should grace the orchestra pit of a theatre was a virtual guarantee of respectability.

> (Cannadine 1992, p. 16–17)

National pride and avoidance of foreign cultural influence was again invoked as an incentive to artistic aspiration. The maintenance of high *English* musical standards was integral to Carte's enterprise. From the outset he declared an intention to create a form which equalled or surpassed that of existing foreign entertainments. The scores of the Savoy operas fulfilled this function admirably. Sullivan's musical allusions to British military bands, patriotic sea-songs, early English madrigals and the English choral tradition (especially the revered Handel) would have seemed both novel and reassuringly patriotic. His clever parodies of grand opera (notably Auber in *The Sorcerer*, Donizetti in *The Pirates of Penzance* and Wagner in *Iolanthe*) would have flattered the musical awareness of the *cognoscenti*, provided artistically satisfying settings for Gilbert's lyrics and reminded the audience that all this was being achieved by a home-grown team (Fig. 3.1).

Fig. 3.1   The Triumvirate: Carte, Gilbert and Sullivan, with Savoy conductor François Cellier in the background. (Alfred Bryan, *Entr'acte* 1894) Public Domain

SUMMARY

The success of the recently commercialised West End in the late Victorian period lay with the ability of managements to specialise and seek out new markets. Part of that process was an understanding of the extent to which a section of the suburban 'middle-class' theatre-going public, who formed the bulk of the West End's clientele, required an entertainment experience which accorded with the cultural and ethical values that affirmed and defined their ideological and social status. But it cannot be said that the predominance of bourgeois values alone accounted for the 'gentrification' of the West End. Certainly, the pre-eminence of the Savoy operas, and their financial success both in London and nationally, attests to the fact that the formula provided by the Triumvirate successfully matched the entertainment needs of the 'middle-classes'. It was supported by the public assertion of 'middle-class' status by the purveyors of such entertainments who, as we have seen, were aware of the need to remove themselves from the 'lower' forms of theatre performance with which they might have been associated, and to recruit performers who had little or no connection with pre-existing popular musical theatre forms. However, economic considerations inevitably ran parallel with more acceptable theatrical forms. Respectable values came to dominate the West End as a result of market forces which favoured those spectators who were prepared to pay more for a seat in a theatre than many of the population could afford. The combination of 'middle-class' ideology and middle-class affluence would seem to have been the primary cause of the 'gentrification' of the West End. While Chapter 5 will explore these economic connections in greater depth, the next chapter will focus on material issues. It will address a specific question. How can an understanding of the experience of attending a Savoy opera—the complete 'theatre event' as enjoyed by spectators in the 1880s—be used to examine ways in which the business of making theatre was connected with the cultural and class-based ideologies of the period?

NOTES

1. 'Victorian slang for a flamboyant disregard of the conventional, the expected and the customary' (Schoch 2003, p. xxxiii).
2. An increased emphasis on long-term private schooling, university education and delaying marriage until means were sufficient to support a family meant that affluent middle-class male heirs were given more freedom from work and immediate domestic responsibility—and therefore more leisure time—than their fathers (Bailey 1998, p. 15).

3. 'Chambermaids, soubrettes and Burlesque Actresses', *Illustrated Times*, 23 April 1864.
4. 'A Word about Our Theatres', *Fraser's Magazine* 57, February 1858, p. 233.
5. *Daily Telegraph*, 15 July 1869.
6. 'Workers and Their Work: Mr W.S. Gilbert', *Daily News*, 21 January 1885.
7. In 1865 prices ranged from 5s to 1s.
8. It should be noted that a certain amount of cross-dressing, which was strictly banned at the Savoy, did take place in the Howard Paul entertainments. Mrs Howard Paul was famous for using the unusually low range of her singing voice to impersonate the famous tenor Sims Reeves. Jacky Bratton remarks that the critical response to this feat was usually complimentary, although the impersonation itself was sometimes thought odd (2011, p. 84). The 'high art' connotations of the impersonation—Reeves was, after all, a renowned oratorio singer—may have assisted its acceptability. However, Rutland Barrington complained about feeling 'oppressed and unhappy' appearing in drag as 'Miss Althea', who appeared in a sketch as one of two 'old maids' when on tour with the Pauls. He adds that he 'very shortly ceased to be womanly in appearance' (Barrington 1908, p. 10).
9. Edmund Yates, 'Bygone Shows', *Fortnightly Review*, May 1866, p. 645.
10. WSG had written at least seven pieces which could be described as burlesques or as 'extravaganzas'—a dramatic form similar to the burlesque, based on fairy tales or fables.
11. *Pall Mall Gazette*, 26 November 1888.
12. Thus *The Sorcerer* was subtitled 'An entirely new and original Modern Comic Opera', *The Pirates of Penzance* 'A new and original Melo-Dramatic Opera', *Ruddigore* 'A new and original Supernatural Opera', etc.
13. Undated leaflet, promoting October and November 1879 tours (DC/TM).
14. Further discussion of notions of 'Englishness' in the Savoy operas can be found in Oost, 2009, pp. 47–51, and Cannadine, 1992, pp. 12–32.
15. After-dinner speech at the O.P. Club, delivered by W.S. Gilbert on 30 December 1906.
16. There are a few necessary exceptions to these provisos. Katisha's make-up in *The Mikado* is exaggerated, but no more so than any of the other 'Japanese' characters therein. Some physical business was allowed by Gilbert, but more often than not 'slapstick' was censured and removed after it had crept into long runs or was discovered in touring productions—see Chapter 7 for a full discussion on interpolated material.
17. *Era*, 9 December 1877.
18. *The Graphic*, 10 April 1880.
19. *Era*, 25 August 1878.
20. Ibid.

CHAPTER 4

Patience at the Savoy

This chapter is broadly structured around a notional evening visit to *Patience* at the Savoy Theatre, perhaps during the late spring of 1882, about halfway through its run of 408 performances. I will use this method to examine some of the material factors surrounding the run of *Patience* in order to further investigate the ideological 'subtext' which informed the expectations and assumptions of both producers and consumers of the D'Oyly Carte brand. The approach is based on the central idea that the material aspects of a production can disclose the social and cultural pre-conceptions of its makers and its audience. A study of material evidence will necessarily unearth ideological attitudes towards class and society which are embedded within this evidence.

The choice of *Patience* is prompted by the amount of contemporary press coverage it received, resulting from the company's operational move from the Opera Comique to the new Savoy Theatre during the initial run of the show.[1] The Savoy was designed by C.J. Phipps (the most prolific theatre architect of the time) under Carte's instructions, specifically for the presentation of the Gilbert and Sullivan operas. As well as providing a larger performance area and vastly improved backstage facilities, the new venue allowed Carte to offer a theatre-going experience which provided the latest standards of comfort, service and environmental aesthetics. Foremost among these was the provision of electric lighting. The Savoy was the first public building, and *Patience* the first theatre piece, to be lit entirely by electricity, and the publicity surrounding its use indicates a level

© The Author(s) 2016
M. Goron, *Gilbert and Sullivan's 'Respectable Capers'*, Palgrave Studies
in British Musical Theatre, DOI 10.1057/978-1-137-59478-5_4

of cultural significance which, as will be argued below, goes beyond that of visual improvement. These extra factors, together with the topicality of *Patience*'s subject matter, a critique of cultural pretensions associated with the currently popular Aesthetic movement in the arts and literature, produced a quantity of extra material. In addition to the normal run of newspaper reviews and listings, gossip pieces and theatre programmes which accompanied theatre events of the time, there are also press releases relating to the opening of the Savoy, newspaper accounts of the new theatre and its facilities and comments on the interior use of electricity.

Information concerning geographical, architectural and spatial aspects of the Savoy Theatre is drawn from a number of contemporary printed sources, but predominantly a descriptive report published in the *Era* on 1 October 1881. For the sake of clarity, I will use the terms provided by Knowles (2004, pp. 62–101) to separate the various locational, architectural and discourse-related elements under discussion. These are primarily: 'geography and neighbourhood' (concerning location and transportation within the urban environment); 'space and place' (concerning theatre architecture, spaces of reception and the auditorium); and 'public discourses around the text' (including theatre programmes and press coverage). Programme content will be discussed in some detail, beyond that of direct relevance to *Patience*, as an indicator of the changing values and preoccupations of Savoy audiences over time. Of course, printed sources are used throughout this chapter and others, and their value as indicators of the ideology of producers and consumers is implicit throughout. This section will particularly consider those printed sources related to the run of *Patience* and the opening of the Savoy.

GEOGRAPHY AND NEIGHBOURHOOD

For the suburban or provincial 'theatrical tourist', the Savoy Theatre was easily reached by public transport. Let us imagine a party from Kent or the south London suburbs arriving at Charing Cross Station.[2] They could, if sufficiently affluent and desirous of protecting the appearance of their expensive evening dress against the vicissitudes of weather and street conditions, finish the journey by hackney cab. The cost was 1s per hire for one or two passengers, plus 6d per extra person (children half price), to the Savoy. This, in addition to the return journey, either from the theatre itself or the nearest cab rank at Burleigh Street, might add considerably to the price of an evening out.[3] A cheaper option was the 'chocolate'-coloured

'Chelsea' omnibus, available from one of the many stops at Charing Cross which, for 3d would drop the traveller off in the Strand (Dickens Jr. 1888, pp. 48, 179–89).[4] Another possible alternative was to walk the half mile to the theatre along the wide, tree-lined Victoria Embankment. This was of fairly recent construction, having been completed ten years prior to the opening of the Savoy as a pleasant alternative to the Strand, and it pro-vided a location for fashionable promenading in the West End (Goodman 2000, p. 19). The Savoy, whose frontage was adjacent to this thorough-fare, would therefore be ideally placed, both in terms of accessibility via public transport and pleasantness of location, to appeal to affluent, well-attired audiences.

Those arriving by private carriage or who had hired a cab would need to alight at the entrance in Somerset Street, which ran parallel to the Embankment and was sufficiently wide to allow the passage of a number of vehicles. Part of the £11,000 cost of the building plot, purchased by Carte in 1880, contained a contribution to the construction of this new roadway.[5] It was presumably in Carte's interest to ensure maximum acces-sibility to the venue for the remunerative 'carriage trade'. Its fascia was designed accordingly. According to the *Morning Post*, 'the space in which carriages can take up and put down is said to be greater than any London theatre'.[6] A pleasantly situated south-facing main entrance 'almost as secluded as a private road',[7] conveniently separated from the busy thor-oughfare of the Strand, would appear to have been expressly designed for a target audience affluent enough to be arriving by horse-drawn trans-port.[8] Here, a view would be afforded, at least from the opposite side of Somerset Street, of the red brick and white Portland stone frontage of the Savoy (Fig. 4.1).[9]

It was, unusually, a detached structure, 'the only theatre in London of which the four outer-walls stand open and in four thoroughfares',[10] rather than a 'facade' theatre, which formed part of a continuous terrace of shops and public buildings. As such, the Savoy could be seen to represent, on a reduced scale, the qualities of what Carlson terms a 'monumental' the-atre, one which asserts its own prestigious identity within the urban land-scape.[11] This function was generally associated with large opera houses, such as Covent Garden (1825) or the Paris Opera (1878), often per-ceived as visible monuments to national cultural achievement and prestige (Carlson 1989, pp. 79–84). The streets which bounded the Savoy to east and west descended steeply from the Strand and were not wide, restrict-ing any real sense of isolated grandeur. Nevertheless, the free-standing

Fig. 4.1   Savoy Theatre, Somerset Street—main entrance. (C. J. Phipps 1881)
Public Domain

position of the theatre, ostensibly inhabiting the grounds of the medieval
Savoy Palace, can be read as a proclamation of its identity as a home for the
new English comic opera (as the Gilbert and Sullivan collaborations were
always known), with the attendant cultural prestige denoted by this term.

The Savoy's riverside position, about half a mile from the Opera
Comique, could also be regarded as an attempt at dissociation from the
burlesque or *opera bouffe* houses (including the Olympic, the Gaiety, and
the Globe) situated further up the Strand or on its less salubrious turnings.
By implication, this positioning might be read as a retreat from the less
wholesome aspects of the types of performance on offer at these theatres.
Burlesque had been Gilbert's stock in trade through the 1860s. The subtle spatial distancing of the new venture from his old theatrical stamping

ground could be read as a public declaration of the elevation of the burlesque to its new, 'higher' form—English comic opera—while providing an opportunity for Sullivan, as doyen of British music,[12] to transcend any connections with 'lower' forms of theatrical entertainment.

THEATRE ARCHITECTURE

Another likely reason for the move to a purpose-built venue was the perception that the respectability of the D'Oyly Carte organisation at the Opera Comique had been compromised by specific structural and locational factors. Entry was via a subterranean tunnel from the Strand, and the building itself, located between Holywell and Wych Streets, the principal locations of London's pornographic book trade[13] (Davis 1991, p. 83), shared its rear wall with the Globe Theatre. The two theatres, so closely conjoined that the actors on one stage were able to hear the dialogue from the adjoining building (Barrington 1908, p. 17), were known as the 'rickety twins' (Ainger 2002, p. 140).[14] The symbolic contrast with the new Savoy, standing clear of any other structure, in a newly developed area (which was nevertheless replete with historical associations), with its main street-level entrance facing the Royal Embankment, could be seen as a deliberate signifier of prestige status.[15]

The existence of quadrilateral public access at the Savoy allowed for 'free and expeditious entrance and exit for all classes of the public'. This comment from the *Era* report casually encapsulates the social segregation inherent in West End theatre of this period, of which the Savoy was only the most up-to-date example. Separate entrances for stalls, pit, circles and gallery seating were employed at the Savoy for reasons of fire safety, and also convenience, in terms of speed of ingress and egress. However, the internal divisions within Victorian theatre auditoria, which split audiences in terms of income and class, were echoed and reinforced by segregated access to those areas. If, as Regina Oost maintains, managerial intention at the Savoy was to create a homogenised, middle-class preserve (2009, pp. 22–34), the four-sided arrangements at the Savoy remained particularly effective in emphasising the *distance* between the widest socioeconomic groupings present rather than their social cohesion. For example, the less well-off but possibly culturally 'middle-class' purchasers of the lower-priced pit seats situated towards the rear of the downstairs auditorium (Davis and Emeljanow 2001, p. 179) *could* have used the entrance lobby in company with fashionably attired inhabitants of the stalls and dress circle. However, from the main entrance, their seats were accessible through pass doors leading to a plain stairwell—perhaps a tacit dissuasion from entering the auditorium in company with higher-paying customers.[16]

The most convenient doors for the 'pittites' and for those inhabiting the less-expensive seating in the upper circle were situated on the Strand to the rear of the theatre and on Beaufort Street on the east side of the building. Beaufort Street was intended for foot trade rather than those arriving by carriage. A contemporary map showing access to the Savoy from surrounding streets indicates a 'one-way system' marked by arrows for carriage routes around the theatre. There are no such indicators for Beaufort Street, which clearly bears the legend 'Entrance for foot passengers to PIT, 1 CIRCLE & other parts' (Wilmore 2013). Customers who frequented the lowest-priced 1s gallery seats were conveniently directed to a completely separate entrance on the other side of the building in Carting Lane. These entrances provided access for the 'undress' parts of the auditorium, where evening wear was not expected.[17] A separate box office for unreserved seats was provided to the rear of the building on the corner of the Strand and Beaufort Street, further assisting the separation of differing income groups immediately prior to the performance.[18] The Savoy's main entrance was primarily intended to accommodate the wealthy.

Such details indicate considerable forethought concerning ways in which different types of patron could be separated, while simultaneously inhabiting the same building. The structure of the theatre, in terms of ingress and egress into both the building and auditorium, along with its internally demarcated zones based on class, income and appearance, would indicate an audience which contained considerable differences in wealth and was highly sensitive to gradations of social acceptability and compatibility within its own ranks. For sound business reasons the satisfaction of the most affluent would seem to have been Carte's chief consideration.

SPACE AND PLACE: SITES OF RECEPTION

Primary access to the foyer with its tasteful decoration and facilities would also have emphasised distinctions of income and status. Those destined for boxes, stalls and the dress circle—we will envisage our representative party among this group—would enter through the elegant Somerset Street entrance. They would pass immediately through a colonnaded covered way 'of 70 feet, giving facilities for taking up half a dozen parties simultaneously and without confusion',[19] and thence into a black-and-white marble paved 'semicircular vestibule', which was the Savoy's central 'place of reception'. Its decorative style provides another indication of the type of patron to whom this theatre was principally targeted. A contemporary illustration shows the foyer resembling the domestic entrance hall of a luxurious home, complete with fireplace and decorated mantelpiece. 'Decorations, furnishings and fittings were subtly designed to suggest a respectable middle class drawing room, a sort of pretence—in case [the audience] still needed a pretence—that they were not really in a theatre at all' (Joseph 1994, p. 79).

Lecturing on 'The House Beautiful' in 1882, Oscar Wilde encapsulated contemporary opinion on the aesthetic advantages of tasteful simplicity in home furnishing.[20] His ideal entrance hall should be tiled, rather than carpeted, should reject artificial flowers in favour of natural blooms, and ornate chandeliers should be replaced by more modest side brackets (O'Brien 1974). All these features were present in the Savoy atrium, signifying initial impressions of highly fashionable, though modestly scaled, domesticity, which might reflect the aspirational standards of the middle classes, rather than the grandeur of the aristocratic 'great house'. Other theatres provided other effects. The St James Theatre, remodelled three years before the Savoy, and at that time presenting a repertoire dominated by adaptations of French farces, presented itself as a 'Parisian mansion [...] the very ticket office has all the appearance of an antechamber sumptuously furnished [with] embossed green and gold wallpaper'.[21] Here, luxuriousness in the French manner counterpointed the style of the drama. In 1881 the Savoy was an up-to-date example of this mode of audience attraction, offering an atmosphere reflecting comfortable but elegant contemporary bourgeois taste. Such particularised variety of decor would indicate that managements were providing a theatre event in which product specialisation was reflected in physical surroundings that complemented the type of show on offer, thereby catering for an audience looking for a complete and specialised leisure 'experience'.

Internal restaurant facilities at the Savoy continued the theme of domestic comfort, providing opportunities for the *Patience* audience to indulge in pre-performance dining and relaxation. All customers were able to obtain refreshments, but the methods of social segregation which affected the auditorium and means of access were also apparent in the location of food outlets and relaxation areas within the building. This was not a recent phenomenon. As early as 1819, the architect Benjamin Wyatt had advocated separate facilities for the 'lower orders', 'for the purpose of attracting all those whom it is desirable to remove from below stairs and keeping them out of the way of the more respectable part of the company' (cited in Carlson 1989, p. 151). Similar arrangements existed in the Savoy. The principal dining area was located below the vestibule and the presence of a smoking room for the gentlemen and a 'boudoir lounge' for the ladies, with their attendant associations of post-prandial 'retirement', demarcated this area as one of relative gentility. Upper circle and gallery were provided with their own self-contained refreshment saloons and lavatories, enabling spectators at ground level to avoid contact with lower-paying clientele.[22]

The significance of on-site dining, which offered the West End theatre-goer a 'packaged' experience, is reinforced by a cartoon by Arthur Bryan, published in the *Entr'acte* of 8 October 1881 (reproduced in Allen 1958, p. 167) two days prior to the opening of the Savoy. It shows Carte dressed as a suave head waiter, a reference to the fact that, rather than rent space to an outside contractor, as had occurred at the Opera Comique, Carte organised the Savoy catering in-house. Internal quality control in terms of dining and drinking could thereby ensure that the entertainment 'package' offered at the Savoy was consistent with managerial and audience expectations.[23] The illustration depicts, in the foreground, Carte inviting the onlooker to enter through a glass door marked 'Savoy Dining Room', while a 'carte', or menu, is pasted to the wall, emphasising the francophone vernacular of the restaurant trade, as well as supplying a punning reference to the theatre manager as food vendor. Behind the door lurk an irate Gilbert and Sullivan, both in chef's attire. The image ironically reduces the Triumvirate and their creative and entrepreneurial endeavours to the quasi-servile status of catering staff in a dining 'saloon'. Librettist and composer are presumably engaged in the hard graft of getting the product 'on the table'. Sullivan wields a baton (there are, perhaps, visual/verbal puns here on the French term for conductor, a '*chef* d'orchestre', as well as a further suggested pun on the proprietor's French-sounding name),[24] while Carte, as 'maitre d'hotel', attempts to lure the reader-as-patron into an establishment which offers comic opera as a literally 'consumable' product. This offers an interesting reflection, intentional or not, on the branding and packaging of West End theatre in this period, and indicates the extent to which targeted marketing to a specific clientele was essential to the success of theatrical entrepreneurship. Carte, the manager and marketer, dominates the three figures in terms of size and definition, suggesting that the cartoonist is aware that promotion, in terms of brand or 'public face', might be assuming more importance than the artistic creations of Carte's collaborators.

Space and Place: The Auditorium

Having enjoyed the Savoy's in-house dining facilities, let us assume that our suburban theatregoers have entered the auditorium from the rear of the first balcony. Here they would have been presented with a mode of interior design which, in terms of moderation of ornament, echoed the style of the foyer and was therefore markedly different from that currently used in West End auditoria. Contemporary press comment[25] and Carte's opening night press release[26] devoted considerable space to describing Collinson and Lock's 'chaste'—in the sense of 'simple' or 'restrained'—decorative schemes, with which the interior was adorned. According to Carte, this style was employed specifically to contrast with the vulgarity of existing internal theatre decoration (which presumably fell short of the aesthetic sensibilities of prospective Savoy spectators) by providing a style which

> I feel sure will be appreciated by all persons of taste. Paintings of cherubim, muses, angels, and mythological deities have been discarded. [...] The main colour schemes are white, pale yellow and gold—gold used only for backgrounds or in large masses, and not—following what may be called, for want of a worse name, the Gingerbread School of Decorative Art—for gilding, relief work or mouldings.[27]

The remainder of the description continues in this manner, lingering over the 'creamy satin' of the front curtain, the 'blue plush of an inky hue' which covered the expensive stall and dress circle chairs, and the 'yellowish silk, brocaded with a pattern of decorative flowers' which embellished the curtains of the private boxes. This deliberate attempt to flatter audience discernment can be read as a desire to attract a class of spectators who are, or imagine themselves to be, able to distinguish between elegance and kitsch. Conspicuous expenditure was also part of Carte's strategy. Several reports, including that of the *Era*, comment on the lavish stage curtain 'of gold coloured satin embroidered with a velvet bottom and a border of Spanish embroidery. This curtain, we are informed, alone cost some hundreds of pounds (Fig. 4.2).'[28]

The fact that discussion of (expensive) decor is so central to this pre-publicity material, and features so prominently in contemporary press coverage, indicates the extent to which internal surroundings were an essential part of the theatregoing experience. House lights were not fully lowered during performances, so the theatre interior was constantly on display. Quality of internal decoration contributed to the atmosphere of an evening at the Savoy, and in a competitive marketplace might have proven an

Fig. 4.2   The Savoy auditorium during Act One of *Patience*. The artist's impression exaggerates the spaciousness of what was an intimately proportioned auditorium. (*Graphic* 1881). Public Domain

important factor in attracting the right kind of clientele. This was enhanced by the provision of free programmes, and the prevention of theatre staff from accepting tips for any services.[29] Ushers who behaved like domestic servants could enhance the comfort and security of those patrons wishing to feel 'at home' at the theatre. The *Morning Post* favourably contrasted the high standard of service at the Savoy with 'some West-End Theatres' where 'the demand for a hat and coat is made in tones which a century ago would not have seemed out of place on Hounslow-heath'.[30]

Patronage could, at times, be of the most eminent type. On 16 February 1882, for example, *Patience* was attended by Princess Beatrice and the Dowager Duchess of Ely.[31] Such an event would have marked one of several occasions during its run requiring utilisation of the royal box, access to which was via a discreet entrance at the corner of Somerset Street and Carting Lane. The royal box remained a feature of Victorian theatre interiors, although the *Era* report makes no specific reference to it at the Savoy. This omission may be significant. Its positioning, at dress circle level, overlooking the forestage, was conspicuous but not overtly so, as it was matched by a similarly placed and decorated box on the opposite side of the theatre, and was part of the middle section of the three tiers of boxes on either side of the stage. This placing could be read as a reflection of a democratisation of interior space in London auditoria and point to the economic and cultural power of the British bourgeoisie. In contrast, aristocratic hierarchies and royal authority are implied by the centrally located royal boxes surrounded by multi-tiered rows of private boxes which filled the vertical spaces of many continental European auditoria (Carlson 1989, pp. 143–8). Royalty could be conspicuously present at the Savoy. But for a predominantly urban and suburban 'middle-class' crowd, whose attitudes towards the aristocracy were not necessarily deferential, the royal box was not the automatic centre of attention in terms of positioning or lines of sight.

The Savoy's internal layout, consisting of a number of private boxes on either side of the stage, a floor space containing stalls, behind which were unreserved pit seats, with three levels of horseshoe-shaped balconies above, culminating in the lowest-priced gallery, was typical of late-nineteenth-century London theatre building.[32] The positioning of the boxes continued to emphasise the visibility of their inhabitants to the rest of the house for reasons of public display. Otherwise, pricing was concomitant with proximity to the stage. Apart from the financial and visual practicalities of such an arrangement, the spatial signification of these divisions can also be understood as an assertion of nineteenth-century British bourgeois identity. It presented a society stratified by wealth and station, in which aristocratic and hereditary power was downplayed in relation to middle-class entrepreneurial and professional ideals. In doing so, it signified an attitude to society in which all grades of person had a place and function, and could share leisure activities, but only as long as distinctions of rank were carefully observed.

The visible signifiers of personal status—costume, jewellery, hair style, deportment and bearing—were rendered more obvious to all inhabitants of the auditorium by Carte's innovative use of electric lighting. Brighter and more revealing than gas light, the new incandescent bulb enhanced the effect of the currently fashionable 'chaste' style of interior decoration, imitated at the Savoy. It also allowed those who attended for social reasons to 'be seen' more clearly by the house. François Cellier reports (with typically deferential effusiveness) how the 'inherent brightness of the fairy-lamps was now called upon to enhance the lustre of the distinguished personages who filled the boxes, stalls and circles' (1914, p. 101).

The *Daily News*, covering the opening night of *Patience*, remarks on the effect of the lighting on the auditorium, noting that 'on the colours in the ladies' dresses in the stalls, and on the appearance of the house, its effect was [...] very striking'.[33] For many spectators, a 'theatre event' could encompass enjoyment of the style and fashions of the well-off as well as the events on stage. Indeed, for one sceptical reviewer, the use of electricity and its effect on personal appearance was the primary attraction of the new house:

> Here they have one novelty in the electric light, which people go to see quite as much as 'Patience' [...] the ladies hurry to the Savoy to see if the electric light is really damaging to false complexions in order to prepare themselves for the introduction of the novel glare into private houses. [...] So the Savoy, owing to the electric light, is, for the moment, the fashion.[34]

It would seem likely that Carte was fully aware of the value of electricity in enhancing the appeal of the Savoy as a place to see, and be seen. The subtlety of its internal decoration is likely to have been conceived with this kind of lighting in mind. The bolder, flashier styles of design of rival auditoria so disparaged by Carte[35] would have been revealed as vulgar by the less flattering electric glow at the Savoy. Bright interior lighting also provides a 'new explanation for the period's emphasis upon clean and decorated auditoria, on stricter audience segregation by degree, and upon their comfort' (Bratton 2009, p. 5), all of which seem to be features exemplified by the construction, decoration and internal arrangements of the Savoy. The enhanced visibility of the attire and behaviour of the 'lower orders', in what was (despite misleading artists' impressions) an intimate auditorium, provided a further reason for their carefully arranged access to, and positioning within, the house.

One of the principal attractions of the new venue as a location was its significance as the first public building anywhere in the world to have been illuminated entirely by electricity. Asa Briggs highlights the Victorian fascination with this new technological development, an appeal which transcended mere practical usage. 'For every theory concerning electricity there was a myth, for every inventor a charlatan, and for every practical invention in its history [...] there was an object of fraud and superstition' (Briggs (a) 1988, p. 396). Carte's 'sales pitch' press release (cited in Cellier and Bridgeman 1914, pp. 95–9), and the subsequent press coverage of the new theatre immediately prior to its opening, capitalised on the newsworthiness and 'PR' value of electric light to a literate and well-informed middle-class audience.

Carte's publicity capitalises on the novelty value of the new technology in enough detail to raise the eager curiosity of any Victorian technophile. He explains the utilisation of in-house electricity generation, the design and installation of the system by Siemans, the type and quality of the 1200 electric arc lights employed, and the reserve gas supply, in case the new technology should fail. In terms of its effect on staging, the use of incandescent bulbs allowed a degree of heightened naturalness, emphasising the lavishness of costume and set, which enhanced the visual appeal of the newly transferred *Patience*, with its specially redesigned dresses and settings. However, a less obvious but equally interesting function of electric lighting, when reading public interior space in terms of attitudes towards class, is its effect on class-based perceptions of health and hygiene.

Considerable reference is made in contemporary comment on the cooler atmosphere and the 'purity' of the air inside the Savoy auditorium—a result of the replacement of gas burners with electricity. Carte refers to the 'foul air and heat which pervades *all* theatres' and anticipates the 'purity of air and coolness' in his new auditorium (my italics).[36] 'The pleasure of sitting in a crowded theatre without being affected by the heat of the gas' and avoidance of 'the dense atmosphere frequently unavoidable in the theatre' is noted by an *Era* correspondent[37] reporting on the Savoy's opening night. Conductor François Cellier, who spent most of his working life in the Opera Comique and Savoy Theatre's orchestra pits, comments on an 'atmosphere free from the foetid heat of Gaslight' (Cellier and Bridgeman 1914, p. 101) at the new theatre. The primary cause of this reaction to large, gaslit interior public spaces was the persistent, conspicuous smell given off by multiple gas jets. But gas also carried with it notions of danger and ill health. Domestic users would have been very familiar with its darkening effect on interior decoration over time. Perhaps more significantly, concerns over gas explosions, poisoning and industrial pollution, as escaping gas supposedly seeped into the ground contaminating soil and water supplies, pervaded perceptions of the use of gas in the Victorian city (Shchivelbusch 1995, pp. 37–40).

As well as provoking thoughts of latent health hazards, the most immediate effect of gas lighting was the generation of considerable amounts of heat. 'During a night in the theatre the temperature measured under the ceiling of the auditorium could rise from 60 F to 100 F (15 °C to 38 °C)' (Shchivelbusch 1995, p. 51).[38] The atmosphere in a full theatre pit, placed to the rear of the auditorium, beneath the 'ceiling' provided by the floor of the dress circle above, 'becomes', according to the *Era*, 'simply awful and comparable only to the famed Black Hole of Calcutta'.[39] As heat inevitably rises, the hottest area of a Victorian auditorium would be the topmost gallery seating—the place where the poorest and least-bathed customers were placed. In an era without modern deodorants, and in which bathing habits were determined by economic advantage, human perspiration added to the odour of burning gas. Busy theatres could be distinctly malodorous places.[40]

Primitive plumbing and the additional concentration of odours result-ing from the overuse of limited toilet facilities would have added to the general unpleasantness, even in relatively upmarket West End venues (Davis 2000, pp. 100–4). Unusually hot summers were often detrimental to box-office receipts as spectators avoided stuffy auditoria. The initial run of *HMS Pinafore* at the Opera Comique in 1878 was almost scuppered by a resultant drop in takings to £40 per performance during a particularly sweltering June. Carte kept the enterprise afloat only by persuading the company to accept a one-third reduction in their wages for the duration of the crisis (Bradley 2005, p. 116). In an age before air conditioning, a cooler auditorium could be a positive business gain, drawing polite society to a more salubrious experience, and away from rival houses.

Tracy C. Davis (2000) presents an intriguing theory concerning inter-nal separation of theatre audiences by social class. She links the heat and often insanitary conditions suffered by audiences within theatres as late as the last quarter of the century with contemporary belief in 'miasma' or 'impure' air as a cause of contagion, and therefore as another reason for segregated auditoria. The better-off (and better-bathed) high-paying cus-tomer needed to be kept away from the unhygienic 'lower orders' (2000, pp. 104–12).[41] Personal cleanliness and its role in the avoidance of dis-ease caused by insanitary conditions were, in the Victorian period, closely connected with issues surrounding class. The occurrence of four cholera epidemics between 1831 and 1867 prompted the intense social and gov-ernmental concern which eventually resulted in Bazalgette's London sew-erage system, completed in 1875. Cholera, transmitted via water-borne microbes, largely affected the poor, to whom clean drinking water was inaccessible (Smith 2007, pp. 279–80). However, before scientific veri-fication that disease was transmitted by microbial infection, the 'bad air' which emanated from the bodies of the poorest urban dwellers was con-sidered to be a cause of infection.

Avoidance of disease also led to an increased public awareness of the necessity of personal hygiene, propounded by mid-century health reformers via a proliferation of monthly magazines, produced and consumed by the literate bourgeoisie. Health commissioners and charity workers noted the physical results of bad hygiene among the urban working classes and a 'top down' movement advocating the provision of public baths for the working classes gained support from the 1840s onwards (Smith 2007, pp. 280–5). As Lee Jackson remarks in his study of Victorian hygiene, *Dirty Old London*, personal cleanliness also demonstrated moral responsibility: 'Mankind was made in the image of God; to be dirty was to befoul that image.' Thus, an unclean home and grubby clothing could denote a failure, particularly on the part of women, to ensure the moral probity of the domestic sphere (Jackson 2014, pp. 138–9). Irrespective of the practical necessity, cleanliness could be regarded as a primary signifier of respectability.

Such class-based assumptions and prejudices, which have been shown to be present in the attitudes of dominant Victorian social groups elsewhere in this study, are likely to have been part of the attitudes of those attending the enclosed public space of the West End theatre auditorium. Better-off theatregoers at the Savoy in 1881, such as our notional visitors from the southern Home Counties, may have retained a perception that protection from impure air remained an effective method of avoiding illness.[42] The journalistic and personal evidence relating to the improved conditions at the Savoy quoted above would suggest a lingering notion that bad smells were more than just a source of temporary inconvenience. Davis goes as far as to comment that 'the segregation that kept gallery from box holders or stalls from pit came to be regarded not just as a matter of […] economic stratification, but a variable governing life and death' (2000, p. 100).

Factors such as these could affect theatre design. From the mid-century onwards, theatre boxes could be considered as potential locations for the entrapment and retention of noxious fumes emanating originally from the cheaper areas, and Davis notes the reduction in provision of boxes in West End theatres through the 1850s and 60s. Higher classes were grouped together in the stalls and dress circle 'where they could exist in a uniformly classed miasma' (Davis 2000, p. 108). Presumably the same reasoning applied to the crowding together of the lower classes in the balcony. This trend seems to have been reversed towards the end of the century. As scientific doubt was cast on the notion of 'bad air', the overall percentage of private box seating in new or converted auditoria began to rise once again, allowing reduced *personal* contact with the potentially infectious members of the lower orders.

Intriguingly, Davis notes that, in comparison with other newly built theatres, an *exception* to this increase in such seating was the Savoy, where proportionally fewer boxes were provided when compared with other recent theatre building (2000, p. 107). Several factors could have affected this particular anomaly. Economic considerations will be considered in more detail in the next chapter. In terms of hygiene, the kind of effective interior segregation present at the Savoy, with separate entrances on four sides for different income groups, would be sufficient to satisfy the exclusivity desired by the better off. It might prevent physical contact between themselves and those likely to carry infection or (for the less scientifically advanced) those emanating it miasmatically through their pores.

In addition, the overall improvement in air quality deriving from the abandonment of gas could have contributed to the decision to limit the use of boxes in an upmarket venue which might otherwise have accommodated increased box trade. The wealthiest customers in the only West End venue to use electric lighting may have been prepared to sit in a more public space (stalls and dress circle) once the overall atmosphere of the auditorium had been improved. This combination of effective social demarcation via entrances and exits, discussed above, with the added comfort and supposed hygiene benefits of electricity encouraged the most profitable use of the auditorium, as a larger number of high-paying customers could be accommodated in the stalls and dress circle than in boxes.

It is, of course, possible that the dangers of contagion were not necessarily uppermost in the minds of late-Victorian theatre audiences. Indeed, such qualms might have been less pronounced at the Savoy, which may, in practice, have contained relatively few members of the unwashed poor. However, it is reasonable to suppose that, in the context of Victorian concerns linking hygiene and class, these fears may have at least contributed to the more generalised desire of the wealthy to remain segregated from their social inferiors. Overall, reduction of heat through electricity seems to have provided a refreshingly novel experience for regular theatregoers. It added to the attractiveness of the Savoy, especially for those who might have harboured doubts about the salubriousness of theatres in general. For the fastidious 'middle classes', an assurance that attending a theatre would be free from personal inconvenience and unpleasantness would have added to its appeal. This may have been especially significant for women. The self-professed probity of Carte's entertainment, together with the emphasis on up-to-date decor and the visual attractions of beautiful female costumes, would have been a major factor in luring middle-class women out of the domestic sphere. *Le Follet*, the smart women's fashion magazine of the period, carried regular updates about events at the Savoy. Wishing to remain comfortable in corsets and evening dress, particularly during the hot summer months, prospective female visitors might have been encouraged by its comments on the 'perfect ventilation' at the Savoy, which

> is an important element of an evening's enjoyment at this season; and when combined with the attractions of Gilbert and Sullivan's aesthetic opera of 'Patience', no one can feel surprised at this theatre being exclusively patronized.[43]

As well as avoiding the noticeable discomfort of hot, smelly auditoria, contemporary perceptions linking electricity with physical well-being could have been an additional motivating factor. In his study of the cultural impact of lighting, *Enchanted Night* (1995), Wolfgang Shchivelbusch postulates that nineteenth-century perceptions of electricity as a physical restorative contributed towards its ready acceptance as a means of interior lighting: 'Electricity did not endanger life or health; on the contrary it was regarded as positively beneficial, almost as a sort of vitamin [...] electricity, energy and life were synonymous' (pp. 71–3).[44]

To the perceived health-giving properties of electricity could be added the important fact that it signified modernity and progress. The Savoy Theatre was the most technologically advanced example of its type, in an age when scientific advancement became a defining feature of Victorian material and intellectual culture (Rhys Morus 2008, p. 457). Before the commencement of the second act of the matinee performance of *Patience* on 28 December 1881,[45] Richard D'Oyly Carte walked onto the stage of the Savoy holding in one hand one of Swan's incandescent bulbs, alight and attached by a cable to the offstage electricity supply. He proceeded to cover it in inflammable muslin and smash it to pieces with no damage either to the muslin or himself.[46] The ostentatious showmanship of this public safety demonstration is indicative of a society in which interest in science was not restricted to the intellectual elite but was part of the regular discourse of the educated classes. As Iwan Rhys Morus observes, 'Both in the metropolis and the provinces, engagement with science through membership of scientific societies, attendance at popular lectures, exhibitions or museums, reading popular accounts or just keeping up with the latest scientific gossip in the press was common' (2008, p. 458). As well as reassuring nervous theatregoers, Carte seems to have tapped into the popular fascination with technology for a 'middle-class' audience for whom science carried considerable cultural capital. As part of celebratory events to commemorate the first anniversary of *Patience* in April 1882, members of the audience were invited backstage to 'inspect all the arrangements for the electric lighting [...] on production of their visiting cards'.[47] Thus the more affluent might satisfy their scientific curiosity by viewing the technical workings, perhaps confirming Carte's promotion of the Savoy as not just the most beautiful and hygienic London theatre, but also as the most technologically sophisticated.

To conclude this survey of the possible cultural significance of electric lighting, some tiny puns in two comic papers suggest an additional reading of the advent of electricity in the Savoy auditorium. The first, from *Funny Folks* (25 February 1882), runs as follows: 'Elec-trickery. Ecclesiastical enemies of the stage should be induced to visit the new Savoy Theatre. Once there they are morally certain to look upon the stage *in a new light*.' The recurrent trope of the propriety of the Carte enterprise, and its consequent appeal to the generally anti-theatrical clergy, is here linked with the new form of lighting. A similar joke had previously appeared in an edition of *Moonshine*: 'Mrs Mifkins, who abominates the sight of her sex in short skirts, announces a determination to visit the Savoy Theatre. She understands that an incan*decent* light is to be found there.'[48] Mrs Mifkins (a credulous, lower-middle-class Mrs Malaprop) became a recurrent vehicle for humorous puns in future editions of this periodical. Her position as supporter of public morality is signified here by her attendance at the Savoy. The atmosphere of the auditorium, dominated by the 'decent' beams of the new lighting system, which will in some magical way expunge any kind of immorality of dress or behaviour, is thus made to appeal to the ultra-respectable matron as well as to the censorious clergy. It is tempting to make a connection between the revealing electric beam and the hygienic improvements which it engendered, with the content and appeal of the Savoy operas and with the Savoy Theatre itself. The new Savoy was a 'clean' auditorium. It was neither malodorous nor unhygienic. And it was also home to a reinvented and morally 'cleansed' form of burlesque. It marked a departure both in atmosphere (in the literal as well as metaphorical sense) and moral tone from the burlesque houses half a mile to the east. It could therefore be seen as a destination for those who regarded cleanliness both of mind and body as synonymous with respectability.[49]

PUBLIC DISCOURSES: THEATRE PROGRAMMES

Having enjoyed the novelty of the electric illumination, and with some time to spare before the beginning of the short 'curtain raiser' at eight o'clock,[50] our suburban spectators may have taken some time to peruse the free programme presented to them by the usher as they entered the auditorium. They may have also obtained a one-shilling copy of the libretto of the main piece, with which to follow the sung or spoken text, or to read afterwards. The back page of the programme advised the musically inclined of the availability of the five-shilling vocal score and three-shilling solo pianoforte arrangement of the *Patience* music, available from Chappell & Co. of New Bond Street (Sands 2008). Thus, spectators could obtain and use adjuncts to the stage performance which might affect their immediate reception, and also allow them to re-experience aspects of the performance through re-enactment, as readers or amateur performers. Such ephemera would also provide them with souvenirs preserving memories of a night at the Savoy, and, if regular visitors, form part of a collection of programmes demonstrating an allegiance to the Gilbert and Sullivan brand.

Printed materials such as these, which form part of the entire 'performance experience' prior to, during and after the show, constitute examples of what Rick Knowles terms 'Public Discourses'. He remarks:

> The cumulative impact of such materials can create discourses of excitement or prestige, exploration or comfort, risk taking or assured quality. It can associate the theatre in audience's minds with [...] outstanding acting or directing, with excellence in design, display or spectacle, as it can evoke nationalist sentiments, or associations with theatrical classics.
>
> (2004, p. 92)

It is probable therefore that the experience of Savoy audiences was influenced by the liberality of the management in providing free, high-quality programmes, as well as by reading favourable press reviews and journalistic comment before and after their theatre visit. But as well as affecting audience reception of a theatre event, the kind of ephemera generated by the

D'Oyly Carte enterprise, together with press releases and critical reviews, can be used to create a reading of managerial intentions and audience expectations which reveals much about the cultural assumptions of both producer and consumer.

Oost (2009) devotes much space to discussion of the cultural significance of theatre programmes and libretti in the promotion of the D'Oyly Carte brand. As a basis for understanding those pertaining to *Patience* in 1881/2, it will be useful to summarise some of her arguments. She interprets injunctions to correct behaviour in West End programmes of this period—for example, Carte's ban on the acceptance of fees by theatre staff for taking care of 'wraps or umbrellas', or requests for audiences to remain seated until the final curtain—as attesting to, and consolidating, 'the status of audience members by establishing theatres as venues for the display of middle-class virtues' (p. 64).

The importance of Savoy programmes, when displayed at home, as prestige items in their own right, demonstrating their purchaser's 'sophistication and economic wherewithal' (p. 69) in attending a fashionable West End theatre, is linked by Oost to the particular attractiveness of their design. She points out that the sometimes lavishly produced programmes typically exhibited Carte's desire to provide a product superior to that of his rivals (pp. 70–4). The fact that, after the opening of the Savoy, programme illustrations often referred back to earlier Gilbert and Sullivan productions exhibits a desire on behalf of a commercially shrewd management to create a sense of 'tradition' and brand identification, tacitly encouraging the desire to become a 'Savoyard' or Gilbert and Sullivan fan (pp. 137–9). From the run of *The Sorcerer* onwards, unique souvenir programmes, printed on card and featuring original artwork depicting scenes from the operas, were issued for special occasions, including first nights. Another such event was the simultaneous 250th performance of *Patience* in London and New York on 29 December 1881. These, together with the regular programmes, became increasingly lavish in terms of size and design as the success of the venture increased.[51]

Oost regards the commercial activities of the Savoy, including its non-performance-based aspects, as attracting a clientele whose 'economic patronage [...] was thus wholly consistent with, and indeed attested to a bourgeois identity constructed upon the dual pillars of respectability and consumerism' (p. 80). Oost's concentration on the extent and success of Carte's marketing strategy is not the focus of intention here. However, examination of surviving *Patience* programmes in the light of her analysis, and comparison with earlier and subsequent programmes, can provide some insight into the 'respectability' of the Carte enterprise and its intended audience.

The programmes for the first night and for much of the run consist of a single sheet folded in two, comprising four printed pages (Sands 2008). Early Savoy specimens consist of a front title page with the name of the theatre placed above and printed in a slightly smaller typeface than the title of the opera, indicating that the importance of the new venue is almost as significant as that of the opera itself. The first three pages are bordered with elegant line drawings of scenes from the show, providing a tasteful artefact which might appeal to the aesthetic sensibilities of those who considered themselves able to appreciate such things. These pages contain information pertaining to the performance: cast list, start times, details of costumes, stage design and refreshment facilities, as well as Carte's injunction against tipping theatre staff. Only the back page contains advertisements. These are exclusively for Chappell of Bond Street and, as mentioned above, 'cross advertise' material relating to the show in the form of the *Patience* libretto and various musical arrangements, as well as promoting unrelated pieces by popular composers of the day.

It is possible that an arrangement with Chappell allowed them the right to be sole advertiser at the prestigious new venue.[52] Perhaps at the start of the Savoy venture, Carte wished to focus the audience's attention chiefly on the Savoy brand and its product rather than on unrelated advertisements for other types of merchandise.[53] What is certain is that an advertisement for products aimed at performance in the home would conform to the tastes and expectations of the respectable 'middle classes'. Regarded as a suitably edifying 'rational recreation', and creating a rapidly expanding market for both sheet music and pianos, domestic music-making flourished during the first half of the century and continued to be popular in bourgeois households (Scott 1988, p. 83; Flanders 2006, pp. 357–66). For whatever reasons, the programme conveys a stylish attempt to present the Savoy and *Patience* in a way which asserts its independence from other products and companies, and which places its readers in a comfortable world of elegance and rational amusement. As the theatre building itself was separated and distanced from rival forms of entertainment, so the programme remains (almost) 'chaste' in its focus on the new theatre and its product.

During the run of the show, the illustrative elements in the programme change or are omitted, but the basic content and structure, including advertising copy, remains the same. However, a *Patience* programme which *predates* the transferral from the Opera Comique shows something rather different (Sands 2008). In common with others from the earlier operas (*The Sorcerer, HMS Pinafore, The Pirates of Penzance*), it advertises a range of goods reflecting the kind of patronage that a Gilbert and Sullivan opera might receive. There are four products mentioned and all are drinks: Wilhelm's Quelle, a 'sparkling table water'; Zoedone, 'a tonic non-alcoholic Champagne'; Vin-Sante, 'the most perfect non-alcoholic beverage'; and Montserrat Pure Lime Juice Cordials, 'guaranteed free from alcohol'.

Then as now, the publisher—in this case the theatre management—is responsible for seeking viable sources of income from potential advertisers. The Savoy management must have been aware of the products likely to appeal to a typical audience member, and therefore of those companies who might buy advertising space. Here, the advertising sought is that most likely to appeal to members of the sober 'middle classes'. It is also important to bear in mind that, prior to the move to the Savoy, programmes were not given free of charge. Thus, the advertising was likely to have been aimed at the majority of audience members likely to buy a programme.

After the move to the Savoy, two types of programme seem to have been provided. These were a decorative sheet bearing advertisements, and a plain card type, containing only information relating to the evening's entertainment. It is likely that the latter was intended for the cheaper, unreserved sections of the auditorium. Thus programme advertising between 1881 and 1896 was aimed at the more affluent spectator. The fact that temperance drinks continued to be advertised to this group indicates the continued presence of 'serious' evangelical and non-conformist audience members. The next chapter will explore the notion that the D'Oyly Carte brand was particularly suited to the preferences of dissenting religious groups. It was among this sector that support for prohibition of alcohol was most prevalent, although avoidance of excess would have been advocated by many of the Anglican middle classes (Thompson 1988, pp. 318–19). Prospective advertisers must have considered that a Gilbert and Sullivan audience was an appropriate market for non-alcoholic drinks, and that Carte wished to promote this image in his programmes. Programmes were also ongoing and self-reinforcing advertisements for the D'Oyly Carte brand, albeit for customers who had visited the theatre at least once. The products found within maintained an image of the company as a purveyor of a set of 'respectable' values held *mutually* by the D'Oyly Carte company, its audiences and its advertisers.

It is important to be wary of over-categorisation of audience sectors and 'target' audiences. Tastes and preferences for products inevitably overlapped. The presence of temperance drinks in advertising does not mean that a Savoy audience consisted entirely of straight-laced abstainers, and programme advertising was not entirely devoted to decent self-restraint. Surviving *Sorcerer* programmes contain sole adverts for Rimmel or Gosnell's perfume, and programmes from the late 1870s contain various luxury products and services. 'Japanese Curtains (51 Oxford Street)', 'Oswald Gudgeon, Russian Cigarette Importer', and 'Krikorian Bros. Rahat Lakoum'[54] all feature in a *Pinafore* programme of May 1879 ([a] Sands 2011). However, more unpretentious products, of the kind alluded to in the *Patience* programme above, also feature during the runs of *HMS Pinafore* and *The Pirates of Penzance*, indicating an awareness that the 'respectable' as well as the 'fashionable' bourgeoisie were frequenting Gilbert and Sullivan performances. Advertisements for 'Tic-Sano tonic', 'Chas. Baker and Co., Clothing at Trade Prices', and 'The Working Man's Mutual Society' (a life insurance firm) indicate that the advertising was aimed at a grouping containing those who prized the essential 'middle-class' ethics of thrift, bodily health and financial security.

After *Patience* and *Iolanthe*, programmes begin to reflect a greater diversity of product and seem aimed at an audience less concerned about abstemiousness, alcoholic or otherwise. While tonics and temperance drinks are still present, a large and colourful ten-page souvenir programme for *The Mikado* in October 1885 ([d] Sands 2011) features products aimed at the luxury end of the market. 'Redfern Ladies Tailor (Braided Coats, Riding Habits and Mantles)—By appointment to Her Majesty the Queen' shares a page with 'The Winter Cruise Office', offering tours to exotic destinations including Natal, India and Madagascar. On other pages are 'Milner's Safes (for the safe custody of diamonds, jewellery and other items of great value)' and 'Herbert Harrison, Stock and Share Broker'. This level of advertising was not common to standard *Mikado* programmes. First nights and special occasions attracted some particularly prestigious advertisers. Nevertheless, an example from earlier in the *Mikado* run (July 1885) contains advertisements for affordable luxuries—'Barber and Company's French Coffee—A luxury unknown in England' and 'T.A. Dickson Flowers—Wedding, Ball and Theatre Bouquets [...] sprays and dress pieces' ([c] Sands 2011).

The move to the Savoy was a successful attempt to reposition the product in the competitive West End marketplace. In business terms, the 'offering' remained the same, but the 'packaging'—the venue, marketing and the 'message' implicit in programme advertising—was somewhat altered. The financial success and popularity of the operas may have reduced the need to appeal so directly to the 'serious' Victorian who otherwise eschewed public entertainment. Programme advertising suggests that the brand remained attractive to these customers, but by the early-to-mid 1880s, it was no longer deemed necessary to target them so directly. If our suburban theatregoers, perusing the advertisements for mineral water in 1882, subsequently became confirmed 'Savoyards', they could, during the run of *Utopia, Limited*, twelve years later, have found themselves examining copy promoting Erard Pianos (Makers to the Royal Family) and Carte's own Savoy Hotel ('The Hotel de Luxe of the World') (Sands 2012).

Significantly, programme content and design can also be read as signifiers of the company's decline. The penultimate original production under Carte's auspices[55] was German and Hood's *Merrie England*, premiered in 1902.[56] One of several attempts to replicate the success of the Gilbert and Sullivan works (in particular *The Yeomen of the Guard* with which it shares a Tudor setting), *Merrie England* ran for a mediocre 120 performances. A programme from December 1902 ([b] Sands 2011) consists of a single sheet folded in three. No longer replete with original artwork, the front page displays the modest black and gold 'ancient coat of arms of the Savoy'. This generic image was used continually from 1897, after the final original Gilbert and Sullivan piece, *The Grand Duke*, had closed after a relatively unsuccessful run. The name of the opera and its composers now appear only on the inside pages, indicating that, after the demise of the Gilbert and Sullivan partnership, the Savoy brand was more marketable than its product. Compared with earlier examples, this programme conveys an impression of waning fortunes. The inclusion of such modest items as Bryant and May matches indicates a need for revenue from any source. The presence of two blank, unsold sections bearing the legend 'This space to let—Apply to Mr J.W. Beckwith Savoy Theatre' reinforces the notion that the company was, to use theatrical slang of the period, 'on its uppers'.[57]

'The Bond Street Fur Company' supplies an example of luxury advertising, but 'Brinsmead Pianos' has replaced the internationally famous Erard brand. Epps Cocoa and Schweppes Table Waters (both regular advertisers through the 1880s) remain as representatives of the soft drink market, but the absence of alcohol is no longer an issue. Significantly, Ind-Coope Draught Ale and Plowman and Co. bottled beers are publicised, and are referred to as being available at the theatre bars. The indication here is

of a greater cultural acceptance of alcohol at the advent of the twentieth century, and a concomitant abandonment of the earlier emphasis on
temperance in the advertising revenue sought. At the midpoint of the
nineteenth century, the respectable classes did not drink publicly at all,
and beer could signify working-class intemperance at its worst. However,
for the upper classes 'social life without alcohol was inconceivable' and the
'middle classes' were divided between those who accepted 'moderate wine
drinking in their own homes' and the teetotal (Thompson 1988, pp. 308–
10, 318). By the time the Savoy opened, alcohol was on offer in theatres
specifically catering to middle- and upper-class needs,[58] particularly when
such venues, like the Savoy, offered full dining facilities.

The fact that beer was prominently advertised in the programme of a
theatre which ten years earlier had been at the height of fashion suggests
a possible alteration in the regular make-up of Savoy audiences. Audience
demographics will be considered in more detail in the next chapter, but it
is worth noting that the patronage of those purchasing the cheaper seats at
the Savoy could have become more valuable as fashionable custom shifted
elsewhere. Beer drinking may have been more common among the inhabitants of the pit and gallery, and it is possible that their continued presence
at the Savoy made such advertising worthwhile for a management finding
it harder to obtain revenue as Savoy opera became less popular with West
End audiences.

Public Discourses: Printed Commentary

Reviews of the original production of *Patience*, which may have attracted
our provincial spectators to its reincarnation at the Savoy, can return us
momentarily to this venue at its most celebrated period. Dramatic criticism
of the premiere at the Opera Comique was, in common with the previous
three Gilbert and Sullivan operas, extremely favourable. Critical reception
of the Savoy opening night focuses on the theatre and its new form of
lighting rather than the merits of the piece, which are taken for granted.
For the purposes of this study, the most noteworthy feature of several
reviews is their reassertion of the essential decorum associated with the
operas, revealing assumptions about morality common to critics, prospective audiences and the D'Oyly Carte organisation. The *Daily News* remarks
on 'the absence of anything approaching to coarseness or vulgarity [...]
visitors to the opera may go away with the double certainty of being thoroughly amused and not in any way offended'.[59] In a similar vein, *The Times*

notes that 'there is not a sentence in the dialogue which [...] "Is calculated to bring the blush of shame to the cheek of modesty", the superiority in this, as in other respects, of the English over French burlesque being again manifested in the most sterling manner'.[60] The critics are clearly signalling the fact that the opera will, like its predecessors, appeal to those who value 'respectable' entertainment.

The lead up to the Savoy opening received considerable press coverage, demonstrating an interest from both press and public in the enterprise. Carte's difficulty in obtaining building permission from the London Board of Works featured in several articles.[61] *The Country Gentleman* kept its readers up to date with various bulletins relating to the new technology. Reports on the 24 November and 8 October 1881 commented on teething problems with the lighting system, which resulted in the postponement of the opening night from Thursday 6 to Monday 10 October. Another piece (25 November) reported complaints from local gentlemen's clubs about the noise made by the Savoy's large external electrical generator, which was situated in a plot of land on the opposite side of Somerset Street. Further articles devoted to descriptions of the new theatre and its novel lighting system appeared just before and after its opening.[62] Many similar commentaries appeared in regional newspapers throughout Great Britain, reflecting an interest in the London activities of a company which had spread its influence through three years of national touring.

Overall, press coverage of the Triumvirate's activities during the run of *Patience*, and throughout their partnership, is too extensive to warrant full coverage here. Numerous reviews, articles, press releases, jokes, cartoons and advertisements are to be found in the pages of contemporary journals and periodicals. Any one of them could be subjected to a reading which explored its relevance to the cultural values of producer and consumer, and this chapter has already considered several examples in preceding sections. However, it is rare but instructive to hear a dissenting voice on the apparent popularity of the Savoy genre. Not all reviews were positive and, as we have seen, cartoons could contain ironic criticism of Carte and his business methods. A piece in the *Sporting Times* recapitulates some of the themes explored in this chapter, concerning the significance of the Savoy's positioning in the urban landscape, its pretensions to social exclusivity and its focus on respectable values.

A week before the opening of the new theatre the *Sporting Times* satirised the perceived odour of sanctity attached to the D'Oyly Carte enterprise:

> It is well known that the Opera Comique has under its present management acquired a reputation for religious and moral sanctity unsurpassed by any other playhouse in London. Consequently we are not surprised to hear that an elegant zinc chapel has been added to the accommodation of the Savoy Theatre. This building, which will probably be dedicated to S.S. Gilbert and Sullivan, will be under the [...] ministration of The Very Rev. D'Oyly Carte, Dean of the Savoy [...] Mr. F. Cellier will be the organist, the church wardens being Messrs. Grossmith and Barrington [...] Deaconess Alice Barnett[63] will occasionally preach, and sisters Bond, Gwynn and Fortescue minister to the wants of the poor in the vicinity. Altogether this chapel idea strikes us as being a great and a good one.[64]

This piece reminds us that the ethos of the Savoy could be seen as ridiculous by contemporary commentators who may have preferred less sanctimonious entertainments, and some of the predominantly male readership of the *Sporting Times* could well have been among them. There is more than a hint of mockery concerning Carte's attempts to lure the theatre-shy by emphasising the propriety of his offerings. Irony is implicit in the idea that the Opera Comique, intended by its original management as a venue for French farce and *opera bouffe*, was now geared towards respectability. Advance publicity concerning the splendour of the Savoy's internal and external decoration is undercut by the implied visual contrast with what is basically a brick or wooden shed with a corrugated metal roof. Carte's promotional interest in the historical importance of the site is manifested in a press release of 6 October where he reminds readers that the Savoy is:

> Built on a spot [...] close to the Savoy Chapel and in the 'precinct of the Savoy' where stood formerly the Savoy Palace once inhabited by John of Gaunt and the Dukes of Lancaster and made memorable in the Wars of the Roses [...] on the Savoy Manor there was apparently a theatre. I have used that ancient name as an appropriate title for the new one.
>
> (cited in Cellier and Bridgeman 1914, p. 96)

Loading the site with historical significance can be seen as an attempt to overlay blunt capitalist entrepreneurship with an appeal to romantic nationalist sentiments. The home of the new 'English' comic opera is one apparently laden with medieval splendour and, as such, a fitting invocation of the patriotic sentiments of English audiences. The nearby Savoy Chapel[65] mentioned by Carte was often used as a venue for fashionable weddings[66] and possessed some of the social exclusiveness to which

Carte's enterprise aspired (Goodman 2000, p. 26). Although published a few days prior to Carte's press release, the reference to a zinc 'chapel' in the *Sporting Times* piece provides an ironically reductionist echo of the presence of the nearby historical monument. Such an edifice is referred to satirically in James Greenwood's *Unsentimental Journeys; or the Byeways of Modern Babylon* (1867), an ironically caricatured, though culturally observant, stroll through London's less salubrious backstreets. Here, 'the Rev. Dapple Mookow, a minister of the Alack-a-day Saints persuasion, and the proprietor of the patent movable corrugated-zinc chapel' bearing the name 'Pewkers Hall', preaches the virtues of temperance to a group of working-class abstainers. Rousing songs such as 'Fill up the Tea Urn' and 'Coffee is my Darling' are performed (Greenwood 1867, p. 170). The notion that a place of Christian worship, and one which proclaimed the avoidance of alcohol with temperance hymns, could be added to a new theatre building devoted to comic opera heightens the absurdity of the joke and provides an ironic reflection on the type of musical entertainment on offer at the Opera Comique and Savoy.

The *Sporting Times* author's ironic sanctification of author and composer, and the transmutation of a financially astute theatrical entrepreneur into a high-ranking churchman, offers an incongruous disparity with prevalent assumptions regarding the moral probity of theatre people. This is compounded by the vision of comedians as church wardens, and pretty soubrettes as religious charity workers. But fundamentally, the overall impact of the joke depends less on the contrast between morality and a false show of decorum than on the potential *truthfulness* of the absurd image. D'Oyly Carte management and practitioners were genuinely engaged in a project which was intended to raise the moral tone of theatre performance, albeit with a strong financial incentive. Carte's desire to maintain high standards of backstage discipline and decency will be addressed in Chapter 6, and his recruitment of artists associated with respectable 'entertainments' and the world of 'serious' music has already been commented on. The piece is a clear expression of contemporary opinion about a company which was remarkable, even in the increasingly respectable West End of the 1870s, as a bastion of moral decency.

SUMMARY

I would suggest that a major reason for the success of the Savoy brand was a correlation in outlook and aspiration between those who were responsible for producing the 'theatre event', those who consumed it and those who commented on it. The Triumvirate, Carte's management team and their chosen architect and designers broadly shared and understood the preferences, concerns and prejudices of 'middle-class' audiences and critics because they were part of that group. This is reflected by the material expectations and aspirations of Gilbert, Sullivan and Carte. It was the profits from *Patience* that enabled them to significantly alter their own standards of living (Goodman 1988, p. 139), evidenced by the improved domestic arrangements of the creative collaborators which occurred in 1881–1883, and that of Carte on his remarriage several years later.

In 1881 Sullivan took leases on two flats in fashionable Victoria Street, for himself and his secretary. His mistress, Fanny Ronalds, advised on interior decoration, which included exotic souvenirs from Sullivan's foreign holidays. 'Persian carpets, silk wall hangings and tapestries, oriental lamps and lanterns, antique Egyptian screens, divans [and] palms [...] other potted plants and a parrot' adorned the apartment. Here Sullivan instituted a regular Sunday *salon*, with eminent guests such as the Prince of Wales, the Duke of Edinburgh and Ferdinand Rothschild (Goodman 2000, p. 21). In 1883, the Gilberts moved to a magnificent purpose-built city mansion in Harrington Gardens, Kensington. Featuring oak-panelled hallways, massive carved chimney pieces and a 'huge stepped gable of nineteen stages', it also boasted oil-fired central heating and electric lighting throughout (Goodman 2000, p. 96). In common with his partners, Carte's Adelphi Terrace house contained a telephone. However, his possession of the first domestic electronic lift in any British private residence confirmed the fascination with the latest technology that had inspired the electrification at the Savoy. Interior decoration by James McNeill Whistler placed Carte's town house at the forefront of London fashion, and his purchase, in 1887, of a private island on the Thames near Weybridge confirmed and proclaimed his social and financial status (Goodman 2000, pp. 139–40).

Display of achievement through material assets reveals the Triumvirate as the societal equivalents of their target audience, the 'carriage trade' who alighted at the Savoy's Somerset Street entrance. They are representative of the late-Victorian upper middle class in terms of earnings, conspicuous consumption and social recognition. Significantly, this success demonstrated that the central entrepreneurial, professional and artistic values of the 'middle classes' could be found among theatre practitioners, reinforcing the validity of this line of business within the status-conscious bourgeoisie. The fact that Gilbert, Sullivan and Carte shared the material, financial and social standing of the more prestigious members of their audience (except royalty or the aristocracy) would in turn have contributed to the cachet of the brand they represented.

However, these conclusions need to be qualified by the fact that the social make-up of a particular audience is equally dictated by the commercial realities of theatre business management, and the incomes of the individuals who make up that audience. It must not be assumed that the Savoy appealed only to a respectable and affluent coterie. In common with many West End theatres, seat pricing was geared towards a wider demographic. If the brand provided principally for the expectations of the wealthy bourgeoisie, how does this square with the fact that 50 per cent of its audience were economically out of this class? The extent to which Savoy audiences were both financially and attitudinally a homogenised grouping will be the primary consideration of the next chapter.

Notes

1. *Patience* premiered at the Opera Comique on 23 April 1881, where it ran for 170 performances, before transferring to the new venue (Rollins and Witts 1962, p. 8).
2. The Underground system 'middle circle' could have transported visitors from suburbs such as Uxbridge in the west, and Notting Hill in the north. The 'outer circle' served the further Willesden, Hampstead and Camden Town vicinities in the north and north-east. Neither ran directly to Charing Cross. Travellers would have had to change onto the 'inner circle' route to access this station. However, the West End was accessible to at least the western and northern London suburbs by train in the 1880s (Dickens Jr 1888, pp. 209–10).
3. Bear in mind that 1s was the price of the cheapest gallery seat at the Savoy.
4. Different routes were colour coded for easy recognition. The 'Chocolate' or Brown bus routes started from Chelsea and made a round trip via Bethnal Green in the east.
5. According to a report in the *Daily News* (24 May 1880), Carte was granted permission to develop the site only on condition that he pay part of the cost of the new roadway. Perceived traffic problems had led to objections to the Savoy project from the Metropolitan Board of Works. See also Joseph 1994, p. 23.
6. *Morning Post*, 11 October 1881.
7. *Morning Post*, 11 October 1881.
8. Carriage access from the Strand was via Savoy Street, which formed a junction with Somerset Street on the south side of the theatre.

9. While the Savoy Theatre continues to operate, modern theatregoers cannot be said to 'know' its original incarnation. Although a theatre exists on the same site that bears the same name, much of the original Savoy no longer stands. The Somerset Street entrance was replaced by a new main entrance in the Strand in 1909, the exterior and auditorium were extensively remodelled in 1929, and much of the auditorium was destroyed in the fire of 1990. It was rebuilt as an exact reconstruction of the 1929 Basil Ionides design and reopened in 1993. To forestall such misconception, I have described the Savoy in the way that would be used to describe any artefact of the past whose remains lie only in visual and written archival sources.

10. *The Times*, 3 October 1881.

11. A more striking example of such a free-standing building is Carte's Royal English Opera House, built in 1891, now the Palace Theatre in Shaftesbury Avenue.

12. Sullivan received a knighthood the year after the opening of the Savoy for his services to music.

13. Rutland Barrington refers euphemistically to the 'celebrated literary emporiums of those days' visible from the upstairs dressing rooms in Holywell Street (Barrington 1908, p. 17).

14. These theatres were demolished in 1899 as part of the Aldwych redevelopment.

15. A domestic corollary could also be implied—the grand, detached domestic residence replaces the terrace or back-to-back slum.

16. *Era*, 1 October 1881.

17. 'Although not *de rigueur* in any part of the theatres […] it predominates in the stalls, especially in theatres such as the Lyceum, the Gaiety [and] the Savoy […] at the Italian operas evening dress is indispensable' (Dickens Jr, 1993, p. 95). The Savoy was the fashionable kind of venue which emulated the dress codes of the opera house, the most expensive and socially exclusive of public entertainments.

18. *Era*, 1 October 1881.

19. *Morning Post*, 10 October 1881.

20. Wilde, a doyen of the Aesthetic movement, was a patron of the Savoy—he attended performances during the run of *Patience*—and, as Wilde's agent, Carte managed his 1882 American lecture series as pre-publicity for *Patience*'s American tour. His lecture 'The House Beautiful' was created for the American circuit and the similarities in decorative good taste between the Savoy and Wilde's ideal home indicates the extent to which the latest fashions in domestic decor were reflected in the internal appearance of Carte's theatre.

21. *Era*, 5 October 1879.

22. *Era*, 1 October 1881.

23. François Cellier remarks that 'in place of the poisonous concoction of fusil-oil, excellent whiskey was provided, and pure coffee took the place of the customary chicory—and all at a reasonable tariff' (Cellier and Bridgeman 1914, pp. 102 – 3). Carte was clearly endeavouring to supply a high level of customer service in all areas.

24. To take this analogy a stage further, there might also be a hint of xenophobia in the association of the francophone name of the Savoy's owner with his nickname in theatrical circles, where he was known as 'Oily' Carte. Although this apparently derived from his suave manner and ability to influence employees, particularly in matters of salary (Joseph 1994, p. 10), there are, perhaps, suggestions here of national stereotyping, in which 'foreigners', possibly those involved in the restaurant trade, might receive offensive epithets, such as 'greasy'.

25. Including the *Morning Post*, 26 September 1881, the *Pall Mall Gazette*, 11 October 1881, etc.

26. *Daily Telegraph*, 8 October 1881.

27. Ibid.

28. *Era*, 24 November 1881.

29. An aspect of service common to other upscale West End theatres, such as the Lyceum and the Haymarket (Oost 2009, p. 64).

30. *Morning Post*, 11 October 1881. Hounslow Heath was, historically, an area frequented by highwaymen, and the 'tones' mentioned here presumably refer to their peremptory injunction to 'stand and deliver'.

31. *Era*, 18 February 1882.

32. The Gaiety (1868), Shaftesbury (1888) and Prince of Wales (1884) theatres, also designed by Phipps, were very similar in layout, as, with few variations, were most West End theatres at this time (Lloyd).

33. *Daily News*, 11 October 1881.

34. *Truth*, 20 October 1881.

35. It was similarly regarded by Oscar Wilde when considering domestic interior decoration (O'Brien 1974, pp. 405 – 7).

36. *Daily Telegraph*, 11 October 1881.

37. *Era*, 15 October 1881.

38. In contrast, *The Country Gentleman and Sporting Gazette* of 29 July 1882 reports a comment made by RDC that, during the current hot spell, 'the temperature was only seventy in the stalls, and seventy-two in the balcony, and that a headache is out of the question at the Savoy'.

39. Letter to the Editor. *Era*, 8 February 1880.

40. However, despite Carte's installation of gas-powered air conditioning in the form of a state-of-the-art 'Strode Sun Burner', conditions even at the Savoy would compare unfavourably with those of the twenty-first century. On rare occasions, temperatures in the Savoy galley could rise to 90 F. One must assume that the foregoing remarks regarding comfort levels were reactions

to the generally inferior auditorium conditions which had hitherto prevailed (Wilmore 2013).

41. The link between notions of impurity, dirtiness and pollution as distinguishing features of an undesirable underclass whose existence was either barely tolerated or explicitly rejected by a dominant group is, regrettably, pervasive throughout human history. See Harari (2014, pp. 154–9).

42. Despite a growing realisation that disease was caused by microbes, Davis notes that scientific verification of the existence of 'germs' did not occur until 1883 and that 'contagionist theory (later supported by proof of microscopic disease-producing organisms) *only slowly won out* over miasmology' (Davis 2000, p. 99, my italics).

43. *Le Follet*, 1 August 1882.

44. Perhaps trading on this perception, a Savoy programme for *Utopia, Limited* (1893) displays an advertisement for an electrically powered health gadget: 'Harness's Electropathic Belts—every weak man and delicate woman should wear one' (Sands 2012).

45. This was the first performance in which electric stage lighting was used. For two and a half months after the opening only the front of house and auditorium received electric illumination.

46. *The Times*, 28 December 1881.

47. *Era*, 22 April 1882.

48. *Moonshine*, 14 January 1882.

49. See also Davis (2000, p. 111).

50. During most of the Savoy run of *Patience*, the curtain raiser was *Mock Turtles*, 'A New and Original Vaudeville' by Desprez and Faning.

51. It is worth noting that the luxurious commemorative programmes issued for special occasions were not provided to those inhabiting the least expensive unreserved seats (Oost 2009, p. 66). Further discussion of significant social distinctions within the apparently 'middle-class' Savoy audience will be covered in the next chapter. The fact that only half the house got the smart souvenir is an indication of who Carte regarded as his target audience.

52. From a financial point of the view, the arrangement with Chappell & Co. was very advantageous to the Triumvirate. Each member shared a portion of advertising revenue, and WSG and AS received royalties from sales of sheet music and libretti which might result from programme advertising (Oost 2009, p. 75).

53. Programmes for the next opera, *Iolanthe*, follow this pattern of sole advertisement. For *Iolanthe*, Liberty & Co. of Regent Street is the exclusive advertiser. Liberty provided the material for the female costumes in the show. This fact is referred to in their advertisement, drawing the attention of the ladies of the audience to the possibility of acquiring the fabrics for themselves. It provided an opportunity for what is known in the twenty-first century as 'synergetic marketing'.

54. Turkish Delight.

55. The D'Oyly Carte brand remained, under the control of Helen Carte, RDC's widow, though William Greet managed the theatre, having bought the lease, though not the freehold, in 1901.

56. From 1892 until the end of the Carte tenure in 1903, the last two G&S works (*Utopia, Limited* and *The Grand Duke*), along with many revivals of old favourites, were interspersed with a number of new productions by different creative teams.

57. *A Princess of Kensington* (1903) by Hood and German was the final 'Savoy Opera'. It ran until May 1903, after which the theatre was closed and taken over by a new management in 1904 (Rollins & Witts 1962, p. 22). Despite a series of prestigious West End revivals between 1906 and 1909, the D'Oyly Carte company was from 1903 essentially a touring organisation. Between 1909 and 1919 the company was absent from the West End. It did not return to the Savoy until 1929.

58. See n68 above.

59. *Daily News*, 25 April 1881.

60. *The Times*, 25 April 1881.

61. For example, *Daily News*, 24 May 1880.

62. For example, *Morning Post*, 26 April; *Daily News* and *Pall Mall Gazette*, 11 October 1881.

63. Alice Barnett created the contralto 'older woman' role of Lady Jane in *Patience*, and Jessie Bond that of Lady Angela. Julia Gwynne and May Fortescue played supporting characters.

64. *Sporting Times*, 1 October 1881.

65. More correctly known as the Queen's Chapel of the Savoy (Goodman 2000, p. 26).

66. RDC married his personal assistant, Helen Couper Black (Helen Lenoir), here on 12 April 1888 (Goodman 2000).

CHAPTER 5

Savoy Audiences 1881–1909

While 'middle-class' material values pervaded the Savoy, it is rather too easy to assume that all Savoy spectators were, economically, middle class. Was this audience a more culturally diverse affair than the 'semi-private club' envisaged by Regina Oost (2009, p. 33)? Few clubs segregate their members into the kind of demarcated and potentially disconnected groupings to be found in Victorian theatre auditoria. While acknowledging social distinctions in access and seating, Oost emphasises a cosy camaraderie engendered by clever branding and a shared interest in 'commonly held beliefs, behaviours and shared anxieties' among the Savoy spectators (2009, pp. 32–3). Although the notion of shared 'middle-class' attitudes and beliefs (a bourgeois 'ideology') is central to this thesis, it does not necessarily follow that a communal engagement with a particular entertainment experience reflects social solidarity either inside or outside the theatre. The intention here is to look into the social composition of the Savoy audience, exploring possible disparities in income, expectation and behaviour. Oost's 'hierarchical' reading, which envisages a unified reception and expression of approval irrespective of economic disparity, will be challenged in the light of evidence suggesting alternative interpretations of attitudes regarding group identity.[1]

How wide was this group, in class terms? Despite the elegant evening dress and codified social behaviour of those inhabiting boxes, stalls and circle, a large proportion of seating in some apparently 'gentrified' theatres, such as the Savoy, remained cheap and unreserved, suggesting a dichotomy of intention underlying the apparent bias towards the promotion of the West End as an affluent leisure area. While Oost (2009 pp. 20–7) is convinced that the 'lower-classes' were excluded from the Savoy, Crowther (2000, pp. 98–9) and Joseph (1994, p. 73) assert a 'working-class' presence in the gallery. Detailed analysis of audience composition, and especially of those in the cheaper seats, is therefore necessary to further scrutinise the relationship between the theatre event and commercial managerial practice. However, there is not a great deal of first-hand information about Savoy audiences. Thus a holistic approach drawing on a number of sources and explanations is required. This inevitably necessitates the use of primary sources, such as memoirs, press articles and contemporary fiction, which deal obliquely or not at all with the Carte enterprise, but which contain information relevant to the investigation. In order to arrive at some provisional answers, informed hypothesis is required to interpret the available data. So the conditional conclusions reached by this chapter should be understood as a proposed interpretation of the evidence rather than a rigid set of solutions.

Between 1881 and 1903, the D'Oyly Carte company played to generally good houses at the Savoy. The danger of oversimplification is attendant on any attempt to interpret the economic, cultural and social make-up of a fluid conglomeration of hundreds of thousands of people over a 20-year period, using limited evidence. Social and cultural factors may well have caused some changes over this time, and the ensuing discussion follows Michael Booth's dictum that 'generalising about nineteenth-century audiences is […] a risky business' (1991, p. 10). Other authors, particularly Davis and Emeljanow and Schoch, have resisted earlier tendencies to assume that West End theatre in the second half of the nineteenth century was the preserve of the bourgeoisie (Davis and Emeljanow 2001, pp. 161–4; Schoch 2004, pp. 343–5). Booth reminds us that 'it is a serious over simplification to picture the nineteenth-century theatre as climbing slowly out of […] working class domination in the early part of the century to reach an eminence of profound Victorian decorum' (p. 10). Indeed, changing tastes reflected by alterations in the content of programme advertising copy were shown in the last chapter to suggest possible shifts in the social make-up of the Savoy audience over two decades.

However, the economics of theatrical management are manifested in seat pricing, and the pricing structure at the Savoy remained more or less intact throughout the D'Oyly Carte occupancy. This chapter will therefore explore the constituency of audiences from the move from the

Opera Comique until the conclusion of the Carte tenure at the Savoy by examining it through three pricing sections: (1) stalls and circles (the reserved seats); (2) the pit; and (3) the gallery (the unreserved seats). Differences in behaviour and response will be investigated to try to identify some tendencies and trends in the make-up of lower-income spectators. This approach will seek to explore ways in which societal change, particularly that which concerned the expanding middle classes, affected leisure provision and consumption at the Savoy and, by implication, the West End, from the 1870s onwards.

PRICING AND SOCIAL DIVISION

First, some essential statistics. The total capacity of the Savoy was 1274[2] and it used a pricing structure which conformed to general West End practice (Davis and Emeljanow 2001, p. 187). The spaciously laid-out stalls contained 175 separate 'arm chairs' in nine rows. The six rows of the dress circle and the five rows of the upper circle accommodated 187 and 178 respectively. Boxes provided for 78 seats. A maximum of 618 seats (48.5 per cent of the total capacity) was therefore given over to pre-bookable, 'expensive' seating. One hundred and sixty-five people could be accommodated in the five rows of pit seats behind the stalls, around 118 could be squeezed into the amphitheatre and 373 more in the topmost gallery benches (Howard 1986, pp. 214–15). Unreserved lower-priced accommodation was therefore available for 659 people (51.5 per cent of the total capacity).

During the opening run of *Patience*, boxes were priced at three guineas and two guineas,[3] and stalls at 10s 6d. The dress circle above was known at the Savoy as 'balcony stalls'. Presumably this was to differentiate its clientele from the lower-paying attendees in the 'circle' above, as the term 'balcony *stalls*' would remind spectators that evening dress was preferred here. Admission was 7s 6d for the front row and 6s thereafter. The circle offered the cheapest pre-bookable seats at 3s. Unreserved seating in the pit was 2s 6d, and the topmost level was divided into two price points—the so-called 'amphitheatre' at 2s, and the rearmost gallery at 1s. Using these figures a full house would take around £271 5s, a figure verified by Dark and Grey, who state that '[t]he Savoy theatre originally held about £270 when quite full' (1923, p. 85), with the higher-priced sections responsible for £219 12s (81 per cent of total takings) and the lower-priced sections £51 13s (19 per cent).[4]

With the more expensive seats accounting for a large proportion of revenue, it might be assumed that the Savoy, like the Prince of Wales, seemed intent on providing an environment and style of entertainment geared towards the moneyed. Squire Bancroft had claimed that the appeal of his theatre was to those 'refined and educated classes [...] as ready as ever to crowd the playhouses provided that the entertainment given there was suited to their sympathies and taste' (Bancroft and Bancroft 1909, p. 83). John Hollingshead, in his 'critical contemplation' of differing audience types, points to discreet patronage by the 'purely fashionable' audience of the theatres of 'Tottenham Street and Sloane Square' (1877, p. 274).[5] As we have seen in the previous chapter, all the material and locational factors of a theatre event at the Savoy seemed geared towards the 'refined and educated classes'. The surprise, then, is the relatively large number of lowest-priced seats. The 1s gallery was the most potentially populated discrete area of the house. The purpose-built Savoy, a third larger in capacity than the Opera Comique, therefore offered the possibility of catering for an increased number of low-paying customers, and its structure enabled the managerial control of the location and movement of those customers within the building to preserve proper social distance between the classes.

It is possible that a demand for unreserved seats at the Opera Comique which exceeded supply had encouraged Carte to cater for such customers at the new theatre. But if lower-priced seats were considerably *less* remunerative in terms of overall receipts, a question arises concerning the reason for their provision, in quantity, at a theatre which was, in its outward characteristics, thoroughly geared towards a prosperous audience. Davis and Emeljanow remind us, in relation to the Prince of Wales, that apparent social exclusivity and a reliance on West End 'theatrical tourism' did not preclude, in reality, the presence of 'a mixed and partially local audience' (2001, p. 162). Attempts to investigate the apparent disparity between outward-facing refinement and the accommodation of a large minority of low-paying clientele will inform this exploration of the Savoy audience.

RESERVED SEATING: STALLS AND CIRCLES

One explanation might be that around 20 per cent of total box-office revenue could be provided by large, low-paying groupings, which inhabited a relatively small proportion of entire space. This would allow the wealthier stalls and circle patrons to enjoy the luxury of spacious seats and wide aisles, and provide a sufficient financial incentive to make such developments worthwhile. Another possible motivation for maintaining a large proportion of unreserved seats was the effect which their inhabitants might contribute to the atmosphere of the evening. Contemporary reports of Savoy audiences refer to the decorous behaviour of the stalls and dress circle. Spectators often followed the performance using a printed libretto, on sale in the foyer. François Cellier recalls 'the chorus of laughter and applause broken by a *frou-frou* rustle, a whish [sic], as the vast audience, greedy to devour every last morsel of our author's humour, turns over the pages of the book of words' (Cellier and Bridgeman 1914, p. 20). For Clement Scott, the atmosphere at the first night of *Iolanthe* suggested the reverence which might accompany attendance at a 'serious' musical event. 'The whole audience was plunged into the mysteries of the libretto, and when the time came for turning over the leaves of the book there was such a rustling as is only equalled when musicians are following a score in an oratorio.'[6]

The inference here is that the type of stalls behaviour demonstrated at the Savoy reflected that of the concert hall rather than that commonly encountered in the theatre. Those in the theatre stalls elsewhere seem to have been less reverential, if not especially demonstrative. In 1877, *All the Year Round* describes the 'scions of hereditary legislators [...] baronets, guardsmen and their hangers on' for whom the West End theatre was a part of an evening diversion or place to be seen rather than the focus of their attention.[7] In the same year, an *Era* article, 'Stalls Swells',[8] focuses on the type of wealthy, fashion-conscious young male theatregoer who habitually arrives late, engages in idle conversation throughout the stage action, ogles the actresses and, if bored, leaves before the end. While recognising the media stereotyping employed by specialist papers serving a theatre-going readership who could find such antics annoying, the essential difference between the Savoy stalls and circle and those of other West End theatres may have been that a particularly attentive atmosphere prevailed. The desire to appreciate the wit of Gilbert's lyrics, which could pass too quickly to be fully grasped without the aid of a printed text, encouraged a more absorbed response from the higher-paying customers. Attitudes in the stalls and 'balcony stalls' (dress circle) seating at the Savoy could be seen to typify the Victorian trend towards 'correct' behaviour and 'rational recreation'. The observance of proper etiquette and behavioural restraint were the external signifiers of 'gentlemanly' and 'ladylike' conduct. Hollingshead comments, with some irony, that the face of the 'ultra-fashionable' West End theatregoer 'is as passionless and undecipherable as the sphinx' (1877, p. 274). Large displays of emotion did not suit high social status. Getting the most out of the experience of a Gilbert and Sullivan opera by assiduously following the book is also redolent of the 'serious' Victorian tourists who would rather carefully follow their Baedeker or Murray's guide than open themselves up to the splendours of Vesuvius or the Louvre (Thompson 1988, pp. 262–5). By the point at which the major retrospective revivals of the operas were presented (1906–1910) this mixture of 'seriousness' and diffidence seems to have epitomised the 'fashionable' West End audience. In 1910, *Our Stage and Its Critics* notes that 'on most occasions comparatively little noise is made in the way of applause or condemnations save from the pit and gallery. The stalls are remarkably frigid though on the other hand, they never, or hardly ever, show any active signs of disapproval' (1910, p. 245).

UNRESERVED SEATING: THE PIT

While this description reflects one aspect of audience behaviour, it should be noted that the 1s cost of a libretto at the Savoy would have added an unacceptable level of extra expense for most spectators in the unreserved sections, whose attention was consequently directed towards the stage rather than the page. The importance of less affluent spectators to the success of a performance is noted by Clement Scott in 1875. He remarks that once theatre pits are removed (as in the Bancrofts' Haymarket) 'the pulse of interest which once vibrated through the theatre ceases to beat. The hum is hushed. The applause is deadened. The entertainments cease to fizz' (Scott 1875, p. 82). It is worth noting that the first four Gilbert and Sullivan operas were premiered at the Opera Comique, which had no pit. The enthusiasm generated by a livelier crowd *downstairs*, mitigating the relative reserve of the stalls, would have been advantageous for overall reception, and may have been instrumental in its inclusion at the Savoy.

Contemporary press commentary has less to say about the activities of the less-affluent sections of Victorian theatre audiences than the wealthy (Davis and Emeljanow 2001, pp. 168–70, 179). Indeed, the term 'galleryite', used to describe those in the topmost tiers, hardly appears in the popular press until the 1860s, an indication of journalistic preference for focusing on the activities of the rich and fashionable.[9] The 'pittites' and the 'galleryites' are often mentioned in tandem in Victorian periodicals, as though those in unreserved seats contributed a single identity. When referred to separately (as they will be for the remainder of this section), those inhabiting the pit, at least as reported in the press, are generally male and appear as lively, garrulous, theatrically well-informed and inclined to barrack a play or players they do not like. The Victorian press enjoyed characterising certain sections of the audience for dramatic effect, and it is unlikely that every pittite in every theatre behaved in this way. However, there must have been enough truth behind the journalese to render even satirical pieces credible to theatre-going readers.

The press debated the value and social acceptability of the pit through the 1870s and 80s. In 1887, the *Era* published an editorial defending the pit against managers who would remove it for the financial benefits to be gained from enlarging the stalls.[10] Avoidance of adverse publicity as well as desire to maintain an important audience sector may have influenced the retention of the pit at the Savoy. In 1880, the restored Haymarket under the Bancroft management abolished it, replacing it with higher-priced stalls seating. This action caused a riot on the Haymarket's opening night, which led Clement Scott to opine that an acting company of such quality should 'be acceptable to the public at large, and not only to the uphold-ers of a fashionable and fastidious exclusiveness'.[11] This article, published in *The Theatre* in 1880, also contains a contribution from Frank Marshall who argued that the pittites constituted the truly appreciative section of the house, devoting 'their whole attention to what is being said or done on the stage, and not, as their more fashionable rivals, to what is being said or done around them'. 'Fashionable' society is seen here as in opposi-tion to the 'worthiness' of the pittites, who appear to inhabit a democratic space containing a group whose commonality was possibly financial rather than related to education or cultural taste. To reject this sector may have incurred similar criticism to that levelled at the Bancrofts, while at the same time removing those patrons who might have been likely to offer the most vociferous appreciation of the elements of social criticism contained in Gilbert's libretti.

It must also be significant that the Opera Comique, built in 1870, had dispensed with the pit from the start (Howard 1986, p. 167). Its 'rickety twin' neighbour, the Globe, built at the same time, contained 560 pit seats to 90 stalls, and so must have been aiming at a less wealthy, or at least 'fashionable', clientele (Mander and Mitchenson 1976, p. 63).[12] The 140 stalls, 320 upper and lower circle seats and 72 boxes of the Opera Comique indicate that it was intended from the outset to be a 'fashionable' house. Unreserved seating was restricted to a gallery which held 330. With a total capacity of 862, the Opera Comique was significantly smaller than the Savoy, but apart from the absence of the pit, similarly proportioned in terms of cheaper accommodation. However, box seating (72 seats to the Savoy's 78) was proportionally larger than Carte's theatre (Howard 1986, p. 167), again indicating the expectation of wealthy patronage.

Press coverage in the *Era* praised the lavishness of the internal decoration at the Opera Comique, and, with a repertoire originally consisting of French operetta and French-language farce, its management presumably intended to target a niche audience. Carte became lessee of the Opera Comique for a short period in 1874, when he (unsuccessfully) attempted to produce a series of English comic operas. Despite this setback, in terms of size, pricing and decor it must, in 1876, have appeared to Carte to be an appropriate location for the first Gilbert and Sullivan collaboration. From a distance of 35 years, François Cellier highlights the negative aspects of the Opera Comique in terms of location and access, suggesting it was far from being a first choice (Cellier and Bridgeman 1914, p. 33). However, Carte was very familiar with the theatre and there were presumably advantages to its use. It was small enough to sustain the risk of appealing to a select crowd, with an experimental style of show. It offered, from the front of house at least, the kind of smart appearance which the Savoy later capitalised on.

The Opera Comique's rejection of pit seating (relatively early in terms of the internal development of later Victorian West End auditoria) indicates a house which, at least at the start of its life, deliberately sought to concentrate affluent, fashionable custom and/or pleasure-seeking bourgeois males in the downstairs seated area.[13] While presumably wishing to capitalise on the patronage of its affluent customers, Carte's original 'PR' campaign, which focused on the wholesomeness of the Gilbert and Sullivan enterprise, may have been necessary to counter unseemly associations connected with the 'French' repertoire at the Opera Comique, and also perhaps discourage some of its former 'fast' clientele.

The newly purpose-built (and in every way respectable) Savoy retained the later Victorian placing of the pit at the rear of the downstairs area. Carte must have considered it both profitable and necessary to the success of his venture. Its importance to the Savoy management was reasserted as late as 1907, when Helen D'Oyly Carte, long-time company administrator and full-time manager after her husband's death in 1901, resisted the growing West End trend to abolish unreserved seating. In an *Era* interview she stated that 'we value the support of our pit patrons to such an extent that we should very carefully consider any suggestion from them, and endeavour to meet their wishes if it were possible'.[14] This kind of appreciation, along with occasional provision of free tea and cakes to first night queues (Cellier and Bridgeman 1914, p. 129), indicates the importance of lower-income custom to the Savoy management. By the early part of the twentieth century, with the growth in popularity of the musical comedy genre, it may have become apparent that, while attendance at a Savoy opera was no longer necessarily de rigueur for the fashionable, those at the lower end of the pricing scale were forming the bedrock of the Gilbert and Sullivan audience.

The fact that the pit at the Savoy was significantly smaller in capacity than the cheapest gallery seating would imply that, while it catered to customers whose income and pretentions to status were lower than the box, stalls and circle crowd, its patrons would have considered themselves a cut above those who were only able to afford the gallery. It is also likely that the 2s amphitheatre might have formed a slightly cheaper alternative to the pit, particularly when the theatre was busy. This could explain the comparably smaller capacity of the amphitheatre (118), which was one-third the size of the topmost gallery (373). Despite their proximity, the 1s price differential between amphitheatre and gallery could signify some elements of social difference, even in these similarly located areas. The Bancroft management at the Haymarket had 'banished' its pittites to an unreserved 'upper circle' at 2s 6d. Would-be pittites at the Savoy might have used Carte's 2s 'amphitheatre' as an alternative if the pit were full (Fig. 5.1).[15]

" WHAT'S THERE TO LAUGH AT?"

Fig. 5.1   A view of a theatre pit. (*Judy* 1877). Public Domain

PIT DEMOGRAPHICS

Other than its relative decorum, it is hard to say whether unreserved seating differed in social constitution from that of other West End theatres. An 1877 illustration in the satirical magazine *Judy* accompanies an article concerning West End pantomime audiences—and, in the view of the author, the poor quality of the comedy on offer. Putting aside the exaggerated solemnity of the resolutely stony-faced crowd, it shows a respectably dressed throng that includes women, children and the elderly.[16] This could have been a plausible combination at the Savoy, especially at matinees, where a similarly respectable 'family friendly' product was on offer. A first night review of *Princess Ida* noted that the Savoy pit was 'as comfortable and more roomy than the stalls of many of our houses',[17] possibly a concession towards anticipated 'middle-class' patrons, who would expect a high level of comfort even in unreserved sections. Memoirs of prominent Edwardians show that middle- and upper-class children certainly attended. The actress Irene Vanbrugh recalls sitting in the upper circle during the revival of *HMS Pinafore* in 1887. Future prime minister Stanley Baldwin was present during the original run (Joseph 1994, p. 73).[18]

The journalistic trope of an overwhelmingly male pit is challenged (albeit implicitly) by an unusual source. In 1888, Beatrix F. Cresswell contributed a short story, 'Beneath London', to *Young Folks Paper*.[19] The back pages of this publication were given over to 'readers' stories', which received guidance and criticism from the editor. Hailed as 'in some respects the most remarkable story that has yet appeared', it is a surreal fantasy, in which a mysterious West End theatre becomes a metaphor for illicit desire and death. Putting aside the temptation to investigate the psychological undercurrents of this intriguing text, several features of the story are significant in revealing the attitudes of a young, middle-class, late-Victorian woman towards theatre in general, and to the Savoy in particular.

The tale opens with the female protagonist, Nancy, and her male medical student cousin, François, searching for the pit entrance to the Savoy, 'a difficult place to find hidden away in the numerous side streets which run from the Embankment to the Strand'. After entering what they believe to be the pit door, they find themselves in a mysterious theatre, clearly different from their intended destination. Scarlet-clad attendants and a red colour scheme create an allegorical hell into which the young people are pulled by an enthusiastic crowd. Once in the auditorium, actors in red costumes encourage willing audience members to participate in a weird but alluring *Danse Macabre*, in which spectators are lured onto the stage and disappear into the wings, never to return. There is also a subplot in which the protagonist's affluent, recently married childhood friend, Francesca, is discovered seated in the stalls. She is accompanied by 'Lord St George', who is not her husband (a plot twist which introduces a theme of forbidden desire), and is encouraged by her aristocratic male companion to join the onstage dance—'On the stage, I am told, nothing is more ravishing.'

Despite the overall impression that the theatre and its urban environs are potentially 'dangerous', especially for a well-brought-up girl, the Savoy, as presented at the start of the story, is clearly an appropriate destination for a young woman accompanied only by a male relative of a similar age. The propriety of some forms of theatre-going for the respectable classes seems not to be in doubt. However, dangers lurk. Those of a sexual nature are personified in the person of Lord St George, who fulfils the common Victorian 'middle-class' suspicion of the idle, pleasure-loving aristocrat. Nevertheless, wholesome bourgeois values triumph when, at the climax of the narrative, Nancy persuades her errant friend to leave both the theatre and the road to perdition represented by a sinister onstage *Danse Macabre*.

The tale implies that the author attended the Savoy, and that young adult 'middle-class' female spectators might be found in the Savoy pit. This might have been even truer of matinee performances in which male attendance would have been restricted by working hours, and when the potential risks of night-time attendance could be avoided (Hollingshead 1877, p. 275). Cresswell exhibits a genuine familiarity with the venue through details such as the description of the pit entrance with 'two shillings and sixpence printed in red numbers on the lamp flaring above it'. 'Beneath London' appeared on 30 June 1888, during the run of *Ruddigore*, and it is possible that the author had attended a performance or at least read reviews. Perhaps the supernatural content of this opera, in which the dead come to life, sparked the imagination of its young spectator. The frequent use of red imagery in the story might have been influenced by, or be a self-conscious reference to, the title of the opera then playing—'Ruddy-gore'. Indeed, whether Miss Cresswell visited the Savoy or not, the presence of this theatre in a narrative intended for publication in *Young Folks* would indicate that it could be accepted as a place of entertainment suitable for the type of children or adolescents who formed its readership. The intention of a respectable young woman to attend the Savoy Theatre without parents seems unexceptionable within the narrative, providing another illustration of the perceived social acceptability of the Savoy among the 'middle classes'.

Equally interesting is the social embarrassment of discovering that Francesca, though possessing a titled husband ('Sir Hubert Walton'), is escorted by a lord, and that, to make matters worse, she is seated in the stalls just a few rows in front of Nancy's pit bench.

> I shrank back. I was ashamed that my rich friend, the fashionable beauty, would see me with my medical student cousin in the pit of the theatre [...]. We were in the front of the pit. I wished myself farther back. I was ashamed of my situation should Francesca turn and see me.[20]

Although the Savoy pit might contain the less prosperous 'middle classes', presence there implies a significant drop in status compared with a seat in the stalls. The perceived social gulf is clear. Through an advantageous marriage Francesca has risen above her friend, who appears in contrast relatively poor. I will return to the notion of tension and fragmentation within the 'middle class' later in the chapter, but Nancy's reaction to her friend's presence in the most expensive seats signifies the extent to which social identity and location within an auditorium were connected. A few yards of carpet might separate the young women, but the notional social distance (with its implied disparity in wealth and status) seems to be far greater.

In simplified class terms, the Victorian theatre pit (and possibly, at the Savoy, the amphitheatre) might have contained, among others, a cross section of the less-well-off, middling sorts. Those who could not afford 'fashionable' seats but who considered themselves, in certain respects, the equals of those who could, such as better-paid clerks, students, those engaged in creative or artistic careers, theatre personnel, young, single professionals, and unmarried 'middle-class' women, may well have been among its inhabitants (Davis and Emeljanow 2001, p. 220). The last two of these groups provide some of the principal characters in another informative literary source—George Gissing's novel *The Odd Women* (1893), Chapter 14 of which contains an intriguing reference to the Savoy (Gissing 1893). Assuming that a realistic novel concerning contemporary social mores needs to be accurate in its depiction of the minutiae of everyday life in order to be credible to readers who share those experiences, this excerpt can be used to offer some useful information on the constituency of Savoy audiences. Everard Barfoot, Eton-educated, but disowned by his family, and consequently relatively 'poor', is conversing with the emancipated Miss Nunn:

'Is there anything very good in the new Gilbert and Sullivan opera?' he asked.

'Many good things. You really haven't been yet?'

'No—I'm ashamed to say.'

'Do go this evening, if you can get a seat. Which part of the theatre do you prefer?'

His eye rested on her, but he could detect no irony.

'I'm a poor man, you know. I have to be content with the cheap places.'

This exchange emphasises the popularity of the operas among the 'middle classes', as Miss Nunn is evidently surprised that Barfoot has not yet seen the opera.[21] He in turn is embarrassed at not being *au fait* with the latest Savoy offering, the reputation of which is so marked that seats might not be had. The dialogue highlights the relative expense of the boxes, stalls and dress circle, to which Miss Nunn presumably refers. Her assumption that he could attend that very evening might suggest that she is, in fact, being ironic, and is aware that he cannot meet the expense of the best pre-bookable seats. Alternatively, she may genuinely be unaware of his financially reduced status.

Although Barfoot's background and manner might indicate to Miss Nunn that he can afford to sit where he pleases, it is his relative poverty which consigns him to the 'cheap places'. He inhabits 'a cheap flat, poorly furnished, in Bayswater' and lives on 'a pittance of four hundred and fifty pounds a year' (Chapter 9). An ironic description, perhaps, as by general late-nineteenth-century standards Everard is well off. His income places him towards the bottom of an income bracket containing those earning between £300 and £1000 a year and who are defined by the Victorian economist R.D. Baxter as 'middle-class' (Perkin 1969, p. 420). In 1901, the *Cornhill Magazine* declared that, for a professional family man living on £800 a year, 'Playgoing must be strictly limited' (cited in Perkin 1989, p. 93). People receiving £450 per year *could*, therefore, be restricted to the 'cheap places'. Dress circle seats, at 6s, could be a financial challenge to the 'reasonably affluent occasional visitor, who formed a sizeable element of the new tourist class' (Davis and Emeljanow 2001, p. 220). One might assume that the 3s upper circle would be a likely destination for an average middle-class suburban family party.

Everard's income is supposedly covering the needs of an unmarried man about town rather than providing for a family. It may be assumed, from figures provided by Baxter's categorisation of social classes, that the inhabitants of the pit would be drawn in part from among those spectators forming the lower end of the middle-class sector, earning between £300 and £1000 per annum (Perkin 1969, p. 420). In terms of social acceptability, this grouping could contain audience members who might have considered themselves similarly educated, mannered and informed as those in the most expensive seats, but who lacked the financial means to join them. One could speculate that a single young man about town like Gissing's Everard, with an evening to spare, might have turned up at the box office for a pit seat rather than going through the pre-booking procedures necessary for stalls or circle, irrespective of his ability to afford them. He might also have preferred the relative informality of the rear seats, free of the need to wear evening dress and observe social niceties.

UNRESERVED SEATING: GALLERY AND AMPHITHEATRE

Had Everard Barfoot wanted to 'slum it' he could have considered a seat in the 'gods'. The provision of around 118 seats at 2s and 373 seats at 1s made the Savoy amphitheatre/gallery the most potentially populated area of the auditorium. While Davis and Emeljanow (2001, p. 190) note the dearth of evidence concerning poorer theatregoers in the Victorian period, they demonstrate that, around the middle of the century, the Victorian gallery contained a working-class presence.[22] From a twenty-first-century perspective, Gilbert and Sullivan's burlesque of contemporary artistic pretensions in *Patience* or their Tennyson parody, *Princess Ida*, may not constitute an obvious entertainment choice for Victorian manual workers. But categorisation of audience inclination in terms of suppositions of class-based preference of entertainment *forms* is misleading, as most West End auditoria had relatively inexpensive upper tiers. Later successes such as *The Mikado* and *The Gondoliers*, with their foregrounding of exotic locations and designs and lessening of literary satire, could have been a more likely attraction to a wider social mix. Upwardly mobile aspirants to 'respectability', as well as independently minded, self-confident members of the 'labour aristocracy', might have enjoyed the operas sufficiently to merit a visit to the Savoy. Higher-ranking domestic servants who 'absorbed middle class values and attitudes' and 'acquired a pastiche of bourgeois culture' through association with their employers (Thompson 1988, pp. 250–1) may also conceivably have frequented the gallery seats.

The few contemporary sources which mention the Savoy gallery indicate a degree of relative propriety. François Cellier remarks that 'there was no "rag, tag and bobtail"' attached to a Savoy crowd. 'The refining influence of Gilbert's wit and Sullivan's convincing music were able to tame the wildest Hooligan from Shoreditch and the East, and to compel every man and woman entering the sanctum of the Savoy to put on company manners' (Cellier and Bridgeman 1914, p. 130). So a working-class audience, albeit one tamed by the hallowed atmosphere of genteel artistic endeavour, *is* apparently acknowledged. However, it is necessary to understand Cellier's subtextual cultural agenda when interpreting such statements. He seems to subscribe to the late-Victorian mythologising tendency to idealise the 'redemptive power of the theatre' (and art in general) as a means of resolving social problems: 'Passivity and obedience [become] desirable qualities' which somehow demonstrate the superiority of the cultural values of the dominant classes over the masses' (Davis and Emeljanow 2001, p. 163). While adjustment of conduct may have been embraced out of personal choice rather than in deference to the 'civilising' influence of Gilbert and Sullivan's art, it indicates the possible presence of a section of the public who could adapt their behaviour as required by social circumstances. They had chosen to engage in an 'upmarket' experience and adjusted their conduct accordingly. This aspect of social modification among the working classes is noted by Peter Bailey. While bourgeois Victorian commentators liked to simplify their world view by dividing the working class into 'thinkers and drinkers' or 'virtuous and vicious' (1998, p. 33), the working classes were adept at embracing and enjoying features of 'respectability' when it was advantageous or desirable to do so (1998, pp. 30–46). Bailey describes this as a 'calculative function' (1998, p. 39) in working-class behaviour, which allowed them to be 'capable of playing at roles as well as role playing'.

Bailey cites Goffman's notion of 'role distance' as a method of developing the role-playing aspect of working-class respectability. While apparently conforming to polite norms, 'the social actor can perform a role with sufficient conviction to meet the expectations of the role-other'—in this case, Cellier and others of his respectable tendency—'while injecting some expression into the performance which conveys his psychic resistance to any fundamental attachment to the obligations of that role' (Bailey 1998, p. 39). This 'resistance' might be observed in a Savoy policy decision to restrict numerous encores—a consequence of overly vociferous audience appreciation. That the most voluble encouragement of encores would derive from those sections of the house least restrained by the demands of fashionable bourgeois social etiquette is attested by Cellier. He comments that encores were curtailed 'because it was found that the enthusiasm of the people in the pit and gallery led to the annoyance of the occupants of the stalls' (Cellier and Bridgeman 1914, p. 161). Displays of enthusiasm by a majority of the lower-paying clientele, which perhaps added to the general sense of enjoyment within the house, could nevertheless be regarded as vulgar and distracting by some of their economic and social 'betters' in the stalls and circle. This suggests a marked variation in reception, predicated by the expectations and behaviour of an audience differentiated by self-definition and income. The curtailment of loud demands for encores as an affront to the decorous manners of those in the stalls and circle might be seen as such an act. The clamour demonstrated enthusiasm for the performance while at the same time causing the kind of (deliberate?) disturbance which ruffled the feathers of those seated below.

The imperative for the restriction on encores may have come from Carte himself. However, the final decision was left to Cellier who, as conductor for all but first nights and special events, would have been in charge of what took place on stage, at least from the musical angle. He seems to have enjoyed his ability to control proceedings. 'If he thought an encore unreasonable or inconsiderate, he had only to shake his uplifted hand, when, lo! as if by wireless telegraphy, the signal was read, the meaning interpreted, and the loudest shouts promptly subsided' (Cellier and Bridgeman 1914, p. 171). Encores were not, as they later became in D'Oyly Carte practice, opportunities for additional, prearranged sight-gags, but simply repetitions of numbers as demanded by the audience. They required no special preparation, and would not have affected the performance in any way other than increasing its running time. Cellier's endorsement of this reduction in encores in his memoirs, and his responsibility for it in practice, places him among those who prioritised the values of the well-mannered and wealthy over those of the enthusiastic but less well off. Art and decorum are seen to guide and direct (literally, in regard to Cellier's gestural control of the audience) the enthusiastic but awkward manners of the 'lower orders'.

Audience Diversity: The 'Lower Orders'

Gilbert had no qualms about the need to appeal to a wide social demographic. Four years after the opening of *Patience* he explained the success of his theatre pieces by using the culinary metaphor of 'rump steak and oyster sauce', a 'dish that will fit the gastronomic mean of the audience' in its appeal to both the 'butcher's boy in the gallery' and the 'epicure in the stalls.'[23] Despite this assertion that the success of a piece depends on a relatively wide social appeal, Regina Oost rejects the notion of a genuinely socially diverse Savoy audience. Referring to the notion of the deliberate marginalisation of a working-class clientele in the later Victorian West End, she argues that such a patron who 'purchased a ticket for the pit or gallery would have found themselves […] snubbed by programme advertisers and alienated by those who applauded characters' disparagement of the lower classes' (Oost 2009, p. 26). While the central theme of Oost's argument—that the Savoy was geared towards the affluent and 'respectable' sectors of society—is almost certainly correct, several of the arguments she uses to support middle-class exclusivity do not wholly convince.

Advertised products in Savoy programmes did tend to be fairly pricey. 'Tic-Sano Vegetable Tincture', priced at 1s/1½d a bottle, might well be out of the range of a 1s 'galleryite' in need of a tonic. However, the 'Miniature Gold Keyless Compensation Lever Watch for Ladies' advertised in the previously mentioned *Ruddigore* programme for £10 (Sands 2009) would have been prohibitive for even Baxter's 'lower middle-class sector' (£100–£300 per annum). These, according to Oost, would have constituted many of the 649 'less illustrious ticket holders' at the Savoy (2009, p. 28)—in fact, more than *half* the actual total capacity of the house. Oost, in her desire to categorise the Savoy audience as affluent, product-hungry, middle-class consumers, appears to ignore the notion that advertised products can be aspirational as well as affordable, and therefore cannot be taken as an exact indication of even the average actual purchasing power of all theatre patrons.

'Those who applauded characters' disparagement of the lower classes' (Oost 2009, p. 26) might have found some cause to chuckle in the early operas presented at the Opera Comique. There is a distinct feeling of working-class 'otherness' in the first few libretti. Jokes at the expense of the 'lower orders' might easily alienate working-class or lower-middle-class audience members, and the presence of such humour would suggest that such audiences were not expected to be present at the Opera Comique. Certainly exchanges such as this from *The Sorcerer*:

ALINE: The working man is the true Intelligence after all!
ALEXIS: He is a noble creature when he is quite sober.

(*The Sorcerer*, Act One)

presuppose an unpleasantly condescending attitude towards the 'working man'. As discussed in Chapter 2, *HMS Pinafore* has class division as its central theme. It presents the working classes, in the form of the Pinafore crew, in a sympathetic (if somewhat patronising) light, but also as easily influenced by their betters, and prone to discontent via agitation within their ranks. The representatives of the working classes in *The Pirates of Penzance* are a chorus of policemen—portrayed as farcically ineffectual cowards—and Ruth, a comically inept 'maid of all work'. Significantly, *Patience* marks the transition both between the two venues and in the way the 'lower orders' are represented. Patience the milkmaid, the only conceivably 'working-class' character in the play, is a focus of pragmatism around which the vanities, follies and pretensions of the other characters revolve. From there on, working-class or petit-bourgeois characters are either absent (*Princess Ida*), or are depicted sympathetically as political pragmatists (Private Willis—*Iolanthe*), resourceful everyman figures (Ko-Ko—*The Mikado*) or staunch defenders of British independence (Chorus of Yeomen—*The Yeomen of the Guard*).[24]

While the intellectual tone of the operas, in terms of social and cultural references, continues in the works written specifically for the Savoy, there are now no laughs at the expense of the lower orders. Direct downward social criticism is, in any case, reduced in the later operas, as their settings become increasingly exotic and removed from contemporary reality. Andrew Crowther marks this transition—certainly from *Princess Ida* onwards—as a concession towards commercial popularism (2000, pp. 154–5). Colourful exoticism in locations unrelated to contemporary Britain may well have ensured the continuing appeal of the Savoy product to a numerically larger and demographically broader clientele. Concomitant with this change of emphasis in the libretti and mise en scène towards the escapist rather than the satirical is the maintenance of low-cost seating capacity in the new theatre. There is good reason to suppose that the D'Oyly Carte brand, in terms of content and accessibility, was directing itself towards a wider audience, in class terms, than it had at the Opera Comique.

There is nothing in the later libretti which might offend members of the socially amorphous 'upper-working' and 'lower-middle' classes who may have constituted the main inhabitants of the amphitheatre/gallery seats at the Savoy. Indeed, the increasing number of workers who had recently risen from manual labour into the lower-middle classes and who wanted to slough off their proletarian origins by shunning 'the overt hedonism of large sections of the working class' (Perkin 1989, p.100) might well have declared their social identity and cultural aspirations by attending entertainments that were branded as 'respectable'. This probability can be reinforced by a rise in lower-middle-class wages in the second half of the century.[25] The fact that 'the incomes around the lower level of taxable income [...] were increasing fastest of all' (Best 1971, p. 83) during the period of West End commercialisation may be reflected in Carte's decision to maintain seating at this lower end of the pricing structure. The lower-middle classes may now have found themselves in a position to increase their leisure spending. A desire for 'cultural capital' as well as an enjoyment of the attractiveness of both venue and product could explain the increased demand for the Gilbert and Sullivan operas (as well as other West End attractions) from this sector.

For the lowest-paid members of society, the Savoy might have provided a less obvious choice. John Pick has calculated that a representative manual worker, earning around £68 per year, would have needed 38.3 per cent of his weekly wage to afford a 10s stalls seat (an impossible proposition), as opposed to 3.8 per cent of his weekly wage to afford a 1s gallery seat (Pick 1983, p. 187). Arthur Morrison, writing in the *Cornhill Magazine* (cited in Perkin 1989, p.106) estimates that, in 1901, a skilled workman on £77 a year could allocate 4s a week for *all* luxury expenditure. A 1s seat was at the bottom end of West End pricing. Outlying theatres, such as the East London or the Surrey, might offer gallery seats at half this price. It is possible that the allure of the West End's most up-to-date entertainment venue might have been sufficient enticement for workers such as skilled artisans earning between £75 and £85 annually (Perkin 1969, p. 420) to spend the extra money, but in terms of affordability, the Savoy would have been a less likely destination for those on such wages. This does not necessarily exclude their presence completely—human nature dictates that people do not always approach spending for pleasure in a rational frame of mind—but it indicates that pricing dissuaded attendance of the lowest paid.

SINGING IN THE GALLERY

So who was most likely to have accessed the relatively large amphitheatre and gallery capacity? Cellier provides a portrait of the 'gods' which confirms its constitution as 'middle class' in manners, if not in income.

It also maintains the idea of distinct, class-related differences within an auditorium which was broadly 'bourgeois' but nevertheless highly stratified. Discussing the impromptu pre-show concerts improvised by those in the upper tiers, he comments that they:

> became such an important part of a Savoy *premiere* that they had the effect of attracting the early attendance of the elite in the stalls and circles. Doubtless the vocal ability of these *premiere* choristers was attributable to the fact that they comprised a large number of members of suburban amateur societies to whom the Savoy tunes were as familiar as [...] 'Hymns, Ancient and Modern.'
>
> (Cellier and Bridgeman 1914, pp. 130–1)

The pre-show jollification of the 'lower orders' (modified by the awareness that those participating would also be conversant with religious decorum) is here interpreted as a means of providing entertainment to their 'betters'. In spite of Cellier's somewhat patronising viewpoint, the galleryites were clearly also displaying their skill. Cellier demonstrates that these improvised concerts were by no means rough and ready:

> So interesting and attractive was the performance taking place 'in front' that author and composer, with some of the principals, forgetting for a moment the responsible parts they were themselves about to play, listened from behind the curtains and joined in the applause that followed each chorus.
>
> (1914, p. 131)

Membership and participation in amateur singing through the glee clubs and choral societies which proliferated in Victorian England was a popular pastime which attracted members of the 'respectable' lower orders (Thompson 1988, pp. 304–5). While Wales and the North of England are often regarded as centres of organised communal singing, London also functioned as a hub of such activity. The capital contributed 1200 voices to the first Handel festival in 1857, and was the home of the Handel Society and the Royal Choral Society (Smither 2000, pp. 282–3). It is significant that religious music was the main repertoire of the choral societies. Sullivan's occasional use of the English choral style, and his faux baroque and renaissance settings, would have been accessible, familiar and performable to singers trained in Handel oratorios. It may be reasonable to suppose that community singing at the Savoy drew from such groups.

From the middle of the century onwards, the musical educator John Hullah and the Congregationalist minister John Curwen promoted the German 'fixed solfa' ('do, re, mi') method of sight singing. According to Hullah, this simplified approach, which bypassed the need for the kind of musical literacy available to the leisured bourgeoisie, allowed 'the lower orders [and] the lower portions of the middle classes' (Hullah 1842, cited in Potter 1998, p. 81) to engage in the morally redeeming practice of church and community singing. John Potter, in his discussion of class, morality and Victorian vocal technique, states that the popularity of the system 'produced an additional audience for choral music as well as choir-fodder' (1998, pp. 81–2). Potter sees this as a 'top down' imposition of bourgeois ideals, as part of a deliberate devaluation of working-class culture (pp. 86–7). This may be so, but the notion that 'elite' styles signified upward social mobility provided the opportunity for those who identified themselves as lower middle class to adopt these styles as signification of their status. This does not necessarily mean a wholesale imitation of the standards of their social 'betters'. The differences in social conduct within the auditorium discussed above attest to diverse modes of reception and response. But a selective adoption of certain aspects of 'elite' performance, an aspirational desire by amateur singers to engage with culturally 'higher' musical styles, and the ability to perform with a degree of competence could have enhanced the popularity of the operas among the 'lower orders'. Performing rights for the first staged amateur performance of a Savoy opera were granted from 1879, when *HMS Pinafore* was presented in the Drill Hall, Kingston upon Thames, by the Harmonists Choral Society (Bradley 2005, p. 115). It is conceivable that, by the mid 1880s, some audience members, including galleryites, had first-hand knowledge of the works as performers.

While members of church choirs were less likely to be regular theatregoers, the promotion of the Savoy as a morally 'safe' place might have attracted patrons who would have avoided the normal run of theatrical entertainments. Choral societies often recruited from church choirs, particularly those of dissenting sects (Thompson 1988, p. 304). The lower middle classes formed the backbone of non-conformity (Best 1971, p. 156), and London contained many non-conformist worshippers. The 1903 census of church attendance recorded that, out of a total of 1,003,361 attendees at Sunday services in central London over a six-month period, 416,977 frequented dissenting places of worship (Mudie-Smith 1903, p. 269). One can therefore argue for at least the possibility of a non-conformist, middle- and lower-middle-class audience base in London. More accurate evidence of Gilbert and Sullivan audience make-up in relation to religious observance can be gleaned from twentieth-century sources. Not surprisingly, practising Anglicans have often been fans and amateur performers of the operas (Bradley 2005, p.104). However, according to Bradley, 'The provincial Nonconformist, lower-middle-class devotees of G&S provided much of the fan base of the old D'Oyly Carte company' (Bradley, p. 108). Some of the provincial popularity of the operas in the late nineteenth century, served by Carte's extensive touring operation, may have relied on Baptist, Methodist and Congregationalist middle- and lower-middle-class attendance, and a similar audience may have been present in London.

The presence at the Savoy first nights of skilled amateur singers in sufficient numbers to make the kind of musical impact described by a professional such as Cellier could indicate the presence of members of amateur choirs. Placed among the galleryites, they suggest a lower-middle- and/or upper-working-class grouping, which, whether drawn from churches or not, were familiar with the expanding Savoy oeuvre as well as aspects of the 'serious' musical culture of the educated bourgeoisie seated below them. As committed fans, galleryites were exhibiting insider knowledge of the operas, and a willingness to become part of the theatre event as performers in their own right. This can be interpreted as a public assertion of upper-working-class and/or lower-middle-class confidence, intended to exhibit self-respect in a demonstrative, though good-natured, way. The influence of choral singing competitions, which were well established by the 1890s, and which were disparaged as typically 'lower middle class' by those above (Potter 1998, p. 85), may have stimulated an element of competition on the part of the galleryites.

The community singing can also be read as a competitive 'challenge' to the restraint of those seated below. The 'lower orders' were demonstrating their ability to enjoy the social pre-show atmosphere of a performance event in a more spirited and active style than permitted by the supposedly superior conduct of those above them in the social scale. 'Well-mannered but not necessarily excessively deferential' is how Thompson characterises the working-class presence in amateur choral groups (1988, p. 304), and it may also serve as a description of at least some of the amphitheatre and gallery crowd at the Savoy. Vociferous but not rowdy, enthusiastic in demanding encores and well versed in the style of piece being presented, the conduct of those in the Savoy upper tiers contrasted with that of patrons in the expensive seats, where exaggeratedly genteel manners and a kind of artistic reverence seemed to prevail.

THE LOWER-MIDDLE CLASSES

In all probability, the celebratory nature of a Gilbert and Sullivan first night might have been one of the few occasions during which the 'middle classes' in their entirety experienced any sense of camaraderie. Harold Perkin (1989) anatomises the late-nineteenth-century English 'middle-class', revealing

> Various layers and segments [which] were mutually and plurally exclusive, with minutely refined gradations of status expressed not only in [...] visible possessions, but in the intangible rules about who spoke or bowed to, called on, dined with or intermarried with whom [...]. From top to bottom, the middle class was riddled with such divisions and petty snobberies.
>
> (1989, pp. 81–2)

To those sitting in the boxes or stalls, grocers' assistants and postal clerks might have been, in general perception, socially indistinguishable from manual labourers and domestic servants. All were of lower status, and, in a West End theatre, separately located. Most prone to a sense of social uncertainty might have been those who, with their wives and families, filled the cheaper Savoy seats: the small business owners, clerks, shop assistants, technicians and teachers (among many other occupations) belonging to the lower middle classes. Londoners who had recently risen to middle-class economic status, or who had non-manual but poorly paid jobs, inhabited a social no-man's land. Living on the margins of middle-class housing while attempting (with difficulty) to maintain appearances on only slightly higher—or in comparison with skilled artisans, sometimes *lower*—salaries than their working-class near-neighbours, they could easily be marginalised by those above them. This social alienation is neatly summed up by the condescending tone of a suburban vicar, who described the clerks newly arrived in his parish as

> Quite quiet, respectable and inoffensive, but on warm evenings they will sit at their open windows in their shirt-sleeves, drinking beer out of a pot, and though they do it quite quietly it is not what I am accustomed to.
>
> (Cited in Perkin 1989, p. 96)

'Too genteel to go to the pub, not genteel enough to pass muster as "proper" middle class' is Perkin's apt gloss on this quote (p. 96). George

Grossmith, who had cut his teeth as a performer entertaining such audiences at penny-readings and YMCA 'entertainments' epitomised attitudes towards the lower middle class. Via his literary creation, the hapless city clerk, Charles Pooter, in *The Diary of a Nobody* (1889), Grossmith focuses on this social group as a possible source of (albeit affectionate) comedy. Pooter's misadventures, social gaffes and cosy conservatism typify the extent to which the type he represents was seen as socially distanced from the established professional or commercial middle classes and therefore a justifiable comic target.

Such humour relies on the depiction of socially recognisable types. Mr Pooter and his like would have become increasingly visible through the second half of the nineteenth century. Statistics reveal a steady rise in male, white-collar employment, with lower-grade roles, such as commercial clerks, railway officials and commercial travellers, doubling between 1871 and 1891 (Crossick 1977, p. 19). The white-collar lower-middle class has been characterised as being jingoistic, domestically focused and morally (and politically) conservative. The bedrock of respectable morality was moving away from those who had constituted the evangelically inspired bourgeoisie and 'slowly and surely retreating into its strongholds among the lower-middle class' (Price 1977, pp. 91–103). Price describes the way in which the need for increased professionalism was encouraging clerks to adopt 'clerkly respectability with the demands of work discipline'. By the 1870s, the cult of hard work, which justified the capitalist expansion of the early-Victorian entrepreneurial class, had filtered down to its lowliest administrative employees. Along with this went the full complement of 'respectable' values outlined in Chapter 3, including the need for self-improving 'rational' recreations. Going to the theatre was not one of them (Price 1977, p. 102). Making Pooter representative of this grouping, Grossmith shows how its members were conforming to idealised behavioural norms which were out of date among the established 'middle classes' of the 1880s. People whose parents may have been poorly educated servants or artisans were now aping the unfashionable mores of the mid-Victorian 'middle class', and could therefore be regarded as doubly incongruous and comic.

Historians have also described a sense of group insecurity among the new lower-middle classes, who, though relatively safe within the confines of their regular employment, feared that an overstocked labour market could cause redundancy, casting them back into the class from which they had emerged (Perkin 1989, p. 100; Price 1977, p. 103). Thus, their identity was based strongly on a desire to 'distinguish and segregate themselves from the working-class in terms of income, appearance, and physical residence' (Perkin 1989, p. 100). I would suggest that their self-consciously imitative respectability, their desire to disassociate from working-class culture and their need to develop a social identity of their own made the white-collar lower-middle classes ideal consumers of the D'Oyly Carte brand.

When, in chapter three of *Diary of a Nobody* (Grossmith and Grossmith, pp. 21–2), Pooter is presented with the opportunity for some free theatre tickets, his thoughts run to the Italian opera, Irving's Lyceum, Beerbohm Tree's Haymarket and (predictably, but perhaps not surprisingly, given the identity of the author) the Savoy. But the point being made here is that operatic high art, Shakespeare (with its appeal to national pride and literary taste), lavishly produced drama, and the comic operas of Gilbert and Sullivan are the most obvious theatrical forms which the ultra-respectable Pooter can envisage. The Savoy (as well as the Lyceum and Haymarket) could provide an accessible and affordable form of 'higher' culture, which might distinguish its lower-income customers from the habitués of the music hall. Certainly the West End revivals of the most popular Savoy operas in 1906 were greeted with particular enthusiasm by the amphitheatre and gallery. On the opening night of the season, *The Yeomen of the Guard* drew a fervent response from the unreserved sections. Its reception serves as a reminder of marked differences in social manners within a broadly 'middle-class' audience: 'They shouted and bravoed and called for speeches, and the applause continued for many minutes after the safety-curtain had fallen and *the occupants of the stalls and dress circle had gone home*' (my italics).[26] The popularity of Gilbert and Sullivan among lower-income groups may have been the defining feature of Savoy audiences as the century drew to its close.

Davis and Emeljanow (2001, p. 209) remark that the nature of the long run and the emergence of the theatre as a tourist industry meant that the West End could not rely on purely local custom. As well as the generally acknowledged, affluent suburbanites, a large and growing lower-middle-class sector lived outside the central areas of town in newly constructed residential areas. Jerry White describes the suburban building boom of the 1860s and 70s, in which over 100,000 new dwellings appeared (2008, p. 83). These included the northern developments of Islington, Camden Town and Mr Pooter's Holloway, and to the south and east, Hackney and Wandsworth. Poorer suburbanites tended to live at the extremities nearest to central London where it might still be possible to walk to work. But anywhere within an hour's omnibus ride or third-class underground or railway journey would have made the West End accessible to lower-middle-class patrons willing to queue for tickets immediately prior to a performance. There appears to be a connection between the proximity of a relatively new 'respectable' audience in the West End and the growth of a type of entertainment which matched their needs. The Savoy was a venue in which the suburban lower-middle classes could raise their 'cultural capital'. They could experience, within their financial means, an artistically 'upmarket' entertainment which conformed to the ideology of their work and life culture, while enjoying the style of surroundings (in terms of decor, costume and facilities) they might admire and to which they might aspire.

Did suburban audiences need to travel to the Savoy to see Gilbert and Sullivan opera? Despite extensive national touring, there were few visits to outer London or home-counties theatres, especially during the initial runs of the most popular shows.[27] Between 1880 and 1885, the years which consolidated the original success of the brand, outer London visits were comparatively rare (Rollins and Witts 1962, pp. 30–57). *The Mikado* was presented four times in Greenwich and for a week in Croydon in 1885, while just eight performances were given in South London venues in 1886 (Rollins and Witts 1962, pp. 58, 60). These figures suggest that suburban *Mikado* performances during the initial West End run of 1885 may have been deliberately restricted to ensure good business. Occasional visits were made during the late 1880s and early 90s, but touring companies playing the most popular operas in repertory around London showed some increase only after the Gilbert and Sullivan collaboration had ended in 1896.[28]

Significantly, as the West End popularity of the Savoy operas waned around the turn of the century, suburban tours became more important. In 1902, a total of 13 weeks were played by the 'C' and 'D' touring companies in Balham, Brixton, Notting Hill, Camden Town, Deptford, Croydon, Woolwich, Stoke Newington, Kennington and Stratford (Rollins and Witts 1962, pp. 115–16). This pattern would suggest that, during its heyday, outer London audiences were generally obliged to visit the Savoy. It would also lend support to the notion that the suburban middle and lower-middle classes (of both the beer-drinking and non-conformist types) became a valuable source of income to the Carte enterprise during the period of the original company's West End decline.

It is, of course, impossible to exactly define the composition of an amphitheatre/gallery audience at the Savoy in the 1880s and 1890s. The incomes of artisans, trades people and clerical workers overlapped, and West End theatres, as well as many cheaper outlying venues offering other entertainments, were accessible to these potential spectators. We can only speculate on how people with limited incomes chose to spend their money. But bearing in mind the arguments I have presented, it would seem that, in terms of income, cultural preference and a desire to identify strongly with 'respectable', 'middle-class' values, the lower-middle-class, white-collar sector could have constituted a significant proportion of those inhabiting the cheap seats at the Savoy. It explains at least in part both the (presumed) demand for and relatively high provision of such seating at an apparently upmarket venue. While admission price was low, the volume of potential custom must have justified the economic and architectural decisions behind providing the quantity of seating at the Savoy's 1s and 2s price point.

MONEY, LEISURE AND CLASS

Turning from demographics to the bald facts of economics, the massive price differential of over 1000 per cent between lowest gallery and highest-priced stalls is the most obvious explanation of the relationship between prices and available seating at the Savoy, and throughout the West End at this time. This disparity reflects economic circumstances in the last decades of the century, in which, according to Harold Perkin, 'the whole scale of income distribution was being stretched so that inequalities were increasing [...] between classes from top to bottom of society' (Perkin 1969, p. 417).[29] Examined from this perspective, seat pricing, and by implication desired social representation at the Savoy, was actually weighted in favour of the affluent, as the proportion of higher seat prices (3s and above), which made up 48.5 per cent of the total capacity of the theatre, were available to less than 10 per cent of a total population able to afford them. There were, comparatively speaking, far fewer moneyed customers to spread around the West End, providing a sound motive, in terms of both economics and audience reception, for satisfying the increased demands of lower-paying customers. However, as 81 per cent of total box office came from the

618 reserved seats, the need to specifically attract audiences deriving from the highest income brackets was essential to ensure maximum profitability. Theatre architecture, internal decoration and customer facilities had to be purposely geared towards attracting a wealthy crowd, even if over half of any given house might have consisted of those on substantially lower incomes.

This largely 'middle-class' audience was, as we have seen, by no means a unified group. Locations within the auditorium seem to have emphasised some diversity in attitude to the performance event as evidenced by different codes of conduct, even if the kind of rowdiness observable in earlier or non-West End venues was usually absent. However, the audience were attending an event from which most of the low-paid labouring classes were priced out, and this may have been part of its appeal. The movement towards class-based exclusivity in leisure pursuits during the latter part of the nineteenth century has often been remarked on (Best 1971, pp. 20–1; Croll 2007, pp. 401–4). As the bourgeoisie moved away from early-Victorian restraint towards the pursuit of leisure, it did so alongside a working class who had gained shorter working hours and improvement in earnings sufficient to enjoy leisure activities which moved them out of the restrictions of their immediate working environment. 'Middle-class' respectability was now challenged by the physical reality of 'the working man (who) left his urban ghetto and trespassed on the privacy of his betters' (Bailey 1998, p. 18). A new and unwanted corporeal proximity, freed from the deference to be found in the workplace or between masters and servants, profoundly disrupted 'middle-class' notions of social hierarchy and superiority (Bailey 1998, pp. 17–19). Culture shock and a consequent reorientation of leisure provision was not confined to urban entertainment districts but extended to other leisure areas. It is present in the social demarcation of the burgeoning seaside holiday resort. Certain resorts such as Eastbourne, Bournemouth and Hove effectively nullified the possibility of unwelcome culture clashes by heightening those attractions which would appeal to 'middle-class' tastes and/or rejecting those which might pull in crowds of rowdy workers (Thompson 1988, pp. 291–3). The kudos of exclusivity, the provision of entertainment more limited in scale but more expensively priced, the admission of the aspirational lower-middle classes who conformed to the behavioural conventions of the 'target audience'—all seem to have been defining features of the Savoy Theatre. By extension they were probably characteristic of other West End theatres and other forms of leisure activity in late-nineteenth-century Britain.

SUMMARY

Reporting on the opening night of *Utopia, Limited* in 1893, *Reynolds Newspaper*[30] comments that 'Mr. D'Oyly Carte has always an exceptional audience and a distinct following amongst it who are not regular playgoers, but who make an absolute duty of witnessing each new Savoy production'. The quotation is intriguing. It informs us that a part of the Savoy audience was of a distinct type and, as a whole, it contained elements which were uncommon to the West End. This criticism is pinpointing the early existence of a 'fan base'—those who have a special affinity with the Gilbert and Sullivan operas but who respond to little else on the late-Victorian stage. Given the existence of the 'G&S' fan and amateur performer throughout the twentieth and into the twenty-first centuries, this would seem a likely surmise. In a similar vein, François Cellier describes among first night audiences 'a corps, more or less independent of the general army of playgoers [...] they like to call themselves "Savoyards"' (Cellier and Bridgeman 1914, p. 128). Regina Oost is clear in her assessment of the cause of this phenomenon. In her view, Carte succeeded in fashioning a brand which created a sense of customer loyalty based on a shared appreciation of attendance at the Savoy as an affirmation of class identity. 'Knowing' the operas, following the texts, collecting ephemera—in other words, becoming a fan or 'Savoyard' (2009, pp. 142–57) — perfectly matched the tastes and preoccupations of bourgeois audiences, while ensuring a steady revenue stream.

Oost provides a convincing explanation of the development of the Savoy *brand* in terms of its focus on the ideology of material consumption. However, the notion that the Savoy *audience* presents an image of social unity bound together by commodity fetishism restricts her investigation of the actual composition of at least the unreserved sections of the auditorium. There seems to have been as much of a desire throughout parts of the house to demonstrate social status through an exhibition of respectability and the attainment of 'cultural capital' as through conspicuous consumption.

One must be careful not to overemphasise differences of response, particularly in a venue which appealed to a 'respectable' clientele, in a theatre-going environment which was becoming increasingly orderly as the century drew to its close. Nevertheless, even at the Savoy, the evidence indicates a far wider variety of audience reaction, based on income and attitude (in other words, 'class') than would be found in many twentieth- or twenty-first-century West End auditoria. To understate the differences in audience demographics is to miss the fragmented nature of the British class system, even in an environment *least* likely to emphasise its dichotomies. Social distinctions within broadly 'middle-class' theatre audiences, even if less obvious than those to be found in earlier or less respectable theatres, remained present at the Savoy. If its audience was unified by anything other than a shared ideological 'respectability' and a mutual pleasure at witnessing the Gilbert and Sullivan operas, it was probably a common desire to distance itself from the labouring poor who were priced out of West End theatres.

The pursuit of respectability—which included a separation from the perceived mores of the labouring classes—could have accounted for the presence of the 'distinct following' mentioned in the *Reynolds Newspaper* report above. It is possible, given the analysis presented in this chapter, to categorise this type of aficionado as a non-theatre-going, possibly religious, self-consciously decent, lower-middle-class, suburban galleryite. While this is, of course, a simplification, Hollingshead, writing six months prior to the opening of *The Sorcerer*, clearly demarcates West End audiences as consisting predominantly of specific *types*, such as the 'fashionable audience; the fast-fashionable audience; the domestic audience; the respectable audience...' (1877, p. 274). While variation in auditoria seat pricing would probably belie such exclusivity in practice, it is likely that Hollingshead's next category, 'the mixed audience', consisting of at least three of the preceding categories, owed its development, in part, to the D'Oyly Carte entertainments. All of these would have responded favourably to the notion that the Savoy performances were unlikely to offend, and that the organisation and its personnel were also (unusually for theatre people) themselves 'respectable'. Ways in which ideological respectability was embedded in the workings of the D'Oyly Carte company, how it affected the lives of individual performers, and how it helped to create a brand identity which ran deeper than that predicated on notions of materialist consumption, will be addressed in the next chapter.

NOTES

1. See Chapter 2 for an explanation of 'hierarchical' readings of class structure.
2. Assessments of capacity and seat distribution differ among sources and within contemporary theatre plans. The variation in capacity is relatively slight—between 1272 and 1294. Kevin Chapple, Savoy Theatre general manager and archivist, echoes the numbers noted in the *Era* of 1 October 1881, which derive from the Savoy management. These figures are at variance with those supplied by Howard (1986, pp. 214–15). Her information is taken directly from architectural plans now held in the London Metropolitan Archive (Public Record Office LC 7/79 9). For this reason, I take Howard's figures to be the most accurate. However, the variance could be explained by the fact that some small alterations in the seating layout took place between the submission of the plans and the final build. This 22-seat discrepancy does not affect the quantitative-evidence based conclusions of this chapter in any significant way.
3. Lack of information has led me to estimate that 11 boxes would be priced at 3 guineas, the topmost 6, which were smaller, at 2 guineas, while I have assumed that the royal box would be generally unused.
4. The 3s bookable upper circle is much nearer in price to the unreserved seats than the 6s dress circle. I have chosen to count it among the 'expensive' seats. However, its proximity in price to seats possibly occupied by a 'lower-middle-class' audience sector could suggest an even greater number of lower-income customers.
5. The Prince of Wales and the Court Theatre where several of Gilbert's early plays were premiered.
6. Illustrated London News, 2 December 1882.
7. All the Year Round, 19 May 1877.
8. Era, 5 August 1877.
9. Use of 'galleryite' as a search term in the British Library's nineteenth Century Newspaper and Periodical collection reveals a single usage before 1865.
10. *Era*, 18 June 1887.
11. *The Theatre*, 1 March 1880, p. 139.
12. Its mixture of popular English comedy, 'French' farce and *opera bouffe*, and melodramatic Dickens and Hardy adaptations might have been geared towards the young, educated, male pit crowd who frequented burlesque performances (Mander and Mitchenson 1976, p. 66).
13. Hollingshead characterises them as habitués of the burlesque—the 'fast fashionable audience [whose] amplitude of shirt front and wristband [and] strident tones and echoing laugh' proclaim them as 'gentlemen whose days

are given to commercial pursuits in the city and whose evenings are entirely devoted to enjoyment at the West-end' (Hollingshead 1877, pp. 274–5).

14. *Era*, 29 December 1906.

15. It is worth remembering that pit, amphitheatre and gallery all contained continuous bench seating rather than chairs and so shared equal levels of comfort. The advantages of the pit were that it was nearer to the stage, less crowded, nearer main entrances and exits, and more or less within proximity of the wealthy.

16. *Judy*, 19 December 1877, p. 102.

17. *Illustrated London News*, 12 January 1884.

18. This was certainly the case in the early 1900s. Rutland Barrington remarks that a matinee performance of *The Mikado* during the 1908–1909 repertory revivals was 'literally crowded with children, whose laughter was something to live for' (1911, p. 30).

19. *Young Folks Paper*, 30 June 1888. *Young Folks* was a weekly children's literary magazine published between 1871 and 1897. It serialised R.L. Stevenson's most famous novels, including *Treasure Island*. As part of its 'Literary Olympic and Tournament', *Young Folks* devoted its back pages to publishing stories and poems contributed by its readers.

20. *Young Folks Paper*, 30 June 1888, p. 414.

21. Presumably, Gissing refers back a year or two to *The Gondoliers*, which opened in December 1889, and ran until June 1891. Although the novel was published in 1893, there was no 'new' Gilbert and Sullivan work until the opening of *Utopia, Limited* in October 1893, which post-dated the publication of the novel.

22. See also Schoch (2003, p. 343).

23. 'The Evolution of "The Mikado"' in the *Pall Mall Gazette*, 24 August, 1885.

24. The staunch republicanism of the eponymous heroes in *The Gondoliers* is, perhaps, an exception. It does raise, albeit in a comically absurd form, an image of social levelling, with aristocrats performing menial duties while their inferiors live in luxury. However, I would maintain that the impact of implied social criticism is reduced by the exoticised romance of the eighteenth-century Venetian setting, as well as the generally ironic approach to issues of equality in this opera.

25. According to Best, taxable incomes above £150 per year (the minimum tax threshold) underwent a 33 per cent rise between 1851 and 1881.

26. *Daily Express*, 10 December 1906.

27. There was one major exception. During the *Pinafore* craze of 1879, the 'Second London Company' played Shoreditch and Camden Town for six weeks (Rollins and Witts 1962, p. 30).

28. This may have been a move to ensure revenue, as the Savoy was running a repertoire predominantly consisting of revivals immediately after the closure of *The Grand Duke*. A similar touring repertoire would have reinforced the popularity of the brand during uncertain times.

29. Perkin estimates that around 10 per cent of families (the broad middle classes) had an income of between £100 and £5000 per annum (1969, p. 420). The remainder of families below this level made do with annual incomes of between £22 10s (those classified as paupers) and an average of £85 6s (clerical and higher-skilled manual workers).

30. *Reynolds Newspaper,* 8 October 1893.

CHAPTER 6

'The D'Oyly Carte Boarding School': Female Respectability at the Savoy*

The Savoy Theatre was at that time the premiere stage in England after Covent Garden, and dare I say the most high-class [...]. On pain of instant dismissal all obscene talk and any such act was forbidden in every room of the house. These articles had for years always been followed so conscientiously and strictly that a high-class mode of thinking and living was instilled into the flesh and blood of everyone belonging to the Savoy Theatre without exception down to the most modest member of the chorus.

(Lamb 1972, p. 417)

This quotation, taken from the memoirs of the Hungarian soprano Ilka Palmay, encapsulates nineteenth-century impressions of the moral tone of the D'Oyly Carte organisation. Palmay played principal roles with the company at the Savoy Theatre in the 1890s, and had first-hand experience of the unusual degree to which moral propriety within the company was enforced by the management. She was also a foreigner to whom an ethos of decency within a theatre company was unusual enough to be worthy of comment. This account, together with the reminiscences of Jessie Bond and George Grossmith, and other contemporary assessments of the company in books and press reports, indicates the existence of a corporate ethic which promoted 'decent' behaviour,

*Goron, M. (2010). 'The D'Oyly Carte Boarding School'—Female respectability in the theatrical workplace 1877–1903. *New Theatre Quarterly*, volume xxvi, part 3.

141

especially among its female members, in a profession which was popularly supposed to be morally suspect. Gilbert himself appears to have been the main promoter of this code of behaviour. His formidable backstage presence is remarked upon by Jessie Bond: 'Gilbert would suffer no loose word or gesture either behind the stage or on it, and watched over us young women like a dragon' (1930, p. 62). Gilbert's attitude to decorum in the theatrical workplace seems to have been characteristic of an ethos which became instituted as company policy and which was maintained with tenacity (Bradley 2005, pp. 32–3). The preservation of a respectable public face was clearly paramount to the success of the organisation, but the impulse to protect and restrict the lives of its female employees was a particularly noteworthy feature of the D'Oyly Carte operation. This chapter discusses two key issues: why were 'middle-class' values concerning the role of women within the public and domestic spheres inculcated into the theatrical workplace? And to what extent was female respectability promoted as a means of presenting a 'brand image' which matched the moral expectations of contemporary audiences?

BACKSTAGE DECORUM

Further verification of the power Gilbert wielded behind the scenes is demonstrated by an incident, recounted by Jessie Bond, which apparently occurred during the original run of *Patience* at the Opera Comique in 1881. She relates that:

> Gilbert happened to be behind the scenes one night when a note was brought to me. 'What's that, Jessie, a love-letter?' he said.
>
> 'Here it is, you can look for yourself,' I replied indifferently, handing it to him.
>
> It was from a party of four young men in one of the stage boxes, inviting me to supper with them after the performance. Gilbert was furious. He went round to the box, rated the young men for insulting a lady in his Company, and insisted on their leaving the house forthwith. Rather drastic treatment, I think now; and of course it got into the papers, the comic papers particularly. They made very merry over our boarding-school discipline, and pitied

me for my nun-like existence. 'Poor little dear, she always has to show her love-letters to her daddy!'

(Bond 1930, p. 63)

Taken at face value, this incident reveals that an apparently intrusive interference into the personal life of a company employee could be considered acceptable and necessary, and also the extent to which an attempt to importune a D'Oyly Carte actress was treated as a matter requiring serious and immediate action. Bond's 'indifference' to an invitation which Gilbert interprets as immoral presents at least an assumption of sexual disinterest on Bond's part, which appears to be the appropriate response from a female D'Oyly Carte Company member, and was the kind of behaviour which gave rise to the notion of the D'Oyly Carte as a 'boarding school'. Bond's acquiescence to Gilbert's intercession suggests that such managerial interference was the norm within the company environment. Her subsequent comment on the ensuing press coverage reminds us that a 'nun-like existence' was not the generally imagined lifestyle of a young actress, and so was sufficiently unusual to be commented on.

One of Gilbert's personal friends, A.E.T. Watson, presents another version of this story, which may have derived from Gilbert. Here, Jessie Bond, having received the note of assignation, appears in a state of 'much indignation'. Gilbert then confronts the sender in his private box and offers him three options. '"You can take your choice. I will go before the curtain if you like, explain what has happened, and say that Miss Bond refuses to continue whilst you are here, or you can go of your own accord, or I can send a couple of commissionaires to carry you." The man chose the second alternative' (Watson 1918, p. 92). The emphasis here is on the indignation of a respectable but helpless female who needs protection. Gilbert's version of the story highlights his credentials as protector of women and upholder of theatrical morality. It contrasts with Bond's version, in which she maintains her status as an independent and self-possessed career woman who treats the matter with indifference.

However, the exact historical veracity of Bond's account is challenged by the seeming absence of any actual references to the incident in the 'comic papers' of the time,[1] as claimed by Bond, and by the existence of a newspaper account which seems to contradict the dating of Bond's story. A report in the *Era*, concerning the Savoy Theatre, recounts that

... it was at this very theatre that a member of the upper classes, who from his private box had sent round a libertine note to a female member of the company, was then and there politely ejected from the house at the risk of a possible action at law.[2]

This article appeared in February 1884, during the first weeks of the run of *Princess Ida*, and relates to an event which took place a few months before—two years *after* the supposed occurrence of the similar story recounted by Bond. It suggests either that Bond was inaccurate in her recollections, or a similar incident occurred to her at a later date. However, these apparent contradictions, in date, if not in meaning, as well as the existence of Watson's version, help to *reinforce* our perceptions of the D'Oyly Carte Company and its attitude to propriety, and point to the value of anecdote in our perception of theatre historiography. Jacky Bratton's understanding of theatrical anecdote in *New Readings in Theatre History* (2003, p. 103) reminds us that a factually attested situation can become the stuff of theatrical folklore. In this case, the imposition of a strict personal code of morals in a West End theatre company, at a time when such a thing was considered sufficiently rare to be commented on in several sets of artists' memoirs, as well as being mentioned in the press, fulfils this folkloric function. It assumes the value of 'inner truth' (Bratton 2003, p. 103), something which, in this case, *encapsulates* the culture of morality in the D'Oyly Carte.

Theatrical memoir is a genre principally intended to entertain, which may therefore reorganise and reinvent apparent 'facts' to suit the narrative or dramatic purposes of the author. This does not deny the usefulness of such sources, which remain valuable indicators of the shared opinions and preoccupations of the authors of these books and their intended audiences. Later in the chapter, further use will be made of Jessie Bond's autobiography to suggest that she presents, at least in part, a version of her life in which she is represented as an exemplar of middle-class Victorian respectability, in order to distance herself from popular perceptions of the actress as moral degenerate.

However, there is a duality to the narrative which is sometimes contradictory. While conforming to bourgeois mores, Bond also presents herself as an independent, even rebellious woman. She is a self-proclaimed 'naughty little puss' who has never learned to 'order myself lowly and reverently towards my betters' (1930, p. 107). At various points in the book she complains about the authoritarian behaviour of Gilbert and

Sullivan and triumphantly records her successful attempts to raise her salary. In one episode, at odds with the general tone of the narrative, Bond describes how, after a command performance of *The Gondoliers* at Windsor Castle, she becomes determined to sit on 'The Golden throne of England'. While attempting to squeeze herself under the spiked barrier which prevented access to the throne, Bond relates how she had to remove her clothes, layer by layer,

> until nothing was left but a skimpy vest to cover my nakedness. Again I spread myself out on the floor, the spikes caught my last remaining garment and tore it to shreds; but what did I care, I was through! I climbed the steps to that golden throne and there I sat almost naked ... I shivered with cold and excitement. I shiver still—but with horror at my own colossal impudence!
>
> (1930, pp. 110–11)

The unexpected and, in the context of the remainder of the book, uncharacteristic eroticism of this anecdote may suggest the intervention of her co-author, Ethel MacGeorge. However, Bond must have colluded in this depiction of herself. Its presence could be related to the need to increase the sales of a book written by an elderly actress who had not appeared before the public for 35 years, and/or an attempt to rekindle memories of her youthful allure. More relevant to the line of argument presented here is the fact Bond *generally* presents herself as the domesticated Victorian woman who happened to be pursuing a theatrical lifestyle. Her attitudes towards sexual morality will be explored in more detail below.

Viv Gardner remarks that, as well as being a record of 'someone whose personality has hitherto been available only through stage performance', the autobiography of the Victorian actress could also be 'part of a process of identity formation that extends beyond individuals to the group or community to which they belong' (Gardner 2007, p. 175). Bond generally appears to ally with respectable women within her society. In common with actress-autobiographers Mary Anderson and Lena Ashwell, Bond recounts early struggles, the stony path to success and the eventual satisfactions of retirement. But she also wants to have her cake and eat it, continually reminding the reader of her 'theatrical' capriciousness and spontaneity. Overall, Bond offers a reflection on the conventional values of her life as a Victorian actress, rather than a vindication of them, viewed from the perspective of a later age when female behaviour was less constrained. Bond is both a respectably domesticated and conformist Victorian *and* a sceptical, emancipated modern. In presenting this duality she provides us with what is probably a mixture of actuality, embroidered fact and fabrication, some of which is likely to have been refashioned by her co-writer, the journalist Ethel MacGeorge. Sifting the truth is an important exercise—it is necessary to establish for the purpose of this investigation that her reports of backstage morality were essentially correct—but her inventions (if they are such) can be equally informative as indicators of the collective mentality of her time.

It is also possible to choose to read theatrical memoirs at face value, and take a more conventional approach by attempting to confirm the truth of the information they provide by comparing it with other, more concrete, sources of evidence. A series of statements concerning the conditions that prevailed behind the scenes at the Savoy are provided by both Bond (1930, p. 62) and Grossmith (1888, p. 102), and these are factual in tone. Both performers mention the backstage segregation of male and female actors as a physical manifestation of the prevailing ethos of respectability. Both writers point out the absence of male visitors to dressing rooms, the fact that notes from male admirers to female performers were a rarity (implying that such decorum was a departure from usual backstage activity) and that 'strict propriety' was observed at all times. Jessie Bond mentions the fact that male and female dressing rooms were positioned at opposite sides of the stage at the Savoy, and she and Grossmith refer to the use of separate staircases for men and women leading from the dressing rooms to the stage. Bond informs us that performers were prevented from lingering and gossiping in groups while not working, and that the green room was the only permissible location for cross-gender encounters during performance times, presumably to forestall the opportunities which poorly lit backstage areas might provide for illicit activity or harassment (Joseph 1994, p. 60). As rehearsals took place on stage (Ainger 2002, p. 289), actors of both sexes worked in well-lit, public environments.

It is important to remember that the Savoy was purpose-built by the eminent theatre architect C.J. Phipps to Carte's specifications. It would be tempting to assume that gender segregation was literally 'built in' to the Savoy Theatre. This is partly suggested by early architectural plans[3] showing smaller dressing rooms nearer the stage (on the ground and first floors), which, due to their size and proximity to the stage, were presumably reserved for principal artists (following conventional theatre practice, in which closeness to the performance area is often dependent on seniority of role within the company). They were placed directly behind, and on opposite sides of, the stage, with a large scene dock between them. Principal dressing rooms were indeed on opposite sides of the stage on the first two levels, which would permit separation of men and women, giving some credence to Jessie Bond's description. Two separate staircases were also present on the extreme left and right of the backstage area. There were larger dressing rooms on the second and third floors, and their size and relative distance from the stage would suggest that these were the chorus rooms. They were not segregated as such, but extended in a row for the full width of the structure. This would indicate a fortuitous use of an existing architectural design, rather than Jessie Bond's naive interpretation of this layout as a *deliberate* attempt to create an environment in which male and female performers could be separately located. However, the presence of male toilets on the extreme left and female toilets to the extreme right on these floors (determined by the presence of urinals in one and not the other), combined with the continuance of the two staircases to the full height of the structure, would make a degree of segregation possible, and further reinforce the veracity of these artists' recollections regarding the spatial use of the building (Figs. 6.1 and 6.2).

Attempts to prevent overfamiliarity between male and female company members through careful monitoring of their backstage activities indicates a clear desire on the part of the management to prevent improper behaviour. However, the Savoy, like most venues which provided the spectacle of nubile female performers, also attracted its share of male spectators who envisaged a more intimate relationship with their onstage favourites. A letter of complaint written to the London County Council in 1899 indicates that other managements were less scrupulous than the D'Oyly Carte in preventing direct contact. The writer here refers to a backstage incident at the Alhambra, an upmarket music hall:

> In one case I know of, a young girl of 16—who had only been in the theatre a week—was spoken to by two men who came from a box in front whome (sic) she was not afraid to speak to & who made her an improper proposal [...] it is by no means an isolated case.[4]

> (cited in Davis 1991, p. 151)

This quote provides an interesting alternative view of the situation in which Jessie Bond appears to have found herself. While these men used a personal approach, another letter of 1889[5] reports that the Alhambra management actually provided paper and writing materials for notes of

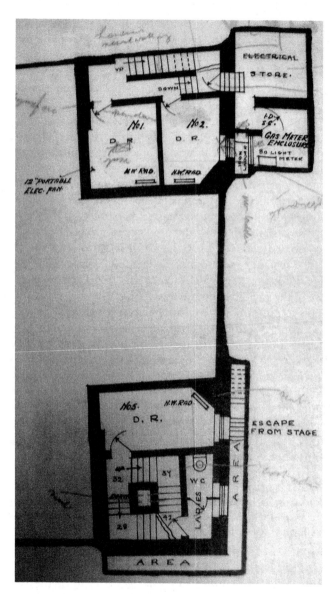

Fig. 6.1   Stage level plan of the backstage area at the Savoy Theatre. Principal dressing rooms separated by open upstage area (C.J. Phipps, Savoy Theatre Plans, 1881 [Metropolitan Archives, London] Photograph by the author)

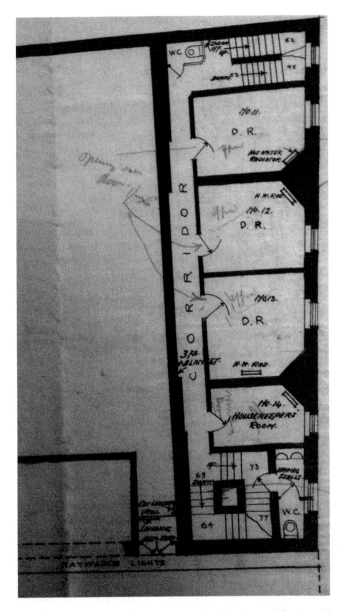

Fig. 6.2 Level 3 plan of the backstage area of the Savoy Theatre. Note three large dressing rooms, with separate stairways and lavatories on either side. This plan was repeated on the floor above, indicating the use of these levels as chorus dressing rooms (C.J. Phipps, Savoy Theatre Plans, 1881 [Metropolitan Archives, London] Photograph by the author)

assignation which could then be delivered backstage by an usher for the price of a tip (cited in Davis 1991, p. 150). Admittedly, there is no direct evidence to attest to such practices in other venues. The atmosphere of the variety house, with its scantily clad ballet girls, and prostitutes frequenting the promenade area to the rear of the auditorium, doubtless added a sexual *frisson* perhaps less evident at a performance of *Patience* at the Savoy. Nevertheless, it might be reasonable to assume, on the basis of the reports relating to the passing of notes at the Savoy already described, that such procedures could have existed in other theatres.

Such occurrences at the Savoy would have taken place in direct contravention of a policy introduced to prevent the transmission of money from audience to theatre staff. When Richard D'Oyly Carte opened the Savoy Theatre in 1881, he was at pains to advertise his opposition to:

> the demanding or expecting of fees and gratuities by attendants [...] any attendant detected in accepting money from visitors will be instantly dismissed. I trust that the public will co-operate with me to support this reform [...] by not tempting attendants with the offer of gratuities.[6]
>
> (cited in Cellier and Bridgeman 1914, p. 99)

Could this suggest a tacit attempt to eliminate the possibility of making backstage assignations via front of house staff? Certainly the threat of instant dismissal for accepting a tip for taking a coat or umbrella seems somewhat harsh. Such action may have been prompted by managerial awareness of the clandestine transmission of notes from auditorium to dressing room, and the illicit rendezvous which might result from such communications. It is, of course, probable that such measures were taken to prevent unscrupulous ushers from charging customers for the often lavishly produced theatre programmes, which were provided gratis at the Savoy. But then it is also possible that one of the reasons the programmes were provided free of charge was to discourage any form of financial exchange between spectator and staff. The forcible ejection of a member of the public for passing a 'libertine note' at the Savoy (an occurrence tacitly encouraged at the Alhambra) is a powerful indicator of the extent of the management's desire to disassociate themselves and their organisation from conventional public attitudes towards the immorality of actresses and, by implication, those who employed them. These practices were not a new invention. Similar measures had been introduced by John Hollingshead to raise the public profile of the Gaiety Theatre some years earlier (Goodman 2000, p. 38). The Gaiety's reputation rested largely on its burlesques, and so it was a venue more susceptible to accusations of immorality (and the probability of backstage assignation) than the Savoy. Hollingshead's veto on the acceptance of tips in a venue where, in all likelihood, the practice had previously occurred, lends further credence to the interpretation of Savoy procedure as a preventative measure.

Finally, some intriguing references within several of Gilbert's libretti suggest that the occurrence and location of such activities were sufficiently well known to be the subject of humour. In *Trial by Jury*, a pre-Savoy piece and one which is somewhat racier in tone than Gilbert's later libretti, the Learned Judge attempts to arrange clandestine romantic assignations with both chief bridesmaid *and* jilted bride-to-be. He does so by passing them written notes of assignation through an intermediate functionary—the court usher. And is it mere coincidence that, in *The Gondoliers*, an opera which reflects the slightly more relaxed moral tone of the late 1880s, Gilbert chooses to name the Spanish Grand Inquisitor, who has a definite eye for young girls, Don *Alhambra*?[7]

THE RIGHT TYPE OF GIRL

A concern for outward respectability has been shown to be an essential characteristic of the D'Oyly Carte management style, and an important ingredient in its marketability. But it does not entirely explain the need to maintain a code of respectability *behind* the scenes. We might assume that, if the characters portrayed by female principals and the ladies' chorus were required to appear genteel, acting ability might suffice to convey this convincingly. However, backstage behaviour appears to have assumed a similar level of importance to the management as the convincing representation of decorous femininity on stage. It is generally acknowledged that there was a significant increase in the levels of middle-class female employment in the theatre in the second half of the nineteenth century. While Tracy C. Davis finds this indicative of a demographic reflection of an overall growth within this particular social sector (1991, p. 14), there appears to be a correlation between the kind of parts being written and the 'type' of person being employed to play them. If the ladies of the D'Oyly Carte were to be convincing as the 'sisters, cousins and aunts' of Sir Joseph Porter in *HMS Pinafore*, the bluestockings of Princess Ida's female University or the aesthetic maidens in *Patience*, then it would make sense for managements to hire performers who could naturally convey these qualities in their manner, deportment and pronunciation.

Good elocution was a generally acknowledged signifier of respectable status in the nineteenth century. In 1839, readers of *Etiquette for Ladies and Gentlemen* were advised that '[t]he moment a woman speaks you can tell whether you are listening to a lady or not'. Vocal tone, accent—especially the increasingly important use of non-regional 'received pronunciation'—along with correct vocabulary, grammar and phraseology were all class indicators (Mugglestone 1990, p. 51). Gilbert's libretti rarely require the use of non-standard elocution, and then only when it is indicated by particular spelling conventions.[8] Thus the predominant stage accent for female characters in the operas is that aspired to or adopted by the middle classes, who formed the predominant constituency of the Savoy audience. Gilbert's concern with appropriate elocution is evinced by his comments on the decline of the burlesque in the 1880s, in which he berated actresses in this type of performance for delivering lines 'with the manners and accents of kitchen maids'.[9] The endeavours of the Savoy operation to disassociate itself from 'lower' forms of performance would have doubtless extended to ensuring that proper diction was employed on stage, by hiring performers (of both genders) who could provide it naturally.

An emphasis on ways in which other attributes such as the appearance, physical behaviour and personality of the performer were perceived to influence their onstage persona is suggested by Percy Fitzgerald in his 1894 book on the operas and their presentation:

> The choruses are formed of refined and mostly pretty girls, drawn from the 'lower middle classes' and are of a very different type from that found in the common opera bouffe chorus. This lends a grace and charm to all they do.

(p. 109)

The combination of grace, charm and refinement, prerequisites for a D'Oyly Carte chorus girl, is equated with social background. The suggestion here is that the level of finesse which distinguishes them from performers in less respectable forms of entertainment is linked to their social origin. Their class background is different from that of 'common' chorus girls drawn, perhaps, from the working classes or the music hall, origins which, presumably, did not guarantee the qualities necessary for the Savoy.

This is further verified by a letter from Gilbert requesting an audition for a prospective chorus member, which indicates the kind of performer the company were looking for:

I have seen Miss Repton & personally I think her a very attractive and interesting girl [...] of course I know nothing of her vocal powers [... but] she
would look most effective in the 2nd Act dresses of the new piece. She is a
total stranger to me (although I know some of her people) [...] but she is a
nice ladylike girl—who has to earn her own living—& is, in short, the sort
of girl one likes to have in the chorus.[10]

'A nice ladylike girl who has to earn her own living' might be the perfect
description of the D'Oyly Carte actress. Here we see a preference for physically attractive female performers of respectable demeanour and reputable
background. The fact that Miss Repton is a 'nice ladylike girl', and that
Gilbert 'knows some of her people', places her within the social circles in
which the upwardly mobile Gilbert chooses to move. It also appears to
take precedence over her musical potential as a reason for employment.
She is obviously the right 'type'. Those outside the company were also
aware of such casting preferences. Responding in 1892 to Ellen Terry's
request for career advice concerning a female acquaintance, the young
Italian soprano Elvira Gambogi, Bernard Shaw remarked:

Do you know D'Oyly Carte, or Mrs. D'Oyly Carte, who was Miss Lenoir?
They always have several Companies touring in a small way with their
Savoy repertory; and they are the only people in the comic opera line in
London, as far as I know, with whom the Signorina's niceness would not be
a disadvantage.

(Lawrence 1965, p. 347)

Given the restrained irony of Shaw's tone (in 1892 the D'Oyly Carte touring operation was by no means 'small'), the implication here is that a
'refined' personality was out of place in the milieu of popular musical theatre, *except* at the Savoy. It gives some indication of the exclusivity of style
cultivated by Carte in comparison to other managements. The 'disadvantage' referred to could derive from the fact that the lady in question would
not 'fit in' to the morally questionable or generally unrestrained atmosphere of most companies. It could also relate to performance style. In his
review of Gambogi's recital, Shaw remarked that 'she has natural refinement, good looks and an engaging personality'.[11] Cultivated demeanour
on stage, or that which was not 'suggestive', was marketable at the Savoy,
but not elsewhere. Shaw's sister, Lucy Carr Shaw, had toured extensively

with D'Oyly Carte companies between 1883 and 1886, suggesting that Shaw had insider knowledge of company requirements.

An instructive comparison might be made with the attitude taken by George Edwardes, who managed the Gaiety Theatre at the time when Shaw was offering casting advice to Terry's protégé. Edwardes's tenure ran from 1885 to 1915, during which time he was the producer of the popular 'Girl' musical comedies, such as *A Gaiety Girl* (1893) and *A Shop Girl* (1894), which were to eclipse the Gilbert and Sullivan operas in popularity with the theatre-going public in the 1890s. Edwardes employed tutors to teach his girls singing, elocution, deportment and social skills, so that 'a refined sexuality was achieved' (Postlewaite 2007, p. 89). This was presumably required because the Gaiety girls were initially employed primarily for their physical beauty and sexual attractiveness, rather than for any particular performing ability, or naturally 'ladylike' qualities (Bailey 1998, p. 178). No such tuition appears to have been required at the Savoy other than that provided by standard rehearsals, as Carte's stringent audition process recruited competent performers who became part of a highly professional workforce.[12] Gilbert's comments regarding Ina Repton show that a pretty face and good figure were important, but they were not the sole criteria for employment at the Savoy. As we have seen, suitable demeanour, deportment and speech seem to have been prerequisite. The 'wrong' type of girl was presumably weeded out during the audition stage.

Edwardes had been part of Carte's management team from the late 1870s until 1885, and had absorbed some of the practices employed by the Triumvirate. Like his mentors at the Savoy, Edwardes monitored the behaviour of his girls, but for notably different reasons. Rather than taking pains to ensure their modesty, he seems to have surreptitiously encouraged them to extend the glamorous aura which accompanied their stage appearances to their everyday lives, promoting their attendance at fashionable restaurants, or at the races (Bailey 1998, p. 178). Any attendant publicity would enhance the glamour of his girls, and increase their appeal to the young, single, lower-middle-class spectators who made up a large part of the audience for this kind of entertainment (Bailey 1998, p. 191). The Savoy and Gaiety managements seemed to be very aware of ways in which the personal behaviour of female employees could affect the public image of their respective organisations, and both managements exercised an unusual degree of control over the behaviour of their female workforce, in order to produce the required effect.[13] In a crowded, highly competitive and profit-driven theatrical marketplace, where specialisation in a particular type of show for a specific audience sector made sound economic sense, 'naughtiness' and glamorised sexuality were good for business at the Gaiety, just as 'respectability', both onstage and off, proved profitable for Richard D'Oyly Carte at the Savoy.

An example of what might be considered typical Victorian double standards, but one which also demonstrates workplace control in action, is to be found in Carte's management of the 'unacceptable' behaviour of one of his female principals, Leonora Braham, Carte's lead soprano from 1881 until 1887. Braham had an alcohol problem which threatened to end her career at the Savoy. In the middle of July 1885, early in the first *Mikado* run, she was drunk on stage, prompting several 'official warnings' from Carte. His concern for the success of his enterprise overrode (though it did not necessarily negate) issues of personal morality. He wrote, 'I am certainly rightly or wrongly under the impression that you do habitually take more than is good for you but that of course is no business of mine so long as it does not unfit you to do your part properly.'[14] For Carte the businessman, what happened behind closed doors was a private matter. It was significant only when it became visible either backstage or in performance—in other words, when it became public and threatened to undermine the quality of the product or the decency of the establishment in the eyes of prospective audiences.

Audiences in the 1890s would have witnessed rather differentiated female stage personae at the two venues. 'Playful gambolling on the verge of indecency' (1897, p. 161) was how William Archer described the Gaiety shows, while Max Beerbohm went further by remarking that '[t]he musical comedies stock in trade was of a wholly sexual order'.[15] The Gaiety's success in the 1890s demonstrates the presence of a large market sector for this kind of entertainment. According to the cultural historian Peter Bailey, female performers at the Gaiety adopted a performing style typified by 'knowingness'. This involved 'the technique of hints and silences that left the audience to fill in the gaps and complete the circuits of meaning, thus flattering them in the sense of their own informed and superior worldliness' (Bailey 1998, p. 105). Any such suggestiveness seems to have been absent in the D'Oyly Carte Company, or was castigated if it occurred. Jessie Bond reports that her attempt to get a laugh from the gallery by wiggling her behind at the audience early in the run of *The Mikado* in 1885 resulted in a reprimand and threat of dismissal (Bond 1930, p. 83). The aura of respectability surrounding female Savoy performers provided a reassurance that the Savoy was a safe location for a respectable audience, particularly the middle-class female matinee-goers, who, from the 1870s onwards, began to frequent theatre performances unchaperoned.

It could be argued, in response to this opinion, that the company did not deliberately publicise its moral ethos, and that any public perceptions of modesty were the result of the press coverage which followed events such as the ejection of the importuning aristocrat mentioned above. However, another piece of evidence might support the idea that the company was concerned about its 'PR' image. At this time, the D'Oyly Carte was largely a touring organisation. A far greater number of performers were employed for regional tours than were to be found in the London company. One of the features of the touring lifestyle was the segregation of personnel into single-sex railway carriages and, as late as the 1930s, male and female performers were required to congregate in separate groups on station platforms, presenting a distinctly outward-facing demonstration of decorum. In the 1880s this spectacle would have been observable to rail travellers on four to six separate provincial station platforms, on a weekly or half-weekly basis, as the touring companies travelled to their next provincial destination. Peter Parker, whose father, Stanley H. Parker, was the private secretary to Rupert D'Oyly Carte (Richard's son), and who, as a boy and young man in the 1930s and 1940s, became personally acquainted with the company, remarks that 'looking back on things I do believe that DOC (sic) did deliberately put on a show of respectability outwardly' (Parker 2008). It is reasonable to assume that measures applied in the 1930s to preclude the stigma of moral laxity attached in the middle-class mind to female performers and chorus girls in particular (Davis 1991, pp. 69–101) would be even more likely in the 1880s. Actresses, like prostitutes, displayed themselves at night, in public, for financial gain, and had regular dealings with men who were not their husbands. If the Savoy girls could be seen to mitigate these disadvantages by acquiring a public reputation for modesty, as well as displaying ladylike 'grace and charm' onstage, then a significant sector of the potential audience could feel secure in the knowledge that they were attending the kind of performance which matched their cultural and moral preoccupations.

The right 'type' of girl was therefore an essential component of the kind of product on offer at the Savoy. Middle-class female aspirants to the theatrical profession might profitably look for work in an organisation whose repertoire was 'middle class' both in terms of the kinds of characters portrayed on stage, and the kind of audience at whom the work was principally aimed. The small amount of information available concerning the social origins of a number of D'Oyly Carte performers such as Jessie Bond, Florence Perry and Emmie Owen place them firmly in the lower-middle classes. Their fathers were respectively a musician and piano maker, a small-scale property developer and a theatrical master carpenter (Bond 1930, p. 11; Joseph 2005, pp. 7, 11). Nevertheless, the fact that all three young women had received musical training before embarking upon theatrical careers or had professional experience in the more socially acceptable realm of the concert hall, would have demonstrated their social credentials (Bratton 2003, p. 104). Many early D'Oyly Carte actresses entered the profession in this way, suggesting a deliberate policy of hiring concert artists for both chorus and principal roles. A high level of musical ability was probably the primary reason for this kind of recruitment, but the kind of social origins that fostered the development of a serious musical career would doubtless have manifested themselves in the personal traits and behaviour of these women.

CODES OF CONDUCT

If the respectable classes considered concert singing to be an acceptable pursuit for a woman, the lifestyle of the theatre artiste challenged many of their core beliefs. For the aspiring actress, reconciling entrenched social prejudice towards the stage with the prospect of a theatrical career was a difficult task. Women from 'middle-class' backgrounds, who were attracted to a profession which now required the personal qualities their class and upbringing had bestowed, could find themselves in an environment completely incompatible with 'middle-class' views of the social function of women in the 'domestic sphere'. It is probable that a further reason for D'Oyly Carte's code of propriety was to provide a workplace which attempted to replicate some of the beneficial features of the Victorian home in order to allow women from such backgrounds to function uncompromised by the hazards which, in other circumstances, might affect young, single women. The worst of these perils was sexual dishonour. Tracy C. Davis comments that:

> Surrendering unmarried daughters to the co-sexual profession of acting (knowing its reputation), was traumatic for parents, especially as chastity was regarded as a prerequisite for female marriage, and marriage (rather than any trade) was *the* female livelihood.

(Davis 1991, p. 172)

The Savoy was not alone in attempting to forestall such disaster. In terms of spoken drama, the Kendals at the St James's Theatre shared similar attitudes to backstage decorum. Indeed, Madge Kendal's company was known as a 'safe' location for young, middle-class actresses. Kerry Powell, in his book *Women and Victorian Theatre*, points out Kendal's intention to apply 'domestic standards of conduct to actors and actresses, and (make) the theatre itself into a home' (1997, p. 61). The morals of middle-class Victorian domesticity were imported into those theatrical environments where managements and practitioners shared such beliefs, in order to combat the dangers perceived to be traditionally inherent in the theatrical lifestyle.

An awareness that '[t]he word "actress" was [...] a euphemism for "prostitute" in the press, where the meanings of the two words were at times indistinguishable' (Powell 1997, p. 33) presumably added to the state of apprehension which lay behind Jessie Bond's initial reaction to the offer of stage work by Carte in 1878:

> The stage was frowned upon by the respectable, and I had been trained in the strict conditions of concert and oratorio singing. Would not such a change in my life mean social downfall, and would not my parents think I had gone to perdition? I dared not tell them of Carte's offer, I knew too well beforehand how strong their objections would be.
>
> (Bond 1930, p. 34)

Bond's fear of parental displeasure in such circumstances would have been a common reaction in the 1870s and 1880s, as would her anxiety concerning her consequent drop in social status. For all its excitement, independence of lifestyle and possibility of financial reward, the adoption of a stage career would have placed a strain on the social identity of a woman in Jessie Bond's position. She faced a typical dilemma: How was it possible to be a stage performer and yet still maintain the distinguishing features of respectable bourgeois womanhood?

In her autobiography, written 50 years after her stage debut in the original production of *HMS Pinafore* in 1878, Bond repeatedly affirms her middle-class credentials, strongly indicating the pervasiveness of the status-related anxieties experienced by a respectable woman entering a theatrical career. She presents herself as a dedicated, industrious professional who is devoted to her calling to the exclusion of other pleasures (Bond 1930, p. 138). She harks back with a degree of nostalgic regret to the spiritual satisfaction provided by the oratorio and church performance which she rejected for the West End stage (p. 86). Bond's time in the Savoy green room is spent in the blameless pursuits of darning and mending, and she performs 'good works' by singing in East End churches gratis, and entertaining the 'poor Jews' of Whitechapel, on her Sundays off (p. 126). She avoids close friendships with her fellow performers (p. 138) and, most significantly

> had no use for love or lovers, and never felt the slightest romantic interest in any man I acted with. I lived only for my work [...] and never once in all those years did I accept an invitation to supper!
>
> (p. 62)

Bond's final gesture towards complete respectability was the eventual abandonment of her theatrical career (having worked successfully and lucratively for over 20 years) in favour of marriage to Lewis Ransom, a wealthy, solidly bourgeois engineer.

If such sanctimony sounds rather forced, the objective truthfulness of these recollections is less important than what they tell us about Jessie Bond's need to assert her innate respectability. Again we find ourselves in the realm of anecdote: stories which tell us a great deal about how a Victorian female performer on the musical stage relates to the social expectations of her age, irrespective of their exact truthfulness. Most pertinent to this discussion is the way Bond negotiates the great pitfall of the actress, attempted seduction. She frequently refers to love letters and poems from admirers, leaving the reader to infer from these the degree of fascination she exerted over her male devotees. However, she pointedly ignores them all. Her rejections culminate with a witty dismissal of the attentions of Europe's greatest playboy, H.R.H the Prince of Wales:

> I am not, and never was, awed by royalty or rank in itself, and had no hesitation in repelling undue advances.
>
> 'May I come to see you, Miss Bond?' he asked me on one occasion.
>
> 'What for, sir?' I asked. 'My mother would be very surprised if she saw *you* walking into our house.'
>
> I had no mother and no house—in London—but that did not matter, and my answer had the desired effect.
>
> (p. 71)

We see Jessie Bond endowing herself with a set of exemplary mid-Victorian virtues: hard work, self-denial in the pursuit of her goals, religious 'feeling' and chastity.[16]

The prevailing ethos of the company could therefore be seen as a response to the need to create an environment in which outwardly respectable women, such as Jessie Bond, could function as employees. To this end, behavioural propriety became enshrined as company policy by including it in contracts of employment. Existing contracts for the original production of *HMS Pinafore* in 1878 contain several clauses which enforce 'proper' behaviour. Most significant is clause 8 which states that:

> Any person being intoxicated, or swearing, or using obscene, abusive or insulting language, *or indulging in unseemly conduct* ... shall forfeit a week's salary or his or her engagement, at the option of the Manager.[17]

While enforcing a code of behaviour which would protect the modesty of female employees by ensuring that male company members refrained from acting in an objectionable way, and also as a general method of ensuring a good working atmosphere, this list of misdemeanours also discloses an assimilation of the received doctrines of middle-class Victorian respectability. Drunkenness, swearing and fornication were anathema to a middle-class mentality derived from the puritan creed of evangelical Christianity, which, in the words of the historian F.M.L. Thompson, sought to preserve 'piety, chastity, sobriety [and] supplied a pattern of total behaviour excellently fitted to the middle-classes, keen to differentiate their status from uncouth lower orders' (1988, p. 251).

Although the severe austerity of mid-Victorian morality had been shaken off by the 1880s, Gilbert, Sullivan and Carte were born into a bourgeois milieu shaped by such principles. These standards were considered integral to the well-being of the Victorian family and, according to Thompson, the implementation of such ideology within the home 'was predominantly the work of the womenfolk' (1988, p. 251). The female members of any family were, therefore, the foundation of its moral integrity, and so it is not surprising to see an organisation which sought to appeal to the middle-class morality of its target audience attempting to reinforce the public probity of its female elements.

Such sentiments are congruent with an implicit managerial policy of inculcating a modified version of the moral values of the Victorian family within the company as a whole. The fact that the D'Oyly Carte organisation was a genuine family business would have both encouraged and furthered such practice.[18] The epithet 'the D'Oyly Carte Family' was commonly used within the company to describe the network of relationships which existed between performers, managers and employees. 'We are all a very happy family,' remarked George Grossmith contentedly in his 1888 autobiography (p. 102). A journalist covering preparations for *Utopia, Limited* in 1893 contrasted behaviour at the Savoy with that of other companies:

> A Savoy rehearsal is indeed a study in propriety of demeanour [...]. What a difference to other theatres, where nothing is done without a quantity of highly-decorated language! In truth, at the Savoy, there is a charming family tone—everyone seems polite and respectful, and there appears to be a genuine feeling of good-fellowship all round.[19]

It is significant that other managements who projected a 'respectable' image—the German Reeds, the Bancrofts and the Kendals—were husband-and-wife acting teams, apparently replicating domestic gender roles within the theatrical workplace. The Savoy functioned in a similar fashion. As a masculine-led institution, which relied on the popularity of its male co-authors to ensure success and profitability rather than the celebrity appeal of married star performers, its leaders, especially Gilbert, appear to have adopted a specifically paternalistic role in enforcing respectable Victorian family values in the theatre. Gilbert and Carte[20] might therefore be seen as surrogate father figures, controlling the potentially unruly behaviour of their 'sons' (male company members) and ensuring they behaved like gentlemen, while protecting their 'daughters' (female performers) from the possible dangers of the working lifestyle. Family values were introduced into theatrical life, not as an evangelical moral crusade, but as a method of enabling a company to co-exist and effectively function in a productive and business-like way while countering any public preconceptions of the immorality of the women it employed.

The occurrence of such immorality would have manifested itself more obviously in the majority of venues, in which no official consideration was given to the personal or moral well-being of female performers. There are few direct reports of sexual harassment in the theatre at this period (Davis 1991, p. 93), but those that do exist suggest that it was not a rare occurrence. Leopold Wagner in his 1899 manual *How to Get on the Stage and How to Succeed There* reports that

With 'ladies of the ballet' and 'show girls' [...] the conditions are by no means favourable. Actors of the lower order do unfortunately expect to have 'a good time' with these auxiliaries, because they are drawn from an inferior class of society and rarely possess the firmness to sedulously shun their advances. Even the scene shifters and 'property men' look forward to the pantomime season as a period of licence, during which they may play havoc among the girls who do not stand on their moral dignity.

(Wagner 1899, p. 179)

This comment clearly places sexual misbehaviour in the context of class. Although sympathetic to the plight of the poor chorus girl, sexual activity, unwelcome or otherwise, is here seen to be connected with those of the 'uncouth lower orders' who either cannot contain their libido, or do not possess the power to resist those whose libido is getting out of control. The entirely middle-class culture of the Savoy would seem to have ensured the prevention of such occurrences. Indeed, the list of punishable offences in the contract mentioned earlier (drunkenness, swearing, fornication) can also be read as a list of faults commonly ascribed by some commentators to the more feckless elements of the working classes. Understood in this way, the Savoy regime may be seen in part to be an attempt to ensure that all performers bought into those notions of middle-class respectability espoused by the management, in the same way that servants in some Victorian households might be expected to attend the churches or chapels of their employers.

It is quite possible that some performers might actually have objected to this degree of control over their personal habits. Although often full of praise for her old employers, Jessie Bond implies more than a usual degree of coercion in the management's treatment of staff:

Looking back on that long connection with the Triumvirate, I see more clearly than ever I did how autocratic they were in their dealings with us, and how they tried to bind us hand and foot [...]. Not that I want to represent us as downtrodden slaves—far from it. They were kindness itself in many ways, but they certainly treated us more as soldiers to be commanded, or even as *neophytes under a vow*, than as human entities.

(1930, p. 141, my italics)

Describing the female workforce as 'neophytes under a vow'—a reference to novitiate nuns in a religious order—suggests that the moral regime was imposed with some vigour, and gives the impression that other nun-like attributes, such as a selfless devotion to duty and an unquestioning response to authority, might have been necessary. The insistence on personal seemliness enshrined in the contract, and our knowledge of Gilbert's, and Sullivan's, meticulous and authoritarian rehearsal methods,[21] would suggest that both of these qualities would have been essential to survival as a chorister and principal performer at the Savoy.

The ethos may also have been largely self-imposed. The punishments for contravention of contractual stipulations were severe: forfeit of a week's wages or dismissal. Losing a position with the D'Oyly Carte Company would have been a severe blow, particularly for a chorister or bit-part player. A major advantage of working at the Savoy was continuity of employment. Choristers in Victorian theatre were usually contracted for the run of a show and not paid for rehearsals.[22] Due to an unbroken run of hits from 1877 to 1891, many choristers and principal performers at the Savoy found themselves rehired for subsequent productions (Davis 1991, p. 32), and as rehearsals for a new work took place during the run of the previous piece, the Savoy chorus were never out of pocket. Bearing in mind an average of 50 per cent unemployment in the theatrical profession at this time, this kind of job security may well have been a great incentive for performers of both sexes to adhere to company regulations (Davis 1991, p. 32). A similar inducement would be the likely realisation by female employees that the necessity of finding alternative employment might expose them to other common perils of the theatrical life. Respectable women elsewhere in the profession were always susceptible to male predation from co-workers or 'mashers' pursuing potential liaisons with actresses.

Such concerns were vociferously aired in public in the 1880s and 1890s. In 1885, Gilbert's professional rival and Sullivan's occasional collaborator F.C. Burnand publicly addressed the 'degrading effect of the stage on young female innocents who attempted to earn a living there' in the the *Fortnightly Review* (cited in Stedman 1996, p. 222), subsequently involving himself, Gilbert and Hollingshead in a war of words concerning theatrical morality. Similar sentiments were expressed in Clement Scott's notorious (and career-changing) 1897 piece *Does the Theatre Make for Good?*[23] He declared that:

It is nearly impossible for a woman to remain pure who adopts the stage as a profession ... The freedom of life, of speech, of gesture which is the rule behind the curtain, renders it almost impossible for a woman to preserve that simplicity of manner which is after all her greatest charm ... These drawbacks are things that render it impossible for a lady to remain a lady ... a woman who endeavours to keep her purity is almost of necessity fore-doomed to failure in her career ... it is unwise in the last degree to expose a young girl to the inevitable consequences of a theatrical life.[24]

(Blaythwayte 1898, pp. 3–4)

If Gilbert, and perhaps Carte, had provided a written manifesto con-cerning the dangers affecting young women in the theatrical workplace, it might have resembled Scott's article, although they would have certainly differed in their conclusions. Scott's opinions concerning the corrupting nature of the theatrical lifestyle demonstrate a condition that Gilbert and the D'Oyly Carte management were doing their best to prevent through the working practices which operated at the Savoy. While the article appeared 20 years after the formation of the D'Oyly Carte Company, Scott had been one of Gilbert's oldest friends and literary colleagues, and we might justifiably speculate that this correlation of idea and practice derives from a parallel standpoint on the issue of female respectability in the the-atre. The gender segregation at the Savoy—which is tellingly referred to in Jessie Bond's memoirs as keeping the 'sheep rigorously separated from the goats' (1930, p. 62)—would indicate a belief on the part of the man-agement that the theatrical environment, with its dangerous 'freedoms' and threat of sexual harassment and corruption, could erode the 'ladylike' manners so necessary for successful performance of the female roles in the operas. Such essential feminine attributes had therefore to be protected by the creation of a working atmosphere in which young women, particularly those of a more genteel or non-theatrical social background, would be safe from the malign influences of theatrical lifestyle, speech and gesture which so concerned Clement Scott. Ladies could remain ladies at the Savoy.

SUMMARY

An examination of evidence in the light of various social and cultural contexts can be seen to demonstrate that the D'Oyly Carte 'board-ing-school' ethos grew out of two significant managerial needs. First, to promote the respectability of a theatrical 'brand' to a spe-cific audience sector in order to encourage that sector to spend its money at the Savoy. Second, to provide an environment conducive to the employment and participation of the middle-class actresses who were essential to the success of these theatre pieces. The emergence of women, particularly middle-class women, into the Victorian workplace, has been seen by historians as a challenge to contemporary male views of their social position (Powell 1997, p. xi; Zakreski 2006, p. 142). The D'Oyly Carte Company's concern for promoting the modesty and respectability of its female employees on stage and off indicates an anxiety to present its female workers as exemplars of conventional female virtues, decorously behaved and compliant with normative gender roles. Working girls they might be, but behavioural codes ensured that they retained those attributes appropriate to their gender and class, both in the workplace and in the public eye.

The preservation of these virtues ensured the respectability of the Savoy 'brand'. which in turn helped to ensure the maximisation of revenue. Middle-class audiences flocked to a type of popular musical theatre which presented a socially acceptable and non-threatening depiction of young womanhood. The enforcement and observation of behavioural conventions within the company benefited middle-class female performers inasmuch as they could pursue their professional career choice in an environment sympathetic to their needs for social acceptability and personal safety. This, in turn, benefited Gilbert, Sullivan and Carte by helping to cement the moral probity of their enterprise. However, the ultimate purpose of these measures was profit, and profit for the Triumvirate was partly derived from their success in altering public perceptions of the musical actress. Until the advent of the D'Oyly Carte Opera Company, wholly respectable musical theatre on a large scale was an anomaly. Attractive female leads and choristers were an indispensable constituent of the Victorian musical stage, but the Savoy Company extended their appeal to customers of both sexes. Beauty, grace and the opportunity to admire gorgeous costumes were as attractive to female customers as demure nubility was for men. The 'refined and mostly pretty girls' of the Savoy, with their 'boarding-school' ethos, contributed to the social acceptability of British theatre-going in the late nineteenth century, and provided a mode of performed behaviour which audiences who aspired to 'middle-class' sophistication could enjoy. The extent to which the external manifestations of 'refined' behaviour in D'Oyly Carte actresses, and 'gentlemanly' behaviour in their male counterparts, may have influenced physical and vocal approaches to performance, and contributed to the distinctive Savoy style, will be explored in the next chapter.

NOTES

1. A search through complete online editions of the comic papers *Punch*, *Judy*, *Moonshine* and *Fun* for the period 1881–1884 (British Library Nineteenth Century Newspaper and Periodical database) has, as yet, revealed no press coverage of this event. This is, of course, not conclusive evidence, as there may have been other papers that ran the story. Similarly, using 'Jessie Bond', 'Opera Comique' and 'Savoy' for keyword searches may be problematic if the characters and places involved were referred to pseudonymously.

2. *Era*, 16 February 1884.

3. London County Council Metropolitan Archive (GLC/AR/BR/19/0047)

4. Greater London Record Office, 5 January 1899.

5. Greater London Record Office, 14 October 1889.

6. Richard D'Oyly Carte's inaugural address, written for the opening of the Savoy Theatre, 6 October 1881.

7. These references were supplied in a private email message on 6 February 2009 by Dorothy Kincaid following my public lecture 'The D'Oyly Carte Boarding School: Gilbert, Sullivan and Victorian Values: 1877–1903', given at the Society for Theatre Research in January 2009.

8. The rustic rural dialect of the chorus of villagers in Act Two of *The Sorcerer* or Dick Dauntless's nautical speech patterns in *Ruddigore* are some examples of deliberately indicated non-standard pronunciation.

9. 'Workers and Their Work: Mr W.S. Gilbert.' *Daily News*, 21 January 1885.

10. Letter from WSG to Helen Carte, 19 December 1895 (DC/TM).

11. *The Musical World*, 6 July 1892.

12. Press interview with RDC, *The Million*, 10 December 1892.

13. It should be noted that Platt (2004) disagrees with Bailey's interpretation of Edwardes's promotional activities, rejecting the notion that 'generalises the musical comedy actress into the victim role, positioned at the mercy of a patriarchal [...] culture' (p. 124). This is perhaps an overreaction. Platt is keen to stress the individual agency of Edwardes's female performers, but cites female *stars*, who inevitably possess greater bargaining power, rather than chorus members, as his examples (p. 125). Regular pay and longevity of employment were likely to have encouraged adherence to managerial injunctions. The manipulation of an image is not necessarily concomitant with the manipulation of individuals outside the workplace, and in any case would partially rely on the willingness of the employee to conform to company policy. Similarly, public image does not determine personal behaviour or opinion when the performer is removed from the workplace.

14. Letter from RDC to Leonora Braham, 18 July 1885 (DC/TM).

15. *Saturday Review*, 30 October 1909.

16. There may have been other, more personal reasons for Bond's amatory reluctance. Early in the autobiography Bond presents a melodramatic account of

her abduction and forced marriage, at the age of 17, to her concert agent, Herr F.A. Schotlaender. She was both attracted and repelled by this Svengali-like figure who managed to convince her that she had been sexually 'compromised' and so must marry him. The marriage was miserable and a son was born who died shortly afterwards. Bond reports how a divorce was easily obtained, allowing her to pursue her career (Bond 1930, pp. 18–22). Despite constant proposals over the years, Bond maintains her aversion to married life, until the point at which she is ready to retire from the stage. What is not reported in her memoir is the fact that that she contracted syphilis from the violent and adulterous Schotlaender. Documents held in the Metropolitan Archive relating to Bond's subsequent divorce reveal that syphilis was the cause of death entered on the death certificate of her son Sidney Arthur Charles Schotlaender, who died aged six weeks in 1871. Her affidavit states that Schotlaender 'knowingly and wilfully communicated to me a certain pestilent and loathsome disease which caused the death of our infant child' (Bond, J., London Metropolitan Archive UK Civil Divorce Records, 1858–1911). Residual symptoms of this illness may account for Bond's frequent indisposition and absences from the stage. Attention was drawn to this archival source by Savoynet contributor Chris Goddard.

17. Contract of Employment between Harriet Everard and the Comedy Opera Company, 1878 (DC/TM), my italics.

18. The leadership passed to Helen Carte's stepson, Rupert, after her demise in 1913. His daughter, Bridget D'Oyly Carte, ran the company after Rupert's death in 1948 until its closure in 1982.

19. 'A Rehearsal at the Savoy: How the New Opera Is Prepared.' *The Westminster Gazette*, 6 October 1893.

20. There is no record of Sullivan personally promoting any kind of 'respectable' behaviour at the Savoy. As a part of the top level of management, we might assume he publicly supported a prevailing moral regime that differed so markedly from his personal habits. See Arthur Jacobs, *Arthur Sullivan. A Victorian Musician* (1984), for information on Sullivan's gambling and womanising.

21. See Grossmith, *A Society Clown*, 1888, pp. 92–4, for a first-hand account.

22. Clause 7 in the contract of employment for *HMS Pinafore* in 1878 stipulates: 'No Artist will be paid Salary for any days on which the theatre is not open, and no Salaries will be paid for rehearsals.' Contract of Employment between Harriet Everard and the Comedy Opera Company, 1878 (DC/TM).

23. The furore surrounding its publication led to Scott's dismissal as theatre critic of the *Daily Telegraph*. See Davies 1991, pp. 93–7, for a considered discussion of the controversy surrounding this article.

24. '"Does the Theatre Make for Good?" An Interview with Mr Clement Scott' (Blaythwayte 1898, pp. 3–4).

CHAPTER 7

'The Placid English Style': Ideology and Performance

In August 1879 Carte wrote to Sullivan regarding preparations for the forthcoming Broadway premiere of *HMS Pinafore*. The letter contains a comment which, when placed in the context of other relevant evidence, offers a fundamental insight into the performance ethos of Carte's company and his collaborators. When reviewing available casting options for the production, Carte contrasted the preferences of American and British audiences. New Yorkers required

> emotional singing and acting. The placid English style wont (sic) do and I assure you that if we took out such a company as the Opera Comique we should make a big failure as likely as not.[1]

Clearly there were good commercial reasons for avoiding a manner of performance which had proved successful in London but which was likely to fail in New York. Indeed, the production, partly recast with American singers, was a hit, outstripping in popularity the numerous unofficial 'pirated' versions then playing throughout the United States.[2] However, the quotation is included here primarily to draw attention to a specific idea– that the D'Oyly Carte Company developed a distinct mode of embodied performance in which 'placidity' and 'restraint' were major ingredients, and that this manner was particularly suited to the cultural preferences of late-Victorian West End theatre practitioners and audiences. Much of the ensuing argument attempts to explore both the cultural and practical conditions

© The Author(s) 2016
M. Goron, *Gilbert and Sullivan's 'Respectable Capers'*, Palgrave Studies in British Musical Theatre, DOI 10.1057/978-1-137-59478-5_7

169

which engendered the adoption of this style at the Opera Comique and Savoy Theatre. In doing so it will also raise several issues, with performance a central concern, but encompassing wider themes deriving from the absorption and expression of 'middle-class' ideology.

Up to this point I have addressed ways in which attitudes towards class and respectability have influenced choice of repertoire, market positioning, theatre building and location, the material elements of the theatrical 'event', audience composition and company ethos. Acting is no less dependent on embedded ideological factors. A manner of playing can be seen as the result of cultural practices which are in turn derived from the absorption and representation of shared attitudes. This chapter will investigate the relationship between the physical signifiers of comic performance and issues of class and social status. How did the notion of embodied 'restraint', in terms of manners and deportment, emerge from the cultural ideology of the 'middle classes'? And in what ways were these 'rules' of etiquette or acceptable social behaviour reflected in the work of D'Oyly Carte artists?

Burlesque represented an ethos of indecorousness and dramaturgical disunity from which the Savoy Triumvirate were eager to escape. Contemporary commentators had already established this opposition, while nevertheless recognising the burlesque origins of the operas. The Savoy pieces 'have nothing in common with the inanities of modern burlesque. Burlesques they are in a way, but free from vulgarity, commonplace, or coarseness', declared the theatre critic of the *Morning Advertiser* in 1882.[3] I will explore contrasts of style and method between Savoy opera and burlesque as a means of highlighting the turn to respectability in the type of musical theatre exemplified by Carte's enterprise. The need to rigorously control comic improvisation and the inclinations of comedians to resist the creative restrictions of the theatre director will be investigated here. This in turn will raise questions concerning ways in which the 'gentlemanly' theatre practitioner was accepted both socially and culturally in the late-Victorian period.

EVIDENCE: THE PRESS

An understanding and evaluation of the approach adopted by early D'Oyly Carte practitioners can be substantiated by a considerable amount of evidence relating to performance style. This includes press reviews, interviews, memoirs, recordings, films, play texts, photographs and artwork. However, apart from some early reviews of *The Sorcerer*, there is little *detailed* description of the work of individual actors. Indeed, the dearth of that type of commentary may in itself be an indicator of style. Well-rehearsed traits of restraint and repose performed by members of a tightly knit ensemble are less liable to receive forthright comment than the characteristics of star performers whose business it was to seize audience attention.

Press reviews are the most accessible and revealing source of information. *The Sorcerer* was the first of the line of full-length operas, and critical consideration of its innovative acting style was presented at length in the press. The general tendency of these reviews is initial surprise at a mode of performance which is unusually decorous and unexpectedly realistic (at least for the musical stage). The style is also characterised by a deliberate lack of awareness of the ludicrousness of the comedy. Thus, the performers do not share with the audience an understanding of the absurd situations in which they find themselves, but instead remain 'in character' throughout. Reviews of the succeeding operas contain less comment about style, as critics and audiences appear to have quickly accepted the Savoy methods. As the popularity of the operas ensured the longevity of the brand, and as a stock company became embedded at the Savoy, there seems to be an understanding that most readers would be familiar with the Gilbert and Sullivan performance style.

Exemplifying the use of restrained and realistic acting was Rutland Barrington's novel rendering of the rural parson Dr Daly. Barrington was hailed by critics for the realism of his portrayal. The *Era*, revisiting the production about a month after its opening, reported that:

> In Mr. Barrington's delineation [...] all the artificial aids of the stage are forgotten at once. The mild, gentle representative of the church in a country village appears 'in his habit as he lived' [...] the life-like manner in which Mr. Barrington depicts some of the harmless peculiarities and mannerisms of a country vicar is positively remarkable. One would suppose he had spent every Sunday of his life in the pulpit, and that his daily life was devoted to the work of a remote parish.[4]

Clearly absent was the kind of self-conscious, 'presentational' style of the typical comedian:

> Mr. Barrington's skill is not burlesque, but faithful reproduction of character, and in every respect the portrait is perfect. The attitudes, the tones, the vocalisation, even the most trifling details, are carefully studied. The actor is never 'out of the character' for a moment.[5]

It is significant that the term 'burlesque' here implies a style which is non-realistic and, by inference, 'non-legitimate'. Its opposite, as demonstrated by Barrington's acting, can be read as an understanding that realism and understatement are indicative of artistic value. Being 'out of character'—in other words, demonstrating a 'knowing' connection between the comic *performer* (rather than the character portrayed) and the audience—is implicitly downgraded. The very fact that the portrayal is not exaggerated attests to its innate propriety and acceptability to a 'respectable' audience:

> But let it not be supposed that there is anything of offensive caricature in this [...]. We hear that several well-known clergymen have already gone to have a quiet chuckle at their reverend brother on the stage.[6]

The presence of a realistically portrayed vicar in a piece descended from burlesque and played in a house originally intended for semi-suggestive French farce and *opera bouffe* could not have been a more perfect representation of the intended moral decency of Carte's venture. What can be deduced from critical comment on Barrington's work, and that of his fellow cast members, is that a lack of exaggeration of any kind is regarded as a virtue. The *Era*'s first night review remarks upon the effectiveness of Barrington's 'air of restraint'.[7] This expression is recurrently used by both critics and D'Oyly Carte practitioners from 1877 to the 1930s when describing the work of the latter. It is often accompanied or substituted by the terms 'refinement' and 'repose', or by words with similar connotations, such as 'blandness', 'discretion' and 'simplicity'. Indeed, the concept of restraint and repose emerges as a common factor describing embodied performance at the Opera Comique and Savoy.

A 'refined' performance, therefore, was one which might avoid vulgarity, be embodied in a stylish manner and exemplify those traits which audiences, performers and practitioners considered estimable. 'Restraint', denoting self-control and moderation, is also a homonym. If a stage performance was to be restrained or 'distanced' in its avoidance of excess, practitioners might also have to be restrained (controlled, inhibited) by a higher authority from giving vent to the tendency towards excessive histrionics. This tension will be explored later in the chapter when considering directorial and managerial control of the creative instincts of performers.

At first sight these descriptions suggest, at least to twenty-first-century tastes, a rather dull manner of presentation. But it would seem highly unlikely that the popularity and success of the operas was due to their perceived insipidity. Instead, critical reception, when expressed in these terms, should be read as an appreciation of the fact that they were anti-thetical to other current modes of performance on the musical theatre stage. What they were *not* was as important as what they were. Some ant-onyms of the aforementioned descriptive terms might be 'excitable', 'cha-otic', 'garish', 'coarse' and 'unnatural'. All are expressions which might be applied by respectable 'middle-class' commentators to those types of entertainment favoured by raffish men about town and the working classes—burlesque and music hall. I will elaborate on the contrasting styles of burlesque and Savoy opera below. However, some necessary discussion of evidence drawn from descriptions of individual performers is required to support the premise of a unified performance style.

George Grossmith's notices conform to the prevailing critical trend. The *Era* remarks on the 'finish and refinement of style [and] unforced and spontaneous style of drollery'[8] which characterised his portrayal of Sir Joseph Porter in *HMS Pinafore*. Grossmith played Major General Stanley in *The Pirates of Penzance* with 'his usual unobtrusive comicality' (*Lloyds Weekly Newspaper*)[9] and 'the blandness and quietude that made the part tell so strongly' (*The Examiner*). His Lord Chancellor in *Iolanthe* was 'rich in quiet, unforced drollery'.[10] Richard Temple, who, with Barrington and Grossmith, was to be one of the mainstays of the original company, played the role of the elderly Baronet, Sir Marmaduke Pointdextre, in *The Sorcerer*. Temple appears to have been a very versatile actor who took pains to put an individual stamp on each role, and his parts in the operas were notable for their dissimilarity. They included the villainous Dick Deadeye, bold Pirate King, dense Prince Arac, and a 'suave, placid' Mikado.[11] In *Iolanthe* he was cast as Strephon, the romantic lead. The *Era*, praising Temple for the veracity of his portrayal in *The Sorcerer*, remarks upon his 'taste and discrimination'.[12] We might justifiably conclude that, like Barrington, his 'skill was not burlesque'. Jessie Bond described her former colleague as 'so much an artist. He knew that the real humour was in Gilbert's words, and had no need to force it out' (Bond 1930, p. 147). Barrington notes that, when some improvised business crept into the orig-inal run of *The Mikado,* Temple disapprovingly 'declared it was not "art"' (Barrington 1908, p. 45).

The notion that a musical theatre performer on any stage other than that which presented grand opera could be regarded as an 'artist' suggests much about the style and intent of the Gilbert and Sullivan productions. By the last quarter of the nineteenth century, the earlier sense of the term 'artistic' as something creative or skilful had been replaced by notions that 'Art' (with a capital 'A') was unworldly, improving and educational. In the upwardly mobile and status-conscious world of the late-Victorian West End it became synonymous with high-minded activities such as Henry Irving's Shakespeare revivals at the Lyceum. John Pick, discussing the effect of this attitudinal adjustment on the theatre, comments that: 'An important effect of this sharp change [...] was that the non-artistic was denigrated. Mere entertainment was seen as a different order of things from theatrical "art"' (1983, p. 65). As will be discussed in more detail below, the burlesque and what it represented was, for some theatre critics at least, not considered to be 'Art' at all (Schoch 2003, p. xix). The Gilbert and Sullivan operas, on the other hand, veered towards high culture in their musical and literary sophistication. Theatre critics applauded D'Oyly Carte performance style most readily when it was least redolent of the kind of acting associated with burlesque and the music hall, and when it embodied the type of behaviour associated with the respectable bourgeoisie.

Press coverage indicates a company whose abilities were focused on a restrained and 'natural' presentation of character rather than the extrovert crowd-pleasing of the Victorian 'low' comedian. While the lack of 'vulgar' caricature by male D'Oyly Carte performers drew praise from critics, an absence of impropriety was also noteworthy in the work of the female performers. This is unsurprising, considering the role of the Savoy actress, discussed in the last chapter, as a representative of backstage decency and domestic moral standards. Again, the vocabulary used by the (presumably) male, middle-class theatre critic emphasises the idea of 'restraint'. This was not immediately apparent. Alice May's portrayal of Aline on the opening night of *The Sorcerer* was originally criticised for overenthusiasm. The *Daily News* noted that she was 'a trifle exuberant in style' while *Figaro* declared that 'she has not yet learned to modify the scale of her accomplishments' (cited in Cox-Ife 1977, p. 42). Significantly, later in the run (perhaps after some additional direction by Gilbert), May had adapted her approach. Revisiting the show in December, the *Era* critic commented on the 'repose in her impersonation [...]. Miss May seeks only to render the character naturally and artistically'.[13] Gracefulness, repose and lack of affectation provide performance traits which apparently conformed to masculinist values of bourgeois womanhood.

Female protagonists came and went in the early years of the company, but between 1881 and 1887 Leonora Braham was the resident soprano lead at the Savoy. Her credentials were impeccable, having been predominantly employed by the German Reeds since her 1874 debut. Gilbert had hired her to play the lead in his New York production of *Princess Toto* in 1879 (Ainger 2002, pp. 88, 196). She was therefore perfectly suited for principal roles in the Gilbert and Sullivan operas. As Patience the milkmaid, Braham was praised for her 'grace and simplicity'[14] and 'perfect simplicity'.[15] As Phyllis the Arcadian shepherdess in *Iolanthe*, Braham was 'charming [...] always graceful, even when most coquettish; and at times earnest without affectation'.[16]

A level of self-possession in the embodiment of the leading female roles seems to have become the expected norm. Braham's Princess Ida was performed with 'refined style'.[17] Her 1887 replacement as Rose Maybud in *Ruddigore*, Geraldine Ulmar, was initially not an ideal substitute. Compared 'with her charming predecessor', Ulmar was regarded as 'a little *prononcé* [...] a trifle more highly coloured than is altogether compatible with the very subdued and refined tone of the general picture'.[18] Ulmar was encouraged to 'moderate her powerful voice and tone down her action' when playing Elsie Maynard in *The Yeomen of the Guard* by the *Times* critic.[19] Such comments indicate that a performing style had become established in the portrayal of the younger female characters in the operas which met with critical and audience approval and was remarked upon when absent. In 1896, Florence Perry, as Lisa in *The Grand Duke*, was warned against a 'tendency to force her small voice and to overact'.[20] Lack of self-control and any propensity to physical and vocal overemphasis among female performers—in other words a deficiency of 'restraint'—received a negative response.

EVIDENCE: VISUAL AND TEXTUAL

While it may be justifiable to arrive at some provisional conclusions about performance style from press commentary, these sources are often limited by the generalised nature of the remarks. As we have seen, critics were willing to mention the overall effect of a performance, or communicate perceived qualities or deficiencies in readily understandable terms. However, there is little detailed description of how the performers used their voices and bodies. To construct a more thorough notion of Savoy performance style (while remaining cognisant that an impression is all it can be), we have to explore other sources.

Visual evidence might appear to offer information about posture, gesture and facial expression. However, Thomas Postlewaite's recommendation that the theatre historian must be wary of the 'unintentional distortions and mistakes' which often serve 'causes other than those of accurate documentation' (Postlewaite 2009, p. 247) should be heeded. Visual sources need to be treated with caution. Photographic records of Savoy artists, though offering useful information on costume, hairstyle and make-up, are of limited reliability when attempting to gain insight into embodied performance. They are invariably posed studio portraits. Although the introduction of new technology in the late 1870s had decreased camera exposure times, it is likely that the early D'Oyly Carte photographs (1877–1880) were taken using the older, cumbersome 'wet-plate' method, which required studio conditions (Langford 1980, p. 28). Using this process, the subject had to remain still for at least 25 seconds (Osterman 2009). Even in the 1880s and 1890s, the stationary style required by earlier photographic methods seems to have prevailed as a fashion. Thus, throughout the period, bodily pose and facial expression were stilted and/or exaggerated. There is little evidence of restraint or repose, at least in the images of the comic characters, in studio photographs from the early years of the company. Physical signifiers appear immobile and uncontextualised when removed from the overall flow of an actor's performance or the mise en scène in which they occurred.

Many contemporary drawings of the Savoy operas appeared in periodicals, often accompanying reviews. They may provide some indication of staging and the posture of performers at significant moments in the action. David Friston's pictures, depicting scenes from the operas, which appeared in the *Illustrated London News* and the *Illustrated Sporting and Dramatic News* during the initial run of premieres, can be used to demonstrate the problems faced when attempting to use illustration as a guide for physical or spatial reconstruction (Fig. 7.1).

The need to present an effective visual composition within the dimensions of the printed page can affect any attempt to establish the proxemics of a particular scene and cast doubt on the veracity of the image as an accurate depiction of stage action. A representative example of this kind of problem is Friston's illustration of the Act Two elopement scene in *HMS Pinafore* (Fig. 12) in which seven of the principal characters are compacted together in what would, I estimate, represent three to four metres of stage space. The moment selected seems to be the revelation of the elopement of Ralph and Josephine. But, according to the text, neither Sir Joseph nor Cousin Hebe (background female face between Ralph and Sir Joseph), who appear in the drawing, are actually on stage at this juncture. A point at which characters *might* have been grouped together in close proximity is the 'Octette'

Fig. 7.1 Scene from Act Two of *HMS Pinafore* by David Friston. (*Illustrated London News*, 1878). Public Domain

following Sir Joseph's banishing of Ralph Rackstraw to a 'dungeon cell'. However, at this moment, Captain Corcoran, who is clearly depicted here with cloak and whip, has left the stage. What we see here is a representative selection of events compressed for visual effect, rather than a trustworthy representation of a single stage picture. Particular poses may convey an indication of individual bearing. Indeed, the postures shown by Friston are redolent of the nautical melodrama on which *HMS Pinafore* was based, and could have been deliberately echoed for parodic effect in Gilbert's staging. However, the illustration cannot be said to represent any specific moment of physical interaction between characters arranged as a group.

A more valuable source of performance information appears in the form of a contemporary text. In 1887, the failure of *Ruddygore*[21] to live up to the expectations of audiences after the triumph of *The Mikado* prompted the only attempt by West End managements to burlesque a Gilbert and Sullivan opera. *Ruddy George* by Percy Reeve and H.F.G. Taylor was presented at Toole's Theatre in Charing Cross on 19 March 1887, ran for 36 performances and received a poor critical reception (Walters 2000). *Ruddy George* is a parody of its source material, containing much intertextual reference to the libretti while lampooning many of the established clichés of the Savoy oeuvre. As such, it provides useful inferential information about Savoy performance style. The punning nature of its title is indicative of its content. The name *Ruddy* (possibly standing in for the expletive 'bloody') *George* can easily be read as a send-up of the Savoy's leading comedian, George Grossmith, who appears as 'Robin Redbreast' in the piece.[22] Rutland Barrington is also parodied, as are the Triumvirate themselves, who are rather mercilessly impersonated in the second act.

Robin's patter song in the first act of *Ruddy George* directly mocks Grossmith's repertoire and onstage presence and, in doing so, conveys something of his mode of performance. Ironically, it attributes Grossmith's success as a performer not to his acting or singing ability, but solely to his facility for memorising complex lyrics:

I know very well that I haven't much voice

But I always know my part.

The characters I play don't afford a varied choice,

But I always know my part.

For the actor that once hesitates

Is lost and this necessitates

A thorough-paced proficiency in art.

And although I don't speak loudly,

Still I must maintain most proudly

That I always know my part.

(Taylor 1887, p. 16)[23]

Grossmith was not a trained singer, and in the company of formally trained professionals, his vocal limitations were apparent to himself (Grossmith 1888, pp. 87, 103) and to critics: 'Without the ghost of a voice, he gave excellent effect to the three amusing songs allotted to him' wrote the

Times' critic of his performance as the Lord Chancellor in *Iolanthe.*[24] The second verse makes reference to his physical technique:

And I pose in limb and feature

As a most eccentric creature [...]

(Taylor 1887, p. 16)

Contemporary photographs and drawings do manage to indicate Grossmith's use of comic physicality, dance and facial expression. He famously improvised a 'quaint run round the stage, brandishing the teapot in which he had mixed the love charm' during the opening night of *The Sorcerer* [25] which was retained in future performances and, according to Rutland Barrington, 'started the series of similar antics in the parts which followed' (Barrington 1908, p. 19).

But the burlesqued Grossmith attests to the accuracy of the press reviews regarding the genuine Grossmith when he is made to declare:

I am always self-contained, and I bite my words out short ...

I never act too much, and I never rant or snort ...

(p. 16)

Here is a clear depiction of the 'restrained' comic style. It was delivered at Toole's Theatre by E.D. Ward, who appears to have successfully imitated Grossmith, an artist known to most of the audience, and whose performance could be witnessed half a mile down the road at the Savoy. Significant is the phrase 'self-contained'. This implies control over an actor's potential to 'rant or snort', to get carried away with excess of emotion—or perhaps more fittingly in a comedy, to mug, gag and over-project to the audience. There is nothing excessive about Grossmith's manner. He 'don't speak loudly' and even his diction is clipped, presumably to properly articulate Gilbert's rapid lyrics. The *Observer* critic remarked that the 'chief merit' of the piece was derived from Ward's '*quiet* burlesque' of Grossmith's manner' (my italics) (cited in Walters 2000, p. 23), providing yet another indication of Grossmith's restrained manner.

It also contrasts with what might have been generally expected from a burlesque company in which 'quietness' and reserve would have been out of place and run contrary to audience expectations. A *Daily News* review of *Ruddy George*[26] suggests that Toole's performers, whose style was likely to have been generally less restrained than that of their targets, were prone to exaggerate for comic effect. Quite how an actor might exaggerate restraint is open to speculation, but both Ward and George Shelton who played the Barrington role—'Sir Gaspard Rougegeorge'— appear to have achieved the right balance. Shelton 'succeeded in giving to a gross caricature a droll suggestion of Mr. Rutland Barrington's portentous manner'.[27] A controlled pomposity is certainly written in to several Barrington roles, most characteristically Pooh-Bah in *The Mikado*, but also Captain Corcoran (*HMS Pinafore*) and the self-obsessed poet Archibald Grosvenor (*Patience*). Gentlemanly reserve appears to have been intrinsic to his stage personality. As King Hildebrand, the 'peppery potentate' in *Princess Ida*, Barrington simply could not provide the requisite anger. His 'acting and singing only recalled the mildest moods of the vicar in *The Sorcerer* [...] of the fierce temper, the blustering tone, the mock heroic and defiant manner there was not a vestige'.[28] The restrained manner is essential during the second act of *Ruddigore*, when Sir Despard is transformed from upper-class scoundrel into a frock-coated, ultra-respectable school teacher.

Ruddy George also indicates the extent to which a parodic style could be employed at the Savoy. Sir Gaspard's spoken idiosyncrasies in the burlesque (taken verbatim from *Ruddigore*) tell us that Barrington parodied the distinctive vocal style and accent of the nineteenth-century melodrama villain:

> Sir Gaspard: Poohoor Chihildren! How they lohoathe meh—meh whose hands are steheeped in infameh, but whose heart is as the heart of a littel chihild!

> (Taylor 1887, p. 23)

Sir Gaspard's Act One song in *Ruddy George* lampoons Sir Despard's opening number in *Ruddigore*:

> Sir Gaspard: Oh why am I moody and glum?

> Chorus: Can't guess.

> Sir Gaspard: And why do I waggle my thumb?

> Chorus: Confess.

> Sir Gaspard: You'll admit that it is rather rum.

Chorus: Why yes.

Sir Gaspard: To have a stiff neck and to stamp.

(Taylor 1887, p. 22).

Its purpose is partly to burlesque Barrington's own melodrama parody. Certain stock physical and facial traits from melodrama appear to have been reproduced by Barrington and were apparently rendered comical through the contrast with his understated delivery. This is suggested by the lyrics given to his impersonator, who was presumably demonstrating each gesture as he described it. The song reveals that Barrington 'wobbles' his eyes, 'works' with his eyebrows and stands with legs astride. But this did not preclude 'restraint'. Stock posturing is contrasted with the physical elegance of the actor himself, suggesting that another aspect of Barrington's stage persona was that of the cultured gentleman:

Sir Gaspard: But why do I walk about *so*—

Chorus: Good shape.

Sir Gaspard: Or stand on one leg and a toe—

Chorus: And drape [...]

And later in the song:

Sir Gaspard: My dancing is graceful and sound—

Chorus: Well, well—

Sir Gaspard: And where are such calves to be found?

Chorus: Pall Mall [...]

(Taylor 1887, pp. 22–3)

This indicates that part of Barrington's comic appeal (like that of the later screen comedian Oliver Hardy) may have been the contrast between his large physical presence and a graceful demeanour.[29] The reference to Pall Mall, the location of many of London's fashionable gentlemen's clubs, locates such elegance within the sphere of refined society. In all of his characters, most of whom are members of the middle or upper classes, Barrington seems to have been projecting a distinctly gentlemanly image.[30]

EVIDENCE: RECORDINGS AND FILM

The single surviving recording of Barrington's voice is regrettably not a Gilbert and Sullivan number but *The Moody Mariner*, a song he performed on the variety stage in 1905.[31] Unlike many twentieth-century performers of the 'Pooh-Bah' line of parts, Barrington is revealed not as an operatic bass but as a light-voiced singing actor with clear diction. Despite portraying an ordinary sailor in the sketch which accompanied the song, Barrington's enunciation is genteel. Like Grossmith, his delivery is laconic and he employs much *parlando*.[32] John Wolfson comments on the 'air of urbane superiority' emanating from Barrington in this recording (Wolfson 1999). From this evidence, the press reviews and his impersonation in *Ruddy George*, we can surmise that, as well as being an accomplished character performer, Barrington, though large in stature, seems to have projected gentlemanly grace. Self-contained pomposity and a refined gentility in both body and voice defined his performing style.

Apart from two cylinders recorded by Richard Temple, no sound recordings exist of artists, male or female, who both worked with Gilbert and Sullivan *and* originated roles in their operas (Temple 1999).[33] However, Walter Passmore recorded a number of the songs created for Grossmith, whose parts he inherited in early revivals from 1895 (Passmore 1996). Like many early D'Oyly Carte practitioners on record, operatically trained or otherwise, Passmore had excellent vocal articulation. His recordings convey a strong but never overstated comic persona, and he sometimes speaks rather than sings. He tends to 'bite [his] words out short' (a description that also applied to Grossmith), rarely elongating a note more than necessary, or lingering on any quasi- or mock-operatic moments written for the comic lead. As well as the 'Grossmith' roles, Passmore played (and recorded) the Sergeant of Police in *The Pirates of Penzance* and the Grand Inquisitor in *The Gondoliers*, both performed by Barrington. Wolfson, comparing Barrington's cylinder to the Passmore recordings, maintains that the latter's recordings 'of Barrington's roles may be as close as we can ever get to what Gilbert actually had in mind' (Wolfson 1999). Passmore's clipped delivery and dry, gentlemanly tone indicates an approach common to both Barrington and Grossmith, and presumably advocated by both Gilbert and Sullivan, in these lines of parts.

The nearest we can come to a fully embodied example of the early D'Oyly Carte performance practice is Sidney Granville's portrayal of Pooh-Bah in Universal Studios' film *The Mikado* (Shertzinger 1939).

This provides the only substantial surviving visual and aural record of a performer who worked both under Gilbert's direction and alongside some of the originators of the Savoy roles.[34] How representative can a 1939 filmed performance be of Victorian stage practice? Conventional wisdom asserts that the performance methods of the D'Oyly Carte Company in the twentieth century reproduced the original productions exactly, but this is not an accurate assessment. Apart from regular updates and changes of style in setting and costume, certain operas, particularly *Ruddigore*, were edited and partially rescored in revival. Others remained nearer to the early staging, but, as will be discussed later, interpretations of individual characters could be radically altered by shifting cultural preferences. Intervening between Barrington and Granville in the role of Pooh-Bah were several other artists, notably Fred Billington and Leo Sheffield, who may have put their personal stamp on the role.[35] Granville did not assume this line of parts until 1928, having played the juvenile baritone roles until this point, so his connection as a performer in the role of Pooh-Bah did not follow directly from Barrington.

However, several factors suggest a high degree of fidelity to original practice in Granville's portrayal. Granville had joined the company as a chorister and small-part player in 1907, during Gilbert's revivals of the most popular operas. When playing the Bosun in *HMS Pinafore* in 1908, he shared the stage with Barrington and Temple, who were reprising their original roles of Captain Corcoran and Dick Deadeye. Granville would have been present as a chorister when Gilbert was directing Barrington as Pooh-Bah in 1909, and appeared on the Savoy stage with him in subsequent performances of *The Mikado* (Rollins & Witts 1962, pp. 21–2). In terms of Granville's continuing career in the company, production standards after Gilbert's death in 1911 until 1939 were maintained under the strict supervision of the stage director, J.M. Gordon. An ex-D'Oyly Carte performer who had worked as Gilbert's stage manager in 1907, Gordon was 'rigidly insistent that every line of dialogue should be delivered exactly as the librettist had prescribed' (Joseph 1994, pp. 206–8). This kind of conformity would probably have been supported by Granville, who was noted for his unbending fidelity to the minutiae of dialogue and stage business. Martyn Green, commenting on the work of his former colleague, noted that each of Granville's performances was 'identical. Each gesture and movement came on the same syllable or word' (Green 1962, p. 643).[36]

In assuming Barrington's line of parts, the need to emulate the work of his predecessors was in all probability expected. Gilbert and Sullivan scholar Ralph MacPhail, Jr comments on the D'Oyly Carte Company's handing on of company style in the early twentieth century: 'that certain way was the way your predecessor did it and also you were expected to do it the same, year in and year out' (MacPhail 2011). Marvin Carlson's theory of theatrical 'ghosting', in which reception of performance is invariably affected by a regular audience's familiarity with dramatic repertoire and actors playing habitually similar roles, was acutely realised in the case of the D'Oyly Carte Company. Here, a production remained in the repertoire for decades, rather than merely for an extended run. Discussing this phenomenon, Carlson comments on the fact that a new actor taking on a familiar role can be sure that 'critics and public alike will begin their reception and analysis of his [sic] interpretation by comparison with the actor he replaced'. He goes on to remark that the result is 'not exactly a new interpretation ... but not simply a repetition of an old interpretation either, since the figure will inevitably bring a somewhat different coloring [...] to the role' (Carlson 2003, p. 74).

While this provides a credible description of the transference of roles within the D'Oyly Carte Company, Carte quickly developed a commercial imperative for creating the notion of a 'tradition' to which a fan base could become attached. As well as attendance rituals, and the retrospective acknowledgement of past productions in programme design, adherence to a performance 'tradition' was expected of the company and its artists (Oost 2009, pp. 135–53). By the mid 1880s, loyal 'Savoyards' would have formed an essential audience sector.[37] It is likely that they required subsequent revisitings of a particular show, and especially revivals of previous operas, to provide them with a recognisably similar experience. Gilbert's acquiescence to perceived audience expectations could even contradict his own artistic instincts. When challenging a piece of business in a revival of *The Mikado*, Gilbert was informed by the stage manager that it derived from the original production. 'Oh, it's classic is it?' replied Gilbert. 'Well we must not interfere with the classics' (Barrington 1908, p. 223). As the D'Oyly Carte had sole performance rights to the presentation of the operas, there could have been minimal variation in the general tone of the individual portrayals, even in touring companies. To habitual 'G&S' devotees, a new performer of Pooh-Bah would automatically be compared with his predecessor. For some spectators, Granville's assumption of the role in 1928 could have provoked memories, not only of Sheffield and Billington, but also, quite possibly, of Rutland Barrington himself. Barrington had last played the role on the West End stage 20 years earlier—well within living memory. Thus, in many if not all cases, a distinct continuity of style can be proposed.[38]

This is attested by several features of Granville's performance in the 1939 film. For example, there is little suggestion of spontaneity in the delivery of lines. Indeed, the portrayal is almost self-consciously premeditated, offering a cosy familiarity which Granville's theatre audiences would have expected and welcomed.[39] Though more suited for stage presentation, and therefore quaintly out of context in a 1930s film musical, Granville's performance is generally unexaggerated. Although his face is mobile, facial expression is rarely overstated and seems to arise naturally from the realities of situation and response. Despite being encased in a heavily padded and built-up costume, he demonstrates an elegant and controlled physicality. Even Pooh-Bah's comically clumsy low obeisance to the Mikado is discreetly choreographed, so that it doesn't convey awkwardness on the part of the actor. Hand and arm movements are graceful and, as Green suggests in his memoirs, closely coordinated with points of dialogue. The controlled and unexaggerated quality of Granville's playing, and his generally premeditated and undemonstrative approach, is redolent of the positive critical comments made about his late-nineteenth-century forebears.

Given his predilection for exact replication of gesture and, one might surmise, vocal inflection (as attested by the studied sound of his dialogue in the film), the essence of Granville's current (1939) stage performance was probably representative of his approach to the characterisation since his assumption of the role in 1928. It is probable that Granville's Pooh-Bah, if inevitably not a replica of Barrington's performance, demonstrates the kind of approach and mode of presentation expected of a D'Oyly Carte principal artist, at least in the first decade of the twentieth century.[40] Several of the players in the 1906–1909 revivals (directed by Gilbert) were the original exponents of their roles, and were inevitably inculcated with the required style. Granville was necessarily influenced, through company policy, by his predecessor's manner of playing. He had absorbed Gilbert's rehearsal methods at first hand and his work thereafter was supervised by the watchful J.M. Gordon. These factors would strongly indicate that Granville's gentlemanly, 'restrained' style, as preserved in the 1939 *Mikado* film, provides a direct link to that found on the Savoy stage 50 years earlier.

COMIC AND VOCAL STYLES

It may therefore be possible, via film, sound recording and press commentary, to achieve a connection to the 'placid English style' remarked on by Carte in 1879 as being characteristic of his company. How and why did the use of the restrained style originate? And to what extent does it reflect a shift of cultural attitude towards comic performance on the nineteenth-century stage? To explore these issues we may turn first to attitudes towards casting in Carte's first Gilbert and Sullivan venture. According to François Cellier, the intended mode of performance of *The Sorcerer* 'would not precisely suit the existing school of actors and singers. There would be too much to unlearn [by] the proud and jealous supporters […] of ancient histrionic traditions' (Cellier and Bridgeman 1914, p. 34). In other words, Cellier is stating that many performers active on the musical stage at this time had the wrong performing credentials. Sullivan's scores were not suited to grand opera's singers, nor were Gilbert's intended methods matched to the majority of actors, who were 'too saturated with the obsolescent spirit of Victorian burlesque and extravaganza ever to become capable exponents of a Gilbert and Sullivan opera' (1914, pp. 35–6). Despite Cellier's retrospective condescension to late-Victorian West End musical theatre, three key factors may be discerned. First, that the requirements of the libretto and score of *The Sorcerer* would require a type of performer whose manner fell somewhere between grand opera and burlesque. Second, those performers would have to be prepared to accept instruction. This would imply that in certain cases the wrong kind of experience might result in intransigence, and relative inexperience could be an advantage. And third, that the perceived vulgarity and sexual provocation of the burlesque rendered its performers unsuitable for the refined tone of the new work.

The background and suitability of several members of the *Sorcerer* cast—Barrington, Grossmith, Temple and Mrs Howard Paul—has previously been considered in Chap. 3, as has the general recruitment of female principals and choristers in Chap. 6. George Power, who replaced the probably less than adequate George Bentham as tenor lead, was a university-educated, Italian-trained opera singer. He also happened to be a member of the British aristocracy. Of all the *Sorcerer* principals, only Harriet Everard, in the comic contralto role of Mrs Partlett, came directly from the world of pantomime and burlesque.[41] As discussed in the previous chapter, a 'respectable' demeanour both on and off the stage was required by the Triumvirate. The target middle-class audience was being catered for by a respectable entertainment brand, which in turn required performers who could convincingly convey the physical, vocal and behavioural signifiers of the respectable classes (Booth 1991, p. 131). This would have precluded the participation of performers who carried with them the style of the burlesque house.

Difficulties experienced as a director[42] when working with established actors and 'stars' had resulted in Gilbert's justifiable suspicion of their willingness and ability to conform to his envisaged performance style.[43] Thus, as well as rejecting performers from the existing 'low-art' musical stage, the D'Oyly Carte management almost always avoided the employment of celebrities.[44] The required combination of realism and restraint was achieved by training a team of relatively inexperienced players over a number of years.[45] It is likely that the development and persistence of the D'Oyly Carte performance style was partly a result of its having to be taught from scratch, or at least positively encouraged in performers to whom it came naturally. Jessie Bond, for example, had never spoken on stage before being entrusted with the small part of Cousin Hebe in *HMS Pinafore*. Over the next few years she developed into a comic performer of stature, being entrusted with more complex and dramatically significant roles as the series progressed.

Once inculcated, Gilbert's methods were protected by his disciples. In her memoirs, Jessie Bond complained about the decline in standards of certain D'Oyly Carte performers of the 1920s. Her inference is that, by this time, the appropriate sense of restraint had, in some instances, been abandoned for more immediate comic and dramatic effect. Among several examples, she cites comic business which had become endorsed during the song 'Were I thy bride' (*The Yeomen of the Guard*), in which Phoebe Merryl attempts to distract the attention of Shadbolt the jailer while she steals his keys. 'The scratching of the jailer's chin, the ruffling of his hair, the ogling of the eyes and all the other "comic" antics which, goodness knows why, are supposed to be funny' are rejected as vulgar and stylistically inappropriate. 'We knew well enough in those days that this so-called humour added nothing to a really beautiful song' (Bond 1930, p. 146). The avoidance of this kind of 'low' comedy is crucial to an understanding of the ethos of the company's early style. François Cellier explains the aversion to the typical comic performer in terms of their presumed inability to adapt:

> It is very easy to [...] pay a handsome salary to a comedian to paint his nose
> red in order to make people laugh [...] but to forbid the cleverest clown to
> decorate his nasal organ—that is where the fun goes and the poor clown
> finds his occupation gone [...] neither Gilbert, Sullivan nor D'Oyly Carte
> wanted their comedians to paint their noses red.
>
> (1914, p. 36)

The 'red-nosed' comedian referred to here is not just the circus or pantomime 'Joey'. He could also be the 'low comedian'—the farce actor who
specialised in the 'low-comic' line of parts in the stock companies of the
eighteenth and nineteenth centuries. Here, character stereotyping maintained 'traditions and customs of performance, as well as a standard set
of characters for dramatists to write for' (Booth 1991, p. 125). Victorian
audiences in London would have been familiar with the range of 'coun-
trymen, servants, street sellers, nouveau rich landowners and working
class eccentrics' (p. 125) portrayed by personality performers like John
Buckstone. He was well known to Gilbert, having mounted seven of
Gilbert's comedies and dramas, and he was celebrated as one of the foremost practitioners of low-comic roles. Buckstone's manner was colour-
fully summarised by a contemporary critic:

> Mr. Buckstone has no refinement. A double entendre lurks in each eye; his
> smirk is the hint of unclean presence [...] he has the true low comedy air in
> his walk and gesture; his face looks dry and red with long roasting before the
> footlights. He is the son of mirth and vulgarity.
>
> (Russell 1888, pp. 385–6)

Here was a presence to gratify the crowd and provoke the censoriousness of
the respectable. Projection of an individual personality through 'playing out'
to the audience, rather than subtlety of interpretation or lightness of manner, was the stock-in-trade of performers like Buckstone and J.L. Toole, who
staged *Ruddy George* in 1887 (Davis 2004, p. 285; Taylor 1989, pp. 65–7).
Toole had also played the lead in Gilbert and Sullivan's burlesque *Thespis* in
1871, and appeared in Gilbert's *La Vivandiere* in 1867. Although one of
the comic stars of the late-Victorian stage, critical appreciation of his work
could be as divided as that afforded to Buckstone. Joseph Knight, writing in
The Theatre (1880), noted that '[t]here is no gift of the low actor which Mr.
Toole does not possess in a high degree [But] the means he adopts to force
a laugh are not always artistic' (cited in Taylor 1989, p. 73).

The general consensus among modern commentators is that the eclipse of this style of playing was a result of the embourgeoisement of audiences, actors, writers and critics (Booth 1991, p. 131; Davis 2004, pp. 285–6; Bratton 2003, pp. 169–70). As theatre practitioners sought to assert their status as members of the respectable middle classes, they needed to distance themselves from indecorous or lower-class entertainment forms. Taylor asserts that Buckstone and his like 'always championed the gallery and pit against the boxes and the orchestra stalls' (Taylor 1989, p. 68). In West End theatres, which sought the revenues provided by the high-end trade and in doing so replicated middle-class behaviour and deportment on stage, the racy obtrusion of the low comedian was out of place. If, as Jim Davis remarks, 'the class conscious innovations of the Bancrofts and others led to the ousting of the low comedian' (Davis 2004, p. 285), the Savoy continued and exemplified this trend. Despite Gilbert's earlier association with the likes of Buckstone and Toole, both his comic aesthetic and the decorous ethos of the Savoy eschewed their forthright style. By personal inclination as members of the middle classes, the artistic decisions made by Gilbert, Sullivan and Carte were likely to have been informed by the desire to project respectability. If so, the same could be said of the approach of the middle-class artists they employed. Thus, D'Oyly Carte performance style can be directly linked to issues of class and social status. As low comedy came to be associated with an old-fashioned, less respectable form of entertainment, it had no part in the Savoy brand.

More appropriate to this change in comic taste was the work of 'light comedians' such as Charles Mathews Junior. While playing alongside the low comedian in the stock companies, the light-comic line of parts was more fitted both to the dramaturgy and taste of the last decades of the nineteenth century. Mathews seems to have typified gentlemanly restraint (Booth 1991, p. 125). His technique was 'quiet, easy, elegant'. He did not project a powerful persona, or eclipse the author, allowing the 'incongruity of the character and the language to work their own laughable way' (Lewes 1968, p. 69). Even when playing burlesque, Mathews did not emulate the conventional tendency to gag or

make grimaces [which] would have been enough to startle the public into laughter at broad incongruities [...] he allows the incongruity of the character and the language to work their own laughable way and presents them with the gravity of one who believed them.

(Lewes 1968, p. 69)

Mathews himself stated that he did not 'pretend to be a farce actor. My only claim is to be agreeable and natural' (cited in Booth 1980, p. 145). It is easy to see how the epithets applied to Mathews correspond to the critical response to the later performances of Grossmith and Barrington. Avoiding vulgarity in both manner and content, light comedy became the acceptable form of comic performance for a respectable middle-class audience towards the end of the century in the legitimate theatre, and Gilbert helped to move it onto the musical stage.

Writing nearly 40 years after his first D'Oyly Carte engagement, Henry Lytton unconsciously echoes Lewes's description of Mathews regarding the avoidance of the low-comic manner in performance. 'Forcing a point' was not encouraged. Lytton illustrates this with a moment from Act Two of *Iolanthe*. Here, Strephon, who is both Arcadian shepherd and hybrid fairy, argues grandiloquently that normal legal procedures do not apply to those like him, who are 'children of nature'. The Lord Chancellor counters by ridiculing his position. He points out the absurdity of 'an affidavit from a thunderstorm or a few words on oath from a heavy shower'. Lytton continues:

> Well you know how the comic man would say that, how he would whip up his coat collar and shiver at the suggestion of rain, and how he would do his poor best to make it look and sound 'funny.' And the result would be that he would kill the wittiness of the lines by 'burlesque.'
>
> (Lytton, p. 48)

Lytton, who first played the Lord Chancellor in 1891 (Rollins and Witts 1962, p. 78), characterises the appropriate style by emphasising the importance of 'deadly seriousness [...] as if the actor believes absolutely in the fanciful and extravagant things he is saying' (Lytton 1922, p. 48). The exaggeration of the 'comic man' is inappropriate and ineffective for the type of comedy Gilbert considered to be 'based upon a grave and quasi-respectful treatment of the ridiculous and absurd' (Crowther 2000, p. 91). An unaffected realism was required to highlight the absurdity of situation and dialogue. Significantly for Lytton, the term 'burlesque' has come to denote a performance style rather than a dramatic genre, and is denigrated as the antithesis of the restrained manner. For Lytton, the avoidance of 'refinement' would be 'foreign to the tranquil atmosphere of Gilbert and Sullivan' (Lytton 1922, p. 102). When the low-comic style intruded into his work, Gilbert was quick to correct the lapse. Witnessing a revival of *Trial by Jury* in 1898, he complained about the small-part player Strafford Moss,

> a 'funny' man who is the bane of true comic opera. He has overacted right through rehearsals &, although I told the 'jurymen' not to make up with wigs &c. he nevertheless took upon himself to appear last night in a grotesque flaxen wig [...]. I suggested that he be put in the back row at the end furthest from the stage—then his exaggerations will not be important.[46]

The deliberate rejection of comic hyperbole connects with the increased tendency towards physically and vocally restrained acting styles, used for serious as well as comic roles, which emerged in the West End in the second half of the nineteenth century (Schoch 2004, p. 334). This development is sometimes ascribed to the emulation of French actors such as Charles Fechter whose realistic restraint was seen as a novelty when it first appeared in London at the St James's Theatre in the middle years of the century. However, other noted exponents were Eton-educated Charles Kean and Alfred Wigan, an ex-schoolmaster with a classical education (Booth 1991, p. 132; Bratton 2011, pp. 161–2). They were self-consciously 'middle-class' practitioners, embodying on stage the physical and vocal traits which typified their social group.[47] Such behavioural signifiers were essential to the success of Tom Robertson's genteel Prince of Wales comedies of the 1860s, which promoted the embourgeoisement of both West End audiences and practitioners. They were, in turn, adopted by Robertson's friend and disciple W.S. Gilbert when he produced his own realistic comedies and dramas, and were maintained in his work for Carte.

If acting style was typified by moderation and control, the practice of singing also seems to have responded to, and reinforced, bourgeois expectations and cultural norms. John Potter traces the connections between the rise of an accepted 'classical' singing style and that of middle-class ideology in the early nineteenth century. He argues that a specific tonal quality was achieved by the adoption of the Italian lower-larynx position, or 'voix sombrée' (1998, p. 63–6). This manner was underpinned by typically Victorian, systematised teaching practice, and given a 'scientific' basis for its adoption and development. Its general acceptance for the performance of Western art music coincided with and, Potter argues, reinforced the need for an 'elite' vocal practice which served the exclusive requirements of the dominant classes.[48] This style contrasted markedly with the 'harsh, ugly, noisy' sounds produced by the uneducated. However, 'with the aid of an enculturing education [...] through the gift of middle-class culture' (Olwage 2004, p. 207), such noise could be refined to suit desired cultural standards. This transformation is reminiscent of the gallery singing at the Savoy mentioned in Chapter 6. The lower orders, after receiving the benefits of 'sol-fa' teaching, and having participated in choirs and music societies, could produce a sound which signified their upward mobility and 'middle-class' status.

In terms of professional D'Oyly Carte performance practice, the argument is not quite as clear-cut. I have noted that, apart from specifically 'comic' performers such as Barrington and Grossmith, Savoy artists were selected from the ranks of socially acceptable, formally trained operatic and concert singers. Musical director François Cellier nevertheless maintained that the vocal requirements of the Savoy oeuvre were 'not suited to the attributes of Grand Opera singers of [...] the intensely melodramatic class' (Cellier 1914, p. 35). Significantly, the development of the 'voix sombrée' also accompanied an increase in the emotional intensity of operatic composition, originating in the works of Donizetti, and brought to fruition by Verdi and Wagner. Previously, operatic or 'art' singing had been characterised by a lighter-toned, agile style which placed emphasis on tonal beauty and articulation of words (Potter 1998, pp. 51–6). Indeed, the 'bigger' style of the new breed of singers was criticised by some English detractors as emotionally exaggerated and technically forced (Potter 1998, pp. 60–1). It also may well have been the kind of 'emotional singing' referred to by Carte in the quotation given at the start of the chapter, preferred by American audiences but alien to the Savoy.

Contemporary journalistic censure of female D'Oyly Carte principals such as Alice May, Geraldine Ulmar and Florence Perry (mentioned above) focuses on moments when they tried to 'force' their tone. This suggests that the resultant timbre was inappropriate for the portrayal of the kind of demure, perhaps vivacious, but unthreatening younger female characters in the operas. Styles and mannerisms suitable for Donizetti's and Verdi's crazed, disturbed or vengeful female leads were ripe for Sullivan's musical parody in *Pinafore*, *Pirates* and *Ruddigore*. However, emulation of the vocal style necessary to perform these operatic roles adequately seems not to have been congruent with what critics or the Triumvirate saw as appropriate for Gilbert and Sullivan's girls. It is instructive to note that the vocally demanding and dramatically 'heavier' eponymous soprano lead in *Princess Ida* was originally intended for an imported star, Lillian Russell. Her dismissal resulted in the promotion of the resident soprano, Leonora

Braham, to the main role. The fact that Braham was not originally selected indicates that her voice was initially considered insufficiently powerful for a female character who embodied authority.

Olwage (2004, pp. 211–12) makes the point that 'soft singing' was encouraged by Victorian vocal instructors, at least when practising or rehearsing. Certainly for choral singers, this kind of vocal restraint 'was claimed to be productive of good tone, and so became an end in itself' (Olwage 2004, p. 212). This once again indicates a culturally dominant consensus about what constituted a refined and artistic manner of delivery, even if levels of volume and tonal fullness might alter with differing musical styles or the type of operatic role essayed. A clear, agile voice which prioritised articulation of texts over emotional and tonal 'weight' seems to have been encouraged at the Savoy for female roles other than the contralto 'older' woman line of parts. Few recordings exist of singers engaged by Sullivan, and none (save Richard Temple) was an originator of their recorded roles. However, one aspect of consistency in subsequent D'Oyly Carte recordings for singers of either gender, until at least the 1960s, is a more or less 'classically' produced vocal style which nevertheless favoured clear enunciation over volume and depth of tone. It is possible that the style used for Savoy opera at the time of its inception had more in common with that used by contemporaries of Mozart and Rossini than with the development of 'emotional' grand opera in the mid nineteenth century.

However, this is by no means certain or indeed probable as a universal description of Savoy singing. Some singers trained in Britain may have been schooled in the earlier manner. Others may have been adept at reducing tonal 'weight' in favour of articulation, while maintaining a quality concomitant with accepted standards of elite vocal practice, irrespective of training methods. For example, Durward Lely, lead tenor between 1880 and 1887, negotiated the vocal requirements of both Savoy and mainstream opera. Lely was Milan-trained, and was presumably an exponent of the heavier 'voix sombrée'.[49] After an early career which included the first performance in Britain of Don José in Bizet's *Carmen* (1879), he went on to play a series of *comic*, although largely gentlemanly, tenor roles, written specifically for him by Gilbert and Sullivan, before returning to a prominent operatic career. His acting and vocal style enabled him to deal with dim aristocrats (the Duke of Dunstable in *Patience* and Earl Tolloller in *Iolanthe*) as well as the bumptious Cyril in *Princess Ida*, romantic lead Nanki-Pooh in *The Mikado*, and Alexis in revivals of *The Sorcerer*. From a contemporaneous perspective, Percy Fitzgerald remarks on Lely's ability to adjust his vocal style to the requirements of the Savoy. 'He sang [...] with a pleasing and melodious voice yet without any of the effusiveness of the operatic tenor. He was the character first' (Fitzgerald 1894, p. 140). Emotional 'restraint' and a foregrounding of character in sung as well as spoken performance are clearly indicated here.

At the other end of the scale of social acceptability in terms of vocal quality were the comic singers of the London music halls. Middle-class probity might vilify the 'glorification of sex and drink' (Bailey 1998, p. 125) offered by male star performers ('Lions Comique') such as George Leybourne or The Great Vance. However, their perceived vocal short-comings could be similarly disparaged as foreign to bourgeois values. The Victorian pedagogue T. Maskell Hardy declared the antithesis of culti-vated singing style to be the 'coarse, harsh and shouting production of voice [...] generally favoured by the "Lion Comique"' (Hardy 1910, p. 4). Apparent moral coarseness had its auditory equivalent in roughness of tone. Conversely, a smoothness, refinement and restraint, typified by both the vocal and physical performance style of Savoy artists, immediately proclaimed their affinity with the cultural values of the dominant classes. As Richard W. Schoch succinctly remarks—and his conclusions are as true of sung performance as of spoken—'acting styles, when viewed as cultural practices ... were part of the mid-Victorian theatre's self-conscious emula-tion of the cult of the gentleman' (Schoch 2004, p. 334).

GENTLEMEN AND LADIES

The 'placid English style' of stage performance can be shown to derive from idealised notions of correct behaviour propounded by Victorian etiquette literature. The notion of embodied 'restraint' was an integral component of 'gentlemanly behaviour' in the cultural ideology of the 'middle classes'. The Victorian gentleman was the product of a rising and status-conscious bourgeoisie who sought to emulate aristocratic models of behaviour in order to enhance their social credentials and differentiate themselves from the lower orders. Michael Curtin, in his study of nineteenth-century man-ners, *Propriety and Position* (1994), describes how the ease of manner and lack of pomposity which characterised upper-class behaviour in the late eighteenth and early nineteenth centuries contrasted with the asser-tive forthrightness of the emerging middle classes. The tendency of the arrivistes to declare their status through 'harshness to inferiors, toady-ing to superiors and keeping up with the Joneses' (Curtin 1994, p. 286) compared unfavourably with the easy aristocratic style with which their increasing wealth and prestige brought them into contact.

Similarly, in an increasingly democratic age, the bourgeois virtues of seriousness, economy and applied knowledge challenged some of the perceived failings of the privileged aristocracy. Curtin describes how a workable compromise emerged between these extremes. While '[t]he easy style [...] was the recognised style of high status, it also appealed to a democratic sentiment because it eschewed some of the formal and explicit advantages of social superiority, and because it could in theory, be emulated by all' (1994, p. 109).

The pervasiveness of idealised behaviour should not be exaggerated. Not everyone was aware of the 'rules' of etiquette, or if they did know them, they could choose to ignore them or reject their discipline (Curtin 1994, p. 5). However, the ubiquity of etiquette books presents evidence of a definite cultural preoccupation in a society in which manners were the means whereby class and social prestige were most obviously exhibited. A restrained mode of social conduct in terms of manners, demeanour, voice and physicality denoted gentlemanly status: 'Nothing marks the gentleman so soon and so decidedly as quiet and refined ease of manner' (Hartley 1860, p. 186). Curtin refers to the instructions of Lord Chesterfield to his son, published in the late eighteenth century but influential throughout the nineteenth. In terms of posture and bearing, 'the man of fashion is easy in every position: instead of lolling or lounging as he sits, he leans with elegance' (cited in Curtin 1994, p. 114). Curtin notes how 'when he walked in the street, the gentleman neither slouched nor swaggered. He was alert, with head erect, shoulders back, hands out of his pockets' (p. 114).

Graceful physicality needed to be matched with appropriate manners. C.B. Hartley, in *The Gentleman's Book of Etiquette* (1860), enjoins his male readers to 'always avoid any rude or boisterous action [...] if you jest let it be with a quiet and gentlemanly wit, never depending upon clownish gestures'. Overt buffoonery was rejected. Gentlemen 'always avoid any rude or boisterous action' (p.186) and 'avoid eccentric conduct'. 'All turbulence, over eagerness, and egotism are to be condemned. A very soft and quiet manner has, at last, been settled upon in the most elevated circles as the best' (pp. 186, 204, 220) (Fig. 7.2).

The consequences of these injunctions on performers and performance style are not hard to deduce. The virtues the light comedian Charles Mathews Junior displayed to his contemporaries—his ability to be 'quiet

Fig. 7.2 The middle-class 'gentleman' actor relaxes among the comforts of home. A portrait of George Grossmith by George Hutchinson (*The Idler*, 1893). Public domain

without being absurdly insignificant, to be lively without being vulgar, to look like a gentleman, to speak and move as a gentleman' (Lewes 1875, p. 62)—would appear to exemplify the connection between performance style and social acceptability. If authors, managers, artists and audiences shared similar cultural and social values, the overt manifestation of such standards in terms of behaviour would end up being emulated on stage. Conduct which was rude, boisterous, eccentric, clownish, egotistical, turbulent, loud, and which emphasised an unrestrained physicality—in other words, features which typified the successful low comedian—would have seemed inappropriate in the Gallery of Illustration, the Prince of

Wales and the Savoy. It is likely that press reviews of the early Gilbert and Sullivan operas welcomed the 'restraint' of performers such as Grossmith and Barrington because it matched the changing tastes of a sector of the West End audience keen to gain some of the 'cultural capital' attached to the Savoy operas.

If gentlemanly restraint on stage reflected and reinforced the social role of the 'middle-class' male, female performers could be regarded as more important personifications of cultural ideology in practice. Modern commentators (Curtin 1994; Langland 1995) have seen the behavioural traits of 'middle-class' Victorian women, like their male counterparts, as a series of necessary 'signifying practices' which delineated the status of a class increased and transformed by the acquisition of wealth. As noted in the previous chapter, women were seen as responsible for the domestic, religious and social manifestations of 'middle-class' identity. Etiquette was 'a protection against the intrusion of those whose abrupt manners and vulgar habits would rend them disagreeable and obnoxious' (*Etiquette for Ladies and Gentleman*, 1862, cited in Langland 1995, p. 27). It enabled women, as the arbiters of social desirability, to distinguish those members of society with whom one should associate in order to assert and maintain rank and social standing.

In explaining the manner in which correct behaviour was absorbed and inculcated, G.A. Foster observes that etiquette guides often exhorted their young readers to 'master the gestures of a controlled actress'. She goes on to point out the paradoxical virtues of 'seeming natural in society, lacking obvious performative gestures' while being 'simultaneously conscious of rules and standards' (Foster 2000, p. 80). This real-life anomaly seems to be exemplified in the type of performative behaviour encouraged on the Savoy stage. Savoy actresses were praised both for their naturalness *and* their control, qualities which might seem antithetical. In doing so they embodied a Victorian middle-class female archetype. If the readers of etiquette manuals followed their injunction to observe actresses in order to learn the tricks of effective presentation, then what better example could they follow than the ladies of the Savoy, whose onstage manner reproduced the accepted and expected modes of respectable social behaviour for women?

In common with the representation of women at the Prince of Wales or St James's theatres, the portrayal of the younger female characters at the Savoy did not arouse 'the anxiety and dread' of male critics towards the potentially powerful figure of the actress. Avoidance of the vocal histrionics of the operatic prima donna has been mentioned earlier, but a similar emotional control also characterised spoken performance. The stage persona of the actress could be unsettling for male spectators. According to Kerry Powell, the dominating impact of performers such as Ristori, Duse and Bernhardt was difficult to reconcile with the domesticated femininity required of the middle-class woman 'who had to be restrained in the interest of relieving male anxiety and preserving the status quo' (2007, p. 63). As well as avoiding the prospect of sexual provocation, the absence of cross-dressing at the Savoy allowed the actress to project 'real' femininity. 'Unhealthy' masculine attributes—the desire for control, a predatory interest in (often younger) members of the opposite sex, and an awareness of violence or punishment appear in the 'older woman' line of parts.[50] Here, the contralto vocal tessitura contributes to their masculinised distance from the higher-voiced girlishness of the soprano lead and soubrette.

There is also an inbuilt camaraderie or 'sisterhood' in many of the younger female roles—'Three Little Maids from School' in *The Mikado*, the Major General's daughters in *The Pirates of Penzance*, the self-created sisterhoods of *Patience* and *Princess Ida*, etc.—which allow the performer to adopt and project a kind of 'sisterly' or non-sexual and non-threatening manner. Powell comments on this aspect of female performance:

> Being a 'girl', a sister—embracing rather than overpowering the audience—was one of the ways in which the actress could demonstrate her solidarity with it. She could enact flattering representations of the public, charming into laughter or tears by dramatizing its most cherished ideals.
>
> (2007, p. 50)

Thus, in the 1870s and 1880s, the women and chaperoned girls in the Savoy audience could observe an idealised version of themselves. Men could rest assured that the incipient rumblings of female emancipation and enfranchisement, and the forthright demeanour which went with them, would, for the most part, be either absent or satirised.[51] Indeed, the possibility arises here of observing the duality between culture and cultural product in action. The Gilbert and Sullivan operas provided theatrical representations which both reflected and embodied contemporary cultural attitudes towards young womanhood. A specific performance style was encouraged by authors, managers and critics. At the same time, the stage presented those values for conscious or subliminal emulation by the audience. This circular process of cultural affirmation would have occurred on other Victorian stages, in the West End and elsewhere. It was also no doubt part of a wider process in which cultural products of all kinds, including artworks, printed images, etiquette books, novels and periodicals played their part. But the particular performance culture of apparent naturalness exercised through self-control noted by critics as occurring at the Savoy seems to serve as an exemplification of this phenomenon. Its popular dissemination could be attested by the success of the 'restrained' style on the West End musical stage as exemplified by the D'Oyly Carte Company, and its replication on a national scale via 25 years of provincial touring.

PERFORMING RESPECTABILITY

In terms of female participation (and much else) the 'meretricious allurements of the *opera bouffe* and the modern or degraded burlesque' signified everything that Gilbert was trying to avoid.[52] Critics were quick to comment on the differences in matters of decorum. A first night review of *Iolanthe* commented that '[t]heir operas have nothing in common with the inanities of modern burlesque. Burlesques they certainly are in a way, but free from vulgarity, commonplace, or coarseness.'[53] Comparison with the mid-to-late-Victorian burlesque can provide an insight into the very different manner of performance employed by Carte's artists. Though requiring an educated clientele who would appreciate the comic inversion of its literary or theatrical targets, the burlesque had often been condemned as 'low art' (Schoch 2003, p. xix). In 1885, its increased focus on the allure of the female body (which, for example, engendered the popular nickname 'Nudity Theatre' for the Gaiety Theatre)[54] drew negative press comment from respectable authors such as Burnand and Gilbert and, unsurprisingly, a defensive counter-blast from the Gaiety's John Hollingshead (Stedman 1996, p. 222). In the midst of this argument, Gilbert declared that 'the meretricious burlesque seems to be, so to speak, on its last legs'. 'Sprawling females in indecent costumes' meant that a once 'charming class of entertainment' had lost its attraction. 'No genuine comedy actress will appear in it [...] now a comedy actress bars burlesque by the terms of her engagement.'[55] Here may be seen a natural bias towards the success of his recent works, at the expense of the competition. But as a perceptive former drama critic, Gilbert must have been aware that the West End burlesque had to alter its style in order to compete. In the following year, William Archer noted approvingly that Savoy operas had caused a fall in demand for 'leg-pieces'. This 'matter for unmixed rejoicing' marked the 'victory of literary and musical grace and humour over rampant vulgarity and meretricious jingle' (Archer 1886, pp. 20–1). As an exponent of progressive writers' theatre, it is no surprise that Archer favoured a type of musical comedy which relied on the perfected style of the established playwright and 'serious' composer, together with a well-rehearsed and carefully styled production.

In contrast, an air of improvisation and ephemerality was intrinsic to the burlesque. It could be, according to Schoch, 'written practically over-night, rehearsed in a week and performed for a month or two' (2003, p. xxii). Updating of topical references and the inclusion of improvised comedy resulted in scripts which, on the page, cannot fully convey the intended theatrical effect. Augustin Filon, reading the text of Burnand's celebrated burlesque *Ixion* (1863) 35 years after its first performance, considers it 'dismal'. However, he reflects that the impact of the genre was reliant on the sensory pleasures of the entire theatre 'event' rather than the surviving scripted 'blueprint'.

> To form any impression of the piece, you must try to picture yourself in the little theatre [...] the *flon flons* of the orchestra, the quivering of gasaliers [...] the diamonds, the gleaming white shoulders and the soft silk tights, the superabundance of animal life and high spirits.
>
> (Filon 1897, p. 95)

'White shoulders', 'soft silk tights' and the 'animal life and high spirits' of the actresses were clearly as important to the reception of the burlesque as the more decorative features of the auditorium.

In providing the direct opposite of this manner of writing and production, the Savoy operas were succeeding financially as well as artistically. Time and money were better invested in producing a long-running product than something which, due to its novelty value, would only play for a few weeks. But such longevity required sophisticated production standards, including better sets and costumes. It also necessitated a durable libretto and memorable music. The former could, on its own merits, withstand subsequent production on tour, and be amusing enough to purchase in printed form. The latter was sufficiently beautiful and well-crafted to invite repeated theatrical and domestic hearing. Most important, when considering embodied performance, is the fact that the kind of comic creativity and invention required by burlesque was antithetical to both the artistic and commercial aims of the Savoy Triumvirate.

Placidity and restraint would have been in short supply in the burlesque house. Henry Barton Baker's description of the typical 'break down' dance, a 'frantic outburst of animal high spirits' in which performers had 'no more control of their legs than the audience had over their applause' (Barton Baker 1904, p. 448), indicates a vigour which at least gave the impression of being exciting and spontaneous. The kind of burlesque familiar to the Triumvirate in the 1870s, and to which Gilbert had contributed from 1866 to 1869, had absorbed 'low art' influences from popular forms. The grotesque 'break down' was an import from black-face minstrel shows, as were hit minstrel songs, which were rewritten to suit their new settings. By the 1860s, music hall numbers were added to a melange of musical styles which also included popular ballads and 'high art' opera choruses and arias (Booth 1991, p. 187). Even when engaged in its production, Gilbert seems to have been keen to distance himself from the genre. In his epilogue to *The Pretty Druidess* (1869), a burlesque on Bellini's opera *Norma*, a sardonic Gilbert has the protagonist entreating the audience to:

[...] forgive our rhymes.

Forgive the jokes you've heard five thousand times:

Forgive each break-down, cellar flap and clog,

Our low-bred songs—our slangy dialogue:

And above all—oh ye with double barrel—

Forgive the scantiness of our apparel.

(Gilbert 1931, p. 180)

While Gilbert is ironically drawing attention to elements of burlesque's appeal, he seems to be putting himself in the position of the respectable 'middle-class' author and spectator who easily recognises (and for the moment tolerates) its obvious shortcomings.

The burlesque may have projected informality. But a description by the Gaiety star Nellie Farren of her preparation for a new role demonstrates the application and skill required of the burlesque lead. According to Schoch, 'While a good measure of a burlesque's humour was written into the script, the success of any production rested primarily with actors who were called upon to execute an impressive range of histrionic skills in a comparatively brief performance' (2003, p. xxix). In an interview, Farren described burlesque as:

> much more difficult and exacting than the drama. In the latter an actress is given a part, and there are stage instructions and business ready for her at hand, which after she has studied, are all plain sailing. In burlesque the actress gets a part. First there is the music, then the words of the song to sing, and next she must make up her mind what to do with the words of the song. Then there will be two or three dances to invent and learn different to anything she has done before. Then comes the part which is frequently very sketchy, and has to be written up as you call it—'gagged' as we say. I think we deserve more credit for our work in burlesque than we get from those who know nothing of how hard we work to make a success.[56]

Essentially, Farren is describing a process in which the principal 'directs' herself. Her achievement is not arbitrated. Interpretive creativity in the preparation of material, and the talent to project it to an audience, are the requirements for success. This process is clearly explained by Farren. After memorising the material, she needs to interpret the song lyric in order to decide how best to convey its meaning and exploit its comic potential. She is also personally responsible for inventing the choreography of each new number, ensuring that material already familiar to her regular audience is not repeated. Finally, she addresses the spoken text—'the part'—where much inventiveness is required. The written material has to be enlarged and elaborated through her individual comic skill. Crucially, Farren uses the term 'gagged' to describe this aspect of her creative practice. 'Gagging' is not merely a method by which a performer increases their prominence and 'pulls focus' by adding extra physical and verbal comedy. It is important to bear in mind that gagging was seen as an accepted and necessary element in the process of creating a comic role. Indeed, attempts to override the instincts of experience through directorial intervention could be regarded with suspicion by artists who were accustomed to working things out for themselves. Having come from the Savoy to Daly's theatre in the 1890s, Barrington noted with surprise that the actors there had 'an inclination to look upon suggestions which concern themselves as almost puerile and certainly ineffective' (Barrington 1908, p. 105).

Carte's company employed an almost diametrically opposed approach. Texts could not be changed, moves were strictly notated and business was vetted and vetoed by Gilbert prior to opening, and subsequently by the management. Although similarly replete with topical allusions, the Savoy operas were the antithesis of the stylistic familiarity or dynamism of the burlesque.

The lengthy and meticulous rehearsal process at the Savoy provides an insight into the emergence of the writer/director in late-nineteenth-century West End theatre as the arbiter of shared cultural tastes.[57] If theatre, and particularly the musical stage, was to be presented as an artistically unified product which reflected and reaffirmed the preferences of its audience, it required a controlling hand. It also needed an environment in which performers followed clearly planned direction and did not stray from its dictates, particularly in the playing of comedy. Clause 16 of Carte's standard artist's contract stipulated that 'No artist shall alter the words or business of his or her part without express permission of the manager or shall forfeit half a week's pay for each and every infringement of this rule'.[58] This meant, according to Cellier, that '[t]he slightest sign of clowning was promptly nipped in the bud'. While Gilbert rarely attended performances of his own work (Barrington 1908, p. 69), in his absence the Savoy stage manager, Richard Barker, 'was always held responsible, and was required to report to headquarters any member of the company violating the Gilbertian 'articles of war' (Cellier and Bridgeman 1914, p. 51).[59]

Discipline extended to the process of rehearsal. If the success of burlesque depended largely on the individual creative contributions of Farren and her colleagues, that of the Savoy operas relied on a well-crafted book and lyrics, a carefully prepared production plan, and talented but respectful artists who would accept the stringent dictates of the author/director or his representative. Rutland Barrington, whose career encompassed various West End managements, regarded Gilbert as the originator and only successful practitioner of detailed and comprehensive direction on the late-nineteenth-century musical (rather than legitimate) stage (Barrington 1908, p. 105). Gilbert's painstaking and doctrinaire rehearsal methods rapidly became enshrined in anecdote and theatrical lore. His practice was partly based on the techniques of the author/director Tom Robertson, whose work at the Prince of Wales he had observed at first hand. According to Gilbert, Robertson 'showed how to give life and variety [...] to a scene by breaking it up with all sorts of little incidents and delicate by-play' (Archer 1904, p. 114). The invention of comic business and variety of characterisation became the responsibility of the author/director rather than the comic actor. 'Most remarkable was Gilbert's facility for inventing comic business. He would leave nothing to the initiative of the comedians,' reports Cellier (1914, p. 51). Grossmith's introduction of a piece of slapstick into *The Mikado* because he 'would get an enormous laugh by it' drew the disapproving retort, 'So you would if you sat on a pork pie.' Low comedy which would impede or which had no relation to the stage action was rejected (Grossmith 1888, p. 107).

Under Gilbert's supervision, *some* unscripted verbal comedy, which emerged during rehearsals or early performances, was endorsed. As a result, several of the funniest lines in *The Mikado* are by Rutland Barrington. Bradley records 29 additions to the original text of *The Mikado*, either performed at various times by Barrington or included at Barrington's instigation (Bradley 1996, pp. 566–8, 574, 578, 580, 596, etc.). Some may have crept in during the original run, but most probably date to the revivals of 1888, 1895 and 1896. The majority of these are spoken, rather than physical gags. An example of the kind of thing Gilbert *rejected*, presumably because it contributes to neither characterisation nor plot is recounted by Bradley. In the Act Two trio, '[t]he criminal cried as he dropped him down',

> Pooh-Bah is interrupted by Pitti-Sing while in the middle of singing the word 'pedigree' and says to her 'I'll give you such a Japanese smack in a minute.' In her notes Helen D'Oyly Carte wrote: 'This was never authorised. It seems to have sprung out of some "business" between Miss Bond and Mr. Barrington' Gilbert's verdict was 'utterly stupid—please omit.'
>
> (Bradley 1996, p. 628)

A similar level of command extended to Gilbert's control of the stage picture. Interviews and recollections reiterate Gilbert's use of a model stage and differently sized and coloured wooden blocks representing male and female performers to pre-plan the stage action and groupings (Archer 1904, p. 129; Grossmith 1888, p. 92). This level of preparation received enough comment in articles and memoirs to suggest that it was remarkable for the time. Similarly remarkable was his insistence that actors conform exactly to his preconceived intentions. An illustrative example of Gilbert's detailed rehearsal practice is recounted by Grossmith:

> Mr Gilbert is a perfect autocrat, insisting that his words should be delivered, even to the inflection of the voice, as he dictates. He will stand on stage beside the actor or actress and repeat the words with appropriate action over and over as he desires them to be. In some instances of course, he allows a little licence, but very little.
>
> (Grossmith 1888, p. 94)

This is graphically conveyed by Decima Moore, the original Casilda in *The Gondoliers*:

He would read a line out clapping his hands between words to emphasise their rhythm thus: 'I've no patience (clap) with the presumption (clap) of persons (clap) in his plebeian (clap) position (clap)!'

(cited in Cox-Ife 1977, p. 47)

As a student singer plucked from the Blackheath Conservatoire at the age of 18, Moore may have required some careful coaching in the delivery of spoken dialogue (Baker, A., 2005). However, as mentioned earlier, many principals were deliberately untried artists, and such treatment may have been commonplace. Contemporary 'common knowledge' seems to have enjoyed characterising Gilbert as a dominant (as well as a domineering) presence at the

The Ironmaster at the Savoy.

Fig. 7.3 'The Ironmaster at the Savoy'. Caricature by Alfred Bryan (*Entr'acte*, 1885)

Savoy irrespective of his actual treatment of personnel. An *Entr'acte* cartoon from 1885, 'The Ironmaster at the Savoy', depicts a gigantic, literally ironclad Gilbert, wielding a riveting hammer, presumably intended to knock everything and everyone into place. A diminutive, anxious Carte hovers around his ankles, perhaps reflecting a perception that Gilbert was the driving force behind the enterprise rather than the entrepreneur and producer (Fig. 7.3).

Less frequently anecdotalised is Sullivan's stringency regarding musical precision. Grossmith comments on the composer stopping full chorus rehearsals to insist that individual choristers observe exact note values (1888, p. 93). Sullivan might select 'some nervous chorister, whose ear was not sensitive and whose reading ability was limited' to 'repeat again and again, as a solo, the note or two on which he had broken down' (Cellier 1914, p. 53). Given some predisposition to exaggerate for effect, Jessie Bond nevertheless conveys the effect of the partners working in combination. Rehearsing *Iolanthe* into the small hours, 'They made me sing my song "He loves", standing up and sitting down and kneeling and with every possible variety of emphasis and shade of meaning, until I was perfectly exhausted' (Bond 1930, p. 121).

For William Archer 'the result was an absolute smoothness and finish of representation which people came to demand in other theatres as well' (Archer 1904, p. 130). Providing a contrast to the relative informality of West End burlesque, the disciplined D'Oyly Carte style seems to have influenced the Gaiety under George Edwardes's management. His first major production after leaving the Savoy was the long-running *Dorothy* (1885), a historical comic opera in the Gilbert and Sullivan mould. Subsequent Gaiety burlesques were refined into a two- or three-act model containing original music, replacing what were often single-act afterpieces, using existing tunes (Booth 1991, p. 198). By the 1890s, the genre had declined as 'increased refinement of middle-class taste had finally driven burlesque into the arms of musical comedy' (Booth 1980, p. 190).

To reiterate the central premise of this chapter, the culture of refinement shared by the 'middle-class' creators, performers and audiences of the Savoy operas was most obviously manifested in embodied performance. Preparation and rehearsal were geared towards the manufacture of a style which, unlike the burlesque, foregrounded genteel restraint, limited individual creativity and removed (or attempted to remove) the possibility of deviation from authorial and directorial intention. 'Gagging' and low comedy represented 'inferior' forms of entertainment. Patronage of the Savoy, and the enjoyment of its offerings, was indicative of 'superior' taste and cultural aspiration.

The cultural significance of the 'restrained' style in the late nineteenth century can be inferred from a series of complaints voiced by Jessie Bond 40 years after her retirement. As mentioned earlier, Bond was entirely a product of Gilbert's stylistic values, at least in terms of her acting. Lamenting the company's decline in standards in the 1920s, she condemns the 'mannerisms, tricks and antics' which would 'never, never have been tolerated for a moment' during her tenure as principal (Bond 1930, p. 143). As well as the comic interpolations in *The Yeomen of the Guard* mentioned earlier in the chapter, she criticises the current Duke of Plaza Toro in *The Gondoliers*. Imitating a 'jumping jack-in-the-box' and pulling faces behind the Duchess, he is contrasted with 'Frank Wyatt, who created the role [and] would have been the last man to be guilty of such a liberty' (Bond 1930, p. 148). Richard Temple's original Mikado was 'every inch a gentleman' who, 'in his quiet refined way' sang in a 'smooth, unforced voice in which every syllable told' (p. 147). She denounces the current incumbent for prancing about 'like a madman, hissing out his lines like a serpent' (p. 147). The 'refinement and polish' expected by London audiences in the 1880s had, in certain cases, been replaced by 'over-acting and low comedy' (p. 148). She blames the influence of touring artists who had become principal players in the single touring company which remained after the disbandment of the majority of the organisation in 1903. For Bond, 'the subtleties of Gilbert's humour may not have been so easily grasped' (p. 148) by provincial audiences, resulting in a broader style than would have been permitted in London. There is an element of metropolitan condescension here from the successful West End star. But it is clear from letters and contemporary writings that the touring circuit, distanced from West End scrutiny, was a breeding ground for the kind of 'gagging' so essential to the low comedian and the burlesque artist, and so discouraged by Gilbert and the London management.

Gagging 'Gagging'

The continuing popularity of the D'Oyly Carte's repertoire ensured its unprecedented success as a large touring concern (Davis 2000, pp. 221–8). The financial incentive of long tours was abetted by a product which was replicable in terms of its artistic content, its production standards and its musical and dramatic text. It did not demand particularly imaginative or inspired 'leads' who could embellish material with their skills and experience. Savoy opera, both in London and the provinces, required a solidly talented group of chorus and principals who could learn to adopt the required discipline efficiently, and who could replicate a product to a high standard for around a year in the West End, or on tour. A team of regular provincial 'stage managers' supervised these productions, using annotated prompt books as a reference source for blocking, chorus grouping and choreography (Joseph 1994, pp. 90–1). While uniform gestures, vocalisations and general acting notes were provided for the chorus, there were few indications in the prompt books, apart from blocking and occasional set gestures, of how the principals should perform. We might conjecture that principal touring artists witnessed the performances of their London counterparts, or that the stage managers were sufficiently familiar with the style to convey what was needed to recruits who were hired for their apparent ability to conform to the requisite manner.

This policy was sometimes ineffective. Continual replication of a limited repertoire, some lack of sophistication among provincial audiences, and the absence of the autocratic author/director may well have encouraged 'gagging' in the touring companies. A series of letters regarding the touring comedian Cairns James reveals the attitudes of both author and management to unsolicited departure from both the text and the required style. For Gilbert, James was 'a confirmed gagger and a very quarrelsome man'.[60] Responding to a request from James, then playing Jack Point and Ko-Ko in the 'B' touring company (Rollins and Witts 1962, p. 69), for promotion to West End roles, Gilbert replied that he had been informed by Carte that James had:

> contracted a habit of 'gagging'—that your attention has been frequently called to the matter, and that you had frequently promised to decline the practice, but that the habit appeared to be inveterate. (Original emphasis) [61]

James seems to have been unable to prevent himself from adding comic material. It was, presumably, as is the case with many natural comedians, integral to his performing personality. The following day, having seen a communication from the 'B' company stage manager to Carte, Gilbert wrote again to James concerning his defiance of the stage manager's admonitions: '... on his remonstrating with you as to your performance of Ko-Ko, you defied his authority. I assure you, in your own interest that such a course of action is most prejudicial to your advancement' (Original emphasis).[62]

Flouting the authority of Gilbert's deputy is evidently synonymous with crossing swords with the highest in the organisation. Gilbert then presents a short manifesto regarding the importance of hierarchical obedience:

> The principle of subordination must be maintained in the theatre as in a regiment. If an unreasonable order is given it must be acted upon ... This is the rule of the Savoy Theatre and no one would be retained on the staff who hesitated to recognise it [...] no actor will ever find his way into our London Company who defies any authority in this respect.[63]

The need for absolute subjugation of individual creativity, particularly in the field of comic acting, was doubtless unusual in the theatre, but Gilbert indicates that D'Oyly Carte performers were no less exempt from the need to obey than any other member of the theatre 'staff'. Presumably, for the Triumvirate, the smooth running of a late-Victorian theatre company was as dependent on authority as any other commercial, civil or military enterprise. Houghton, in his exploration of the Victorian *mentalité*, ascribes the deferential 'habit of mind, partly inherited, and partly acquired which made reliance on authority a natural tendency' to the hierarchical Victorian class system in which the aristocrat retained the real power. He maintains that 'the concept of equality never won any general acceptance—least of all from a middle class eager to preserve the social distinctions it was struggling to attain' (Houghton 1957, p. 103). If awareness of status and hierarchical structures on the individual level became part of the ideology of the dominant classes, then it was eventually bound to manifest itself within the field of theatre production and performance. The comic *dramatist* may choose to satirise social institutions, but his social inferior, the comic actor, cannot presume to distort the intentions of the author by adding subversive material of his own invention. Gilbert and James (and no doubt Barrington and Grossmith) would have regarded themselves as middle-class gentlemen, displaying the 'dichotomous' or 'us and them' attitude to class described in Chapter 2. But in 1889, as part of the creative and managerial Triumvirate, it was Gilbert who held the power over the errant touring principal.

Gilbert's letters to James make clear that his authority is paramount in artistic matters. But there is also the implication that this authority is invested in Gilbert's position as the author, rather than as the director. Gilbert discovers that James has not in fact added to the dialogue, but has instead introduced physical 'business'. While this is no less an infringement of authority, it is less offensive to Gilbert. In another letter Gilbert admits to being 'misled in saying you had gagged'.[64] Gilbert takes 'gagging' to refer to *textual* addition, and to a literary author this was the greater of the two crimes. I would suggest that the critical issue here is that Gilbert saw himself and wanted to be regarded as a member of the circle of elite professionals in the creative and artistic fields. Reflecting on his knighthood the previous day, Gilbert wrote on 16 July 1907:

> I found myself politely described in the official list as Mr. William Gilbert, *playwright*, suggesting that my work was analogical to that of a wheelwright, or a millwright, or a wainwright, as regards the mechanical character of the process by which our respective results are achieved. There is an excellent word 'dramatist' which seems to fit the situation [...] you never hear of a novel-wright or a picture-wright, or a poem-wright; and why a playwright?
>
> (cited in Dark and Grey 1923, p. 196)

Gilbert biographer Andrew Crowther rightly points out that his subject 'was objecting here to being described by implication as craftsman rather than an artist' (2011, p. 51). However, Crowther then goes on to remind us that, when commenting on his own work, Gilbert generally prioritised technical and commercial aspects over 'artistic considerations'. Why, then, on the morning after a knighthood had conferred irrefutable acceptance into high society should Gilbert be complaining? It would seem that social attitudes towards the status of his calling were causing doubt. Unlike the novelist, artist or poet, whose vocation makes them 'gentlemen', Gilbert's work is still that of the artisan, or 'wright'. In other theatre companies, the author might command less respect than the leading comedian. Rutland Barrington makes the point that, in his later work for George Edwardes, the playwright might be the *last* person called upon to make a decision concerning the development of a difficult scene (Barrington 1908, p. 105). Gilbert had achieved far greater power and reputation. However, although his fame and celebrity status were incontrovertible by 1907, this letter reveals some residual insecurity about his position as a member of the elite professional class. In one of many business-related complaints he made to Carte during their working relationship, Gilbert accused his colleague of regarding him as 'a hack author' supplying 'pieces on certain terms'.[65] Can a 'middle-class' 'man of letters' also be the producer of popular West End entertainment?

Significantly, Gilbert's knighthood and his sardonic reflection on it coincided with a period in which he was particularly obsessed with the prevention of gagging, and adherence to the letter of his text. The West End revivals of the most popular of the Savoy operas between 1906 and 1909 saw Gilbert no longer a member of a business partnership, but as a hired hand redirecting his old shows. A long and acrimonious correspondence between Gilbert and Helen Carte (manager since her husband's death in 1901) occurred throughout this period. Apart from criticising casting decisions over which, to his chagrin, Gilbert had no control, the main target of Gilbert's fury was gagging. *The Mikado*, which went into rehearsal in March 1907 (a few months before his knighthood), and *The Gondoliers* were the operas most prone to alteration. C.H. Workman, who had toured in the principal comic roles from the late 1890s, privately informed Gilbert that, since the author's active involvement in the company had ceased, all the pieces were extensively gagged on tour (Ainger 2002, p. 421). An acerbic battle of words with Helen Carte ensued in which Gilbert asserted that his work, once again to be exposed to the full view of the metropolitan audience and critics, was being tampered with by unruly artists.[66]

I would suggest that Gilbert was angry for two reasons. First, he objected to those he considered insubordinate in a hierarchy which he had helped to establish at the Savoy. This pecking order reflected the social distinctions within what Harold Perkin calls 'the riven middle class' (1989, p. 78) whose offstage equivalent was physically manifested in the use of public space within the Savoy Theatre described in Chapter 4. In this hierarchy, the composer and the librettist—who, along with the entrepreneur, was also a profit-sharer—were at the top. Second, if the dramatist was to be regarded as a respectable, gentlemanly 'man of letters', his work needed to be regarded as on a par with that of the literary author. Gilbert's main claim to fame in 1907 was as one half of a partnership which produced morally cleansed and highly lucrative upscale burlesque. Whatever artistic value might be apparent in this (admittedly very popular) genre could not be challenged by what Gilbert referred to in one of his letters as the 'embroideries with which [...] buffoons are in the habit of decorating my work'.[67] In other words, the input of interpretative rather than creative artists could not be allowed to intrude on the work of an author who, despite the evidently 'popular' nature of his work, aspired to be recognised as the equal of the successful poet, painter or novelist.[68]

Implicit in Gilbert's hatred of unsanctioned gagging is a suspicion that it undermines his literary and social credibility while maintaining an approach to performance which retains some of the excesses of the low comedian. Low comedy had been exorcised because it was morally dubious and did not conform to the commercial aspirations of a company which sought 'respectable' patronage. This caused an inevitable tension, as the Victorian comic actor, whether of the 'low' or 'light' variety, existed to provoke laughter and would instinctively embellish existing material. Gilbert's intention was to restrain this instinct, or consent to its results only when they conformed to his dramatic sensibilities.

We can only speculate on the satisfaction of those touring artists who managed to get away with the kind of gagging which was censured at the Savoy and (sometimes) curtailed on tour. A taste of the rebelliousness of the frustrated comic is, however, present in the memoirs of a practitioner not usually associated with the Savoy or its output. An anecdote included in the autobiography of the music hall comedian Arthur Roberts (1852–1933) demonstrates the contest between a culture of artistic control and the freedom of the popular low comedian to improvise. Roberts's rise to fame in popular musical theatre coincided with the flourishing of the D'Oyly Carte enterprise. While *HMS Pinafore* was at the height of its popularity at the Opera Comique, Roberts was touring the London halls with a repertoire of risqué songs (Baker 2005, p. 50). During the 1880s and 1890s, he played the Dame in Drury Lane pantomimes and lead roles in a series of Gaiety burlesques and musical comedies. The worlds of low comedy and refined comic opera apparently collided at some unspecified date during 'the reign of Gilbert and Sullivan' when Roberts participated in a charity performance of *Trial by Jury* at the Savoy. To make a good impression, Roberts adopted a dress style suitable for Savoy rehearsals— 'silk hat, one frock coat, ditto trousers'—and assumed a 'very sober face'. Gilbert was nevertheless appalled that 'so low a person as Arthur Roberts had dared to enter the sacred portals of the Savoy Theatre' (Roberts 1927, p. 39). Annoyed at this reception, Roberts proceeded to rag Gilbert, who in turn lost his temper.[69]

The comedian decided to exact revenge on the author, who also happened to be appearing in *Trial by Jury* in the silent role of 'the advocate'. Roberts describes with relish how, in front of a celebrity audience, he embarked on a series of unrehearsed low-comedy visual gags. These included placing a pair of old boots outside the jury box while chalking the phrase 'call me at seven' on its door, slowly consuming a plate of whelks while watching the court proceedings, and juggling with a stick. Roberts revels in Gilbert's growing aggravation, as, while in character, the director could do nothing to stop this travesty of his working methods.

> He could not swear. He could not storm. All he could do was to watch me and suffer while he saw my muddy boots trampling on the sacred traditions of the Savoy and kicking the susceptibilities of his own idiosyncrasies [...] Gilbert's eyes never left me. They blazed with anger, but I am sure there was actual fear in his heart—fear at what I was going to do next.
>
> (Roberts 1927, p. 42)

Eventually Gilbert succeeded in getting a stagehand to remove Roberts, who casually placed an empty beer mug on the edge of the jury box.

> The opera was in suspension. The audience were in hysterics [...] I discovered a coin in my pocket, took it out and tossed it in the air.
>
> 'Heads I lose' I ejaculated.
>
> I examined the coin.
>
> 'Heads' I exclaimed.
>
> With a sigh I got up [...] and ambled off the stage with the depressed air of one who has unfortunately been sent to fetch the supper beer.
>
> (Roberts 1927, p. 43)

Perhaps regrettably, this story is almost certainly untrue. Roberts took part in an 1887 benefit performance for the actress Amy Roselle at the Lyceum (rather than the Savoy) which included *Trial by Jury*. He played the small, silent role of the 'Associate'.[70] Although this performance was directed by Gilbert, the author did not appear on stage. In 1896, a benefit performance for Kate Vaughan again included the operetta, this time featuring Gilbert as the Associate. In this case, Roberts, while on the same bill, did not appear in *Trial*.[71] Press reviews for these performances make no mention of any unscheduled comic disruption of the piece by Roberts.[72] It is possible that the comedian took umbrage at Gilbert's directorial style during preparations for the 1887 performance and fed his resentment into an effective anecdote, which appeared in his 1927 autobiography, *Fifty Years of Spoof.*

Irrespective of its veracity, the anecdote provides a telling example of the low-comic ethos reacting against the discipline of the author/director. Gilbert is caricatured as the irascible tyrant, held to ransom by the disruptive creativity of the low comedian. The censorious control of the professional 'stage manager' is ridiculed by the comic improviser, who refuses to be limited by a single controlling hand. Militaristic drilling is shown to be of little value when Gilbert's carefully prepared production can be disrupted in an instant by some unscheduled gags. Even Roberts's exit appears to be the result of mere chance, depending as it does on the toss of a coin. According to Roberts, his solo turn provoked hilarity from 'the poor audience who probably knew the opera backwards' (1927, p. 43). There is some envy here at the continuing success of the D'Oyly Carte brand. A carefully developed fan base that enjoyed the repetition of the kind of innocuous material which ran counter to Roberts's background and style signified a move towards respectability which, at least in the 1880s, marginalised the low comedian.

Crucially, issues of class are also implicit in Roberts's story. The entertainer who started his career as a Covent Garden busker and seaside entertainer (Baker 2005, p. 49) is stamping a pair of figurative working-class 'muddy boots' over Gilbert's 'sacred traditions'. He reaffirms the negative view of the Gilbert and Sullivan operas as the theatrical version of a religious rite aimed at the puritanical bourgeoisie. Gilbert, as purveyor of a consciously upmarket product is (at least in Roberts's wish-fulfilment fantasy) not only trounced by a popular comedian, but by one who is able to reduce Gilbert's apparently respectable and affluent audience to 'hysterics' by low-comic clowning. Presented here is a tale in which the rude and unrestrained humour of the whelk-eating, beer-drinking commoner triumphs over the refinement and decorum of the dominant class. The fact that Roberts's early successes—his appearances in Gaiety burlesques and musical comedies—took place in the same highly commercialised West End which generated the Savoy operas does not figure in his implied social criticism.

It is worth a slight digression to demonstrate a similar 'anti-respectability' trope which recurs later in Roberts's autobiography (1927, pp. 44–51). Here, Mrs Bancroft, the former 'sprightly, rather saucy' burlesque performer, is ridiculed for abandoning 'the merry bohemianism of her early days'. At the Prince of Wales, where Roberts has been recruited for another charity performance, she has become 'a figure of solemn and conscious dignity' possessing 'a fanatical faith in propriety and respectability'. According to Roberts, Bancroft and her like regarded music hall performers as second-rate interlopers. The insubordinate clown got his 'revenge' by ingenuously insisting to the frosty Mrs Bancroft that the last moments of the evening's entertainment (a performance of Edward Bulwer Lytton's *Money)* be enlivened with a guest appearance by Roberts's (invented) troupe of performing goats. Even in 1927, Roberts is clearly irritated by the 'turn' to respectability in the late-nineteenth-century West End as represented by Gilbert and Sullivan and the Bancrofts. It infects the theatre of the present day in which '[t]he Variety Theatre has become the sanctuary of respectability' and the drama 'has been drugged with a sense of dope' (p. 44). Roberts fabricates or enlarges events to make his point clear. He projects himself as an outsider to those involved in the 'legitimate' stage and revels in his deflation of their attachment to textual adherence, rehearsal discipline and bourgeois manners.

SUMMARY

For the purposes of the argument presented here, Arthur Roberts's uneasy (if probably fictionalised) involvement with a Bulwer Lytton play is serendipitous. Jacky Bratton reminds us that it was Bulwer Lytton who was prominent in the attempted gentrification of London theatre in the 1830s and 1840s, a process which continued to the end of the century, and was exemplified by the Savoy operas (2003, pp. 88–91). Bulwer Lytton spearheaded the move to link the emancipation of theatrical free trade with the enfranchisement (and resultant sense of empowerment) of the middle classes after the passing of the reform acts. As mentioned in Chapter 3, the resulting 1843 Theatres Act removed the 'aristocratic' monopoly of the patent houses, theoretically allowing the proliferation of smaller theatres while removing the embargo on the performance of purely spoken drama previously restricted to Covent Garden and Drury Lane. In practice, 'the theatre was increasingly appropriated to the middle-class voice in Britain' (Bratton 2003, p. 90). The newly enfranchised bourgeois intelligentsia propounded a theatre which foregrounded the leadership role of the male writer rather than the theatre manager or actor-manager (male or female). As 'popular entertainment was the enemy of the verbal perfection of the text' (2003, p. 88), the divide between theatre as Art and theatre as entertainment became more defined. It led to the segregation of the vulgar, the creation of music hall and of the musical theatre—the whole world of burlesque and extravaganza. The notion of 'the popular' as opposed to 'the Drama' [...] turned all the exuberant life of the theatre of the early-nineteenth-century into 'entertainment.'

(2003, p. 169)

I would argue, on the basis of Bratton's analysis, that the intention of the Triumvirate, and especially Gilbert, was to turn what had become 'entertainment' in the mid-century West End back into Art—or, at least a form which had enough 'Art' about it to satisfy those members of the bourgeoisie desirous of acquiring 'cultural capital'. There is nothing particularly novel about this trend in the sphere of the spoken drama—Irving, the Bancrofts and the Kendals, among others, were engaged in this process at the same time, using classics or new texts suited to the sensibilities of their intended audience. However, the Savoy team succeeded in presenting a form of *musical* theatre which was acceptable to the 'respectable' and 'serious' middle class. One of the many reasons why such audiences responded enthusiastically to the Gilbert and Sullivan works was because they embodied in performance a restraint and control of manner which had become associated with 'respectable' conduct and bearing in social and domestic life. This style was exemplified in the work of Barrington, Grossmith and Braham, and may still be experienced in Passmore's recordings, and in Granville's filmed rendition.

'Placidity', 'restraint' and 'repose' were popularly regarded as the signifying features of high-status groups. By focusing on these and their associated terms, positive contemporary critical reception of the Savoy operas infers a welcome absence of their opposites: 'low comedy' in general and, for actresses, any kind of exuberant, over-intense or 'unnatural' manner of performance. Burlesque and its associate forms became progressively less popular with the 'middle-class' West End audience partly because their excess and high spirits began to be associated with a demeanour which did not accord with normative 'middle-class' social practice. It became, by implication, 'lower', and therefore suitable for those with less cultivated, even working-class tastes. 'Victorian' values moved the low comedian from the spoken drama to the music hall, killed the burlesque, and replaced it with a style of performance which emphasised and reinforced bourgeois values. Thus, what actors did on stage at the Opera Comique and Savoy Theatre between 1877 and (at least) 1896, derived ultimately from an aesthetic embedded in the ideology of the 'middle classes'.

NOTES

1. RDC to AS, 26 August 1879 (DC/TM).
2. 'It was quickly appreciated that this was the real *H.M.S. Pinafore* [...] the orchestrations had a breadth, colour and tone which had been completely missing in the home-made products. It was found that under Gilbert's careful training the lines had a wit and a meaning the very existence of which had hitherto been unknown' (Prestige, 1971, p. 113). Prestige's chapter provides a comprehensive guide to the production and reception of the first American D'Oyly Carte tours.
3. *Morning Advertiser*, 27 November 1882.
4. *Era*, 9 December 1877.
5. Ibid.
6. Ibid.
7. *Era*, 25 November 1877.
8. *Era*, 25 August 1878 (G&S Archive).
9. *Lloyd's Weekly Newspaper*, 4 April 1880 (G&S Archive).
10. *London Morning Advertiser*, 27 November 1882 (G&S Archive). Although a restrained actor, Grossmith seems to have relied on his own personality rather than an ability to transform himself. Gilbert remarked of Grossmith that 'I used to invent a perfectly fresh character each time [...] but he always did it in his own way [...]. It arose from the fact that his individuality was too strong to be concealed' (*St James Gazette*, 23 June 1883, p. 5).
11. *Era*, 21 March 1885, p. 14.
12. *Era*, 9 December 1877.
13. Ibid.
14. *Morning Post*, 25 April 1881.
15. *The Standard*, 25 April 1881.
16. *Daily News*, 27 November 1882.
17. *Daily News*, 7 January 1884.
18. *The Times*, 11 May 1887.
19. *The Times*, 4 October, 1888.
20. *The Times*, 9 March 1896.
21. *Ruddygore* was the original spelling. It was altered to *Ruddigore* about a week after opening night in response to criticisms of implicit vulgarity.
22. Grossmith's *Ruddigore* costume included a red ('ruddy') waistcoat. The character's appearance must have been sufficiently familiar to the intended audience at Toole's Theatre to warrant the reference in the title.

23. Quotations derive from the version prepared and published by Simon Moss (Taylor 2012), from the original licence copy filed in the Lord Chamberlain's Office. See Walters, 2000, p. 21.
24. *The Times*, 27 November 1882.
25. It is effectively reproduced by Martin Savage, playing Grossmith in Mike Leigh's film *Topsy-Turvy* (1999).
26. *Daily News*, 21 March 1887.
27. Ibid.
28. *Era*, 12 January 1884.
29. Photographs show the 24-year-old Barrington inclining to stoutness in his first Gilbert and Sullivan role, Dr Daly in *The Sorcerer*, and growing stouter thereafter.
30. This was an area of high-level homosocial gathering. Sullivan was a member of the Marlborough Club, 'by far the most exclusive', according to Goodman. He was proposed by Prince Christian and the Duke of Edinburgh. Gilbert belonged to the Junior Carlton Club. Both were situated in Pall Mall (Goodman 2000, pp. 84–5).
31. Barrington performed this topical comic song, with lyrics by himself and music by Walter Slaughter, at the Coliseum for eight weeks in 1905 (Barrington 1908, pp. 128-128)
32. *Parlando* is the technique in which the singing voice is made to approximate to speech.
33. Temple's 1902–1903 renderings of the Pirate King's first act solo and 'My object all sublime' from *The Mikado* suggest a performer vocally past his best—breath control and high notes are not perfect. However, the performances are notable for focused tone, impeccable diction and palpable projection of character and personality. My observations depend on the recently refurbished private transfers of these cylinders made by Anthony Baker, which correct the speed errors of the commercially available CD transfers.
34. In 1926, the D'Oyly Carte Opera Company made a short promotional film of *Mikado* excerpts in which Henry Lytton as Ko-Ko and Leo Sheffield as Pooh-Bah appear. Both artists had been directed by Gilbert, but not in these roles. The excerpts, though providing a valuable guide in matters of design and blocking, are too brief to be used for the analysis of individual characterisations.
35. Billington, a mainstay of the touring circuit during the 1880s and 1890s, took over these roles in the main company from 1903. He was succeeded by Sheffield in 1917.
36. Green goes on to provide an amusing anecdote in which Granville as Don Alhambra in *The Gondoliers* failed to bring on a prop snuff-box used to punctuate a certain speech. This resulted in a complete breakdown in his ability to remember either his dialogue or the subsequent song (Green 1962, p. 643).

37. See Chapter 5, above.
38. Such fidelity to original performance practice did not always pertain. Granville's D'Oyly Carte co-star in the 1939 filmed *Mikado*, Martyn Green as Ko-Ko, seems to have embodied an evolution of a G&S role even within the restricted parameters of the company style. There were departures from Gilbert's intended manner among some of the earliest performers. For example, Carte seems to have allowed George Thorne in the first Broadway production more liberty than Grossmith was permitted in London, presumably to avoid 'the placid English style' (Stedman 1996, p. 234). Thorne rose to the task by introducing a number of physical gags. During the early twentieth century, Ko-Ko assumed the characteristics of licensed clown. Unlike other characters in the oeuvre, a good deal of physical comedy was added to the playing of the role, often consisting of pratfalls and other sight-gags which bore little relevance to the text or dramatic situation. These may be witnessed in various forms in both the 1939 film under discussion and in the 1966 film of the then current D'Oyly Carte production.
39. There are, of course, departures from stage practice necessitated by the expansion of the stage picture to the wider and more lavish requirements of a feature film. Blocking and proxemics are often not those of the stage productions, although some cases, notably the positioning for the Act Two trio, 'The criminal cried', are very close to the blocking recorded in the earliest D'Oyly Carte prompt books. Granville is given a costume similar to the then current design by Charles Rickets, but with a high, stiff, round collar. This encouraged some recurring business which could not have been achieved in the D'Oyly Carte costume of either the 1880s or that of the 1930s. In moments of uncertainty or embarrassment, Granville's head retracts comically into the top part of his coat, like a tortoise going into its shell.
40. However, they employed different singing styles. Granville's vocal production is that of the operatic bass, unlike Barrington's untrained *parlando* style.
41. Subsequently cast as Little Buttercup in *HMS Pinafore*, she seemed to have been intended as a comic female counterpart to Barrington and Grossmith. An industrial accident during rehearsals for *The Pirates of Penzance* curtailed her stage career (Barrington 1908, p. 28).
42. For the sake of clarity, I am using the modern term 'director', rather than the Victorian 'stage manager', or slightly later 'producer', for the person who performed this function.
43. A good example would be Gilbert's feud with the actress Henrietta Hodson. Having crossed swords during Gilbert's *Ought We to Visit Her?* in 1874 over her refusal to follow his direction, Gilbert discovered in 1876 that she had been employed as the female lead at the Haymarket where several of Gilbert's plays were to be staged. There ensued what Jane Stedman calls 'an

episode in the contest between actors and dramatists for control of the stage' (Stedman 1972, p. 149). The upshot of this struggle for supremacy between leading lady and director was Hodson's publication and distribution of a 22-page pamphlet which related the *Persecutions which She has Suffered from Mr. William Schwenck Gilbert, a Dramatic Author* (London 1877). Gilbert replied in print shortly afterwards. It is perhaps significant for the future casting of the operas that the agreement to work on *The Sorcerer* was made at the latter end of this dispute. See Crowther 2011, pp. 111–13, 125–8 and Stedman 1996, pp. 145–9.

44. The attempt to cast the American singer and actor Lillian Russell, who had made a name for herself in the Gaiety operettas of the early 1880s, as Princess Ida in 1883 was beset with problems. Unwilling to conform to Gilbert's rehearsal techniques, she was fired from the production and replaced by the resident artist, Leonora Braham.

45. Most of the performers were young, even those playing somewhat 'older' roles—Grossmith and Temple were 30 and Barrington only 24. As for the 'older' female characters, the 'veteran' Mrs Howard Paul was 44 and Harriet Everard 34, only a few years older than the juvenile lead, Alice May, who was 30. Her replacement, Giulia Warwick, was 20 and the tenor lead, George Power, was 31.

46. WSG to Helen Carte, 26 August 1879 (DC/TM).

47. WSG was familiar with Wigan's style. In an interview with William Archer he mentioned Wigan along with Mathews as admirable exponents of the mid-century burlesque (Archer 1904, pp. 106–31), prior to that genre's later 'debasement'. Gilbert's own burlesque, *Robert The Devil* (1868), formed part of a Gaiety bill under Wigan's management.

48. It is, broadly speaking, the darker, full-sounding and often vibrato-rich 'operatic' timbre which predominated from the mid nineteenth century and which is still prevalent in the early twenty-first.

49. In an interview in the *Musical Herald* in 1891, Lely remarks on his use of the 'mixed voice' or head voice in the high register, rather than falsetto, which strongly indicates training based in the 'modern' style. 'Mr. Durward Lely'—*Musical Herald*, 1 May 1891. See also Potter (1998, p. 56).

50. Ruth in *The Pirates of Penzance* attempts to entrap the younger Frederic in marriage. Lady Jane in *Patience* is the 'leader' of the female acolytes, and pursues the younger Bunthorne, a situation which recurs, albeit with less ridicule, in *Iolanthe*, where the Fairy Queen is attracted to, and gets, Private Willis. Katisha in *The Mikado* vengefully chases the young Prince, Nanki-Poo. Dame Carruthers (*The Yeoman of the Guard*) and Dame Hannah (*Ruddigore*) are both formidable figures who have solo numbers which deal with violence and torture. The Duchess in *The Gondoliers* has 'tamed' her ineffectual husband, etc.

51. As has been mentioned in Chapter 2, the operas did move with the times to some extent in their reflection of changing attitudes. *Utopia, Limited* (1893) contains an ambiguous sung description of the New Woman, even though such a character does not appear on stage. The forthright and assertive Julia Jellicoe in *The Grand Duke* (1896) presents something of a departure for Gilbert, at least in the operas. She is a strong-minded, career-orientated actress whose calculating self-interest is no more or less admirable than the characteristics of most of the other characters of either gender in the piece.

52. 'Workers and Their Work: Mr. W.S. Gilbert.' *Daily News*, 21 January 1885, p. 3.

53. *London Morning Advertiser*, 27 November 1882.

54. 'A Theatrical Manager on the Morals of the Stage.' *Pall Mall Gazette*, 15 February 1885, p. 11.

55. 'Workers and Their Work: Mr. W.S. Gilbert.' *Daily News*, 21 January 1885, p. 3.

56. 'Topical Interviews. No. 88. Miss Nelly Farren.' Unattributed newspaper clipping, bound in *The Theatre* (July–December 1880), Folger Shakespeare Library, Washington, D.C.

57. 'How They Write Their Plays: Mr. W.S. Gilbert.' *St James's Gazette*, 23 June 1893, p. 5. 'As to rehearsals, there are in all three weeks for the artists to study the music; then a fortnight's rehearsals without the music; finally, another three or four weeks' rehearsals in position and with the music. The principals are not wearied with rehearsals until the chorus are perfect in their music.'

58. Contract between George Grossmith and Richard D'Oyly Carte, 1877 (DC/TM).

59. Commercial reasons could also have influenced Gilbert's stringency. The text, available for purchase in the theatre, needed to correspond with what was spoken on stage. Audiences were buying Gilbert's wit, rather than that of his performers, as part of the entertainment 'package'.

60. Letter from WSG to Helen Carte, 29 August 1893 (DC/TM).

61. Letter from WSG to Mr James, 10 December 1889 (DC/TM).

62. Letter from WSG to Mr James, 11 December 1889 (DC/TM).

63. Ibid.

64. Letter from WSG to Mr James, 13 December 1889 (DC/TM).

65. Letter from WSG to RDC, 1 June 1885 (DC/TM).

66. This argument is covered in some detail in Ainger (2002, p. 404–15).

67. Letter from WSG to Helen Carte, 13 December 1906 (DC/TM).

68. Nevertheless, it would be unjust to suggest that Gilbert was a snob. In an interview given to William Archer he sincerely praises the work of burlesque writers and actors of the past ('Real Conversations', 1904, p. 118). In a subsequent newspaper interview with Bram Stoker, Gilbert recognised the skill and professionalism of music hall performers. ('The Tendency of the

Modern Stage: A Talk with Sir W.S. Gilbert on Things Theatrical.' *Daily Chronicle*, 2 January 1908, p. 8.)

69. Gilbert's contemporaries often remark that, in rehearsal, he expected very high standards and, although occasionally sarcastic, was never discourteous. Enforcement of the kind of stage discipline adopted by only a few practitioners at this time seems to have contributed to the myth of Gilbert as theatrical tyrant, as did Henrietta Hodson's slanderous pamphlet (see n43, above). Walter Passmore recalled in 1930 that 'Gilbert, who has such a name as a martinet, was never bullying or rude. His sarcasm, at its worst, was mild compared with what one hears today' (Passmore 1930, p. 152). According to Cellier, writing three years after Gilbert's death, 'He never for a moment adopted the methods or language of a bullying taskmaster' (Cellier and Bridgeman 1914, p. 50).

70. *Era*, 18 June 1887.

71. *Morning Post*, 8 June 1896.

72. Also *Era*, 13 June 1896.

CHAPTER 8

Conclusion

Respectability was harder to achieve in the theatrical sphere than in other professional fields. The theatre had little formalised career regulation, was tainted in the public imagination with immorality, and suffered, in terms of public perception of its propriety, from the rather indefinable social status of its inhabitants. The attempts of some theatre practitioners to acquire and demonstrate the trappings of respectability (or to display what they might have considered to be their innate respectability) described throughout this book exhibit a desire to redress this perceived inequality in public acceptance. In his attitudes towards theatre-making, Gilbert was reflecting and reasserting current bourgeois ideology. In their collaborative assent, cooperation and therefore tacit assertion of these principles, Sullivan and Carte were following the same line.

It is worthwhile reiterating Raymond Williams's definition of social ideology. He describes it as 'the characteristic world view or general perspective of a class or other social group, which will include formal and conscious beliefs, but also less conscious, less formulated attitudes, habits and feelings, or even unconscious assumptions, bearings and feelings' (1982, pp. 26–7). The ideology of dominant Victorian social groups has been linked in Chapters 6 and 7 to notions of authority, hierarchy, deference and the display of class-related signifiers within the D'Oyly Carte company both on and off the stage. The theatrical representation of young women

© The Author(s) 2016   223
M. Goron, *Gilbert and Sullivan's 'Respectable Capers'*, Palgrave Studies
in British Musical Theatre, DOI 10.1057/978-1-137-59478-5_8

as non-threatening and 'self-controlled' has been taken into account as a factor in the reception of the operas. The semi-publicised moral virtue of Savoy actresses has been considered as a component of the theatrical 'branding' of respectability. 'Middle-class' preoccupations with physical signifiers of decorum such as demeanour can also be seen to inform signifying features of the Savoy theatre building and its public spaces, as discussed in Chapter 4. Physical proximity to, and separation from, those who were or were not one's chosen social peers, in an environment both conducive to bourgeois comfort and hygiene and removed from less salubrious surroundings, was provided by the internal design and geographical location of the Savoy. It expeditiously permitted a diverse social grouping to attend a long-running series of theatre events which, in terms of their high production values, artistic merit and moral correctness, attracted a wide audience: the fashionable, those who held most theatre attendance to be morally dubious, and the aspirational in search of 'cultural capital'.

I have argued in Chapter 5 that, while solidly aimed at the financially comfortable bourgeoisie, the Savoy theatre event appears to have held particular appeal for certain sections of the lower-middle classes. As we have seen, this does not necessarily indicate homogeneity of response or an amicable inclusiveness within the composition of the Savoy audience. But it does suggest a broad acceptance of social hierarchy from all its sectors, including the less affluent. The sometimes conservative ideological outlook of the lower middle classes, when combined with the serious or evangelical turn of mind higher up the social scale, provided potential for the development of a form of musical theatre which belied anti-theatrical prejudice. 'Middle-class' distancing from the working classes and from morally dubious theatrical forms resulted in the rejection of 'lower' forms of cultural expression. Instead, Carte appropriated existing models of 'respectable' performance (the 'entertainments') and business methods (the 'long run') to create a brand which provided a wholesome alternative to the *opera bouffe* and burlesque for family audiences, and women in particular.

It is important not to underestimate the extent to which the propriety of the Savoy operas, in terms of content and mode of presentation, influenced their success. Until it ceased to be a novelty, press reports frequently remarked on the suitability of the Savoy operas for children, young women and members of the clergy. Gilbert summarised this essential point in a speech to the Dramatic and Musical Sick Fund in February 1885.[1] While contrasting the moral tone of English and French drama, Gilbert is inadvertently providing a description of the level of refinement which characterises his contemporary musical theatre offerings. He focuses on a hypothetical 'young lady of fifteen. She is a very charming girl—gentle, modest, sensitive [...] an excellent specimen of a well-bred young English gentlewoman'. Gilbert goes on to emphasise that the 'moral fitness' of any stage work must not offend her

> eyes and ears [...]. It must contain no allusions that cannot be fully and satisfactorily explained to this young lady; it must contain no incident, no dialogue that can, by any chance, summon a blush to this young lady's innocent face.[2]

Women are seen as moral arbiters, and appealing to young, innocent women is the epitome of theatrical good taste.

Of course, this is a generalisation. Communal possession of demure sensibilities among Victorian teenagers can be questioned by Beatrix Cresswell's gothic fantasy, discussed in Chapter 5. However, Gilbert is presenting conventional affirmations of moral probity—unsurprising, considering the author's characteristically Victorian propensity towards chivalric paternalism. This tendency is echoed in the prevailing culture of the company, as the work of the Triumvirate seems to have been driven by the need to create the kind of entertainment experience which matched, in various ways, their ideological preoccupations.

The extent to which their intentions were deliberate actions, or simply manifestations of the 'unconscious assumptions, bearings and feelings' (Williams 1982, pp. 26–7) of the Victorian bourgeoisie, is difficult to distinguish. While the entrepreneurial ideal and the desire for the social status concomitant with personal wealth seems to have driven each of the partners, cultural and artistic motivators endemic within the 'respectable' value system are also observable. Nationalism and the redemptive power of art can be seen as typical attitudes of the Victorian dominant classes. Carte seems to have had a genuine desire to create a new, indigenous form of musical theatre which could match and surpass that of foreign competitors. Nationalistic pride and a desire to edify the British public through the provision of an 'artistic' theatre experience are demonstrated not only by the Savoy operas but also by Carte's (unsuccessful) attempt at creating a school of English grand opera.

Sullivan, while craving recognition as a composer of 'higher', more culturally worthy, musical forms, nevertheless lent his talents and personal reputation as a leader in the sphere of serious music to the creation of 'tasteful' light opera. Gilbert brought many of the concerns of the 'middle classes' to bear on his work. His desire to create a theatrical organisation which was palpably 'respectable', both on and off the stage, seems less calculatedly commercial than Carte's public declarations of morality, although the actions of both would indicate an adherence towards 'middle-class' norms. Gilbert's 'gentlemanly' defence of women, his concern for professional recognition, and his sense of discipline and hierarchical observance are all symptomatic of nineteenth-century bourgeois ideology. Gilbert's 'middle-class' values permeate his work at the Savoy.

Circularity of influence, in which cultural production is both the result and a reinforcement of ideology, has been argued throughout the thesis. I would suggest that the Savoy operas obtained a particularly high level of ubiquity in the consciousness of the 'middle classes' during and long after their initial success in the West End. This special pervasiveness can be ascribed at least in part to the extensive tours of new operas as they appeared, alongside a travelling repertoire of previous favourites. They were available to a geographically widespread audience, often on an annual basis. It is further attested by their continuing popularity within 'Middle England', which led to the longevity of the D'Oyly Carte as a professional operation throughout much of the twentieth century, as well as the corresponding tradition of amateur performance, which continues to the present day.

It is admittedly harder to observe the cultural effects of the D'Oyly Carte Company outside the theatre than to trace the transmission of values 'across the footlights'. Certainly, advertisers used Gilbert and Sullivan-related images and catchphrases at the height of their popularity as a means of drawing special attention to their products (Oost 2009, pp. 78–9), and photographic portraits of Savoy stars were available as souvenirs (Joseph 1994, p. 76). However, a specific and revealing early example of cultural cross-fertilisation in practice can be found in a *Daily News* report from 1 June 1892. Entitled 'Gilbert and Sullivan Bazaar', it records a three-day summer charity fundraising event (31 May–2 June) which took place in the East London suburb of Stratford. We learn that it was opened by the Marchioness of Salisbury, and that its object was 'to build a new church in the district of St Peter's, Plaistow'. The event's newsworthiness seems to have depended on its 'novel and artistic' theme, 'the stalls being arranged to represent the various Gilbert and Sullivan operas.' The article goes on to describe the stands, each of which corresponds to one of the existing corpus of works:

Mrs. Smith-Rewse, as Iolanthe in gold armour and helmet, sold fancy articles, assisted by the Rev. J.F. Smith-Rewse, garbed as a peer. Ruddigore was
tended by Dame Hannah, in Quaker garb, and Rose Maybud with flowers
to match her name in her hat [...] the Three Little Maids from School,
dressed in correct Japanese costumes, sold Oriental art wares at the Mikado
stall [...] Princess Ida's goods were literary, as was appropriate [...] The
Trial by Jury stall [...] like all the rest [...] was draped with pale, cool, artistic tints, a pleasing contrast to the usual red and white ... Dairy produce
was served at the Patience stall, which was aesthetically arranged in yellow
and white, with grasses and sunflowers [...] Mrs Durrant as Mabel, and St.
Peter's ladies, served under The Pirates of Penzance, disposing of such innocent wares as needlework but assisted by swarthy pirates in costume, even to
the ear rings in their ears [...][3]

Entertainment was provided by 'The Ladies' Venetian String Orchestra'
who played selections from the operas in the afternoons. There were further celebrity guests. Lady Brooke opened the proceedings on Wednesday,
and Mrs W.S. Gilbert officiated on the final morning.

This report reveals much about the cultural impact of the operas in
the final decade of the nineteenth century. Clearly, by 1892 (the year following the closure of The Gondoliers after 554 performances), they were
sufficiently embedded in 'middle-class' popular consciousness to be an
immediately recognisable thematic device. Organisers, customers, the
newspaper reporter and Daily News readers were apparently conversant
enough with the oeuvre to make any detailed explanation of the references
unnecessary. For example, the casual comment that the items sold on the
'Princess Ida' stall were literary, assumes familiarity with the academic setting of a work produced eight years earlier, which received less than whole-
hearted critical praise and which was overshadowed by both the more
successful Iolanthe, which preceded it, and The Mikado, which followed.
The physical appearance of the leading characters was well-known enough
to be replicated by amateurs and immediately recognisable to the public.
In an age before electronic media distribution, this shared awareness of
Savoy opera imagery, presumably deriving from memories of West End
and touring performance, ephemera and amateur performance, attests to
significant cultural absorption.

But perhaps most noteworthy is the fact that musical theatre works are
regarded as an unexceptionable theme for an event intrinsically connected
with the church. This indicates a change in attitudes to theatre among
the devout. Carte's deliberately 'respectable' image-making and the moral

acceptability of the Savoy performance style, along with positive press coverage, seems to have achieved a widespread acceptance of the propriety of at least some types of musical theatre entertainment. By 1892, the active, costumed participation of a clergyman and his wife (the Reverend and Mrs Smith-Rewse) in an event commemorating West End popular entertainment is perfectly permissible when fundraising for a religious cause. Some considerable distance seems to have been traversed since 1878 when the Reverend Stewart Headlam was dismissed from his curacy at St Matthews in Bethnal Green for preaching tolerance towards the theatre (Sanderson 1984, p. 146).

The presence of several prominent members of the aristocracy, along with Lucy Gilbert as celebrity guest, suggests this was an event of some social significance. Their gender, and the fact that the event partly occurred during the working day, is a reminder of the predominantly female participation and organisation of the occasion. This is not surprising as charity work was organised at the grass-roots level by middle-class women (Thompson 1988, pp. 252–3). However, the connection between an event planned and presided over by women and its chosen theme demonstrates an association between the operas and a female spectatorship. I have discussed the high standards of decor, comfort and hygiene of the Savoy auditorium in Chapter 4, features likely to appeal to conventionally minded 'middle-class' women of the time. Certainly, good housekeeping was an essential component of the successful management of the domestic sphere (Smith 2007, pp. 284–5), and the Savoy's combination of fashion, cleanliness and helpful service provided an environment likely to appeal to the Victorian homemaker. The subtly shaded decoration of the Savoy interior is echoed in the description of the St Peter's bazaar where 'pale, cool, artistic tints' provide 'a pleasing contrast to the usual red and white' of market stalls. A design ethos common to late-Victorian cultivated taste in interior design connects this with the Savoy, and (especially) its female patrons. As audience members and participators in the associated activities of domestic music-making,[4] women would seem to have been important both as consumers of the D'Oyly Carte brand and receivers and disseminators of the values it represented. Overall, the Stratford bazaar serves to demonstrate a moment of cultural symbiosis. A morally reputable and 'tasteful' product, purveyed by a West End company for whom female respectability was a priority, has been absorbed into a bourgeois culture of female 'fandom' and social involvement.

The extent of the Triumvirate's achievement was connected with an innate understanding of shared attitudes towards issues such as these. Other West End theatre managers in the 1880s needed to be flexible in order to compete with the D'Oyly Carte offerings. While John Hollingshead successfully negotiated this period by leavening the Gaiety's menu of burlesque with distinguished foreign companies and upmarket amateur theatricals, it was the enterprising Charles Edwardes who led musical theatre into the new century by responding to changes in audience taste with the hugely popular series of 'Girl' musical comedies. The reduction in quality of Gilbert and Sullivan's work after 1891, the inability of succeeding composers and lyricists at the Savoy to replicate their artistic and commercial achievements, and Carte's failure to adjust to changes in public response (which he had judged so acutely in the 1870s) resulted in the company's decline as a viable West End concern. Despite some successful attempts to move with the times by modifying its ideological emphasis as social values altered during the late 1880s and 1890s, by 1903 Savoy opera was failing to chime with subtle changes in the thinking and behavior of the majority of the broad 'middle classes'. Shows which made fewer demands on intellectual sophistication, and veered away from 'Art' in their musical content, appealed to an audience containing an increasing number of young, lower-middle-class spectators (Bailey 1998, p. 191; Platt 2004, p. 7).[5] The Gilbert and Sullivan works retained a fan base, and were preserved by a single provincial touring company and by amateur performance. However, despite the nostalgic delights of the 1907–1909 repertory seasons, the operas were replaced by musical comedy as the mainstream, middle-class, 'light' entertainment of choice in the Edwardian and prewar West End.

Nevertheless, the period between the opening of *The Sorcerer* in 1877 and the closing of *The Gondoliers* in 1891 saw the Savoy Company and its repertoire triumphantly exemplifying the culmination of 'middle-class' ideological ascendancy. I have proposed the idea that a congruence of 'respectable' Victorian ideals influenced all aspects of the company's onstage work, the working lives of its personnel, and the material and practical issues which related to its physical location and everyday organisation. It also may be argued that audience reception of D'Oyly Carte performances disseminated and enhanced these values in the wider social sphere. In every sense, the 'theatre event' which characterised the work of the D'Oyly Carte Company in the production of the Gilbert and Sullivan operas was shaped by the ideological preoccupations of the company's creators, its participants and its audience.

Notes

1. *Era*, 21 February 1885.
2. *Era*, 21 February 1885.
3. *Daily News*, 1 June 1892.
4. 'The Ladies' Venetian String Orchestra' was perhaps a group of amateur musicians recruited for the occasion. I can find no reference elsewhere to an ensemble of this name.
5. William Archer, in an article of 1896, remarks that the majority of the audience for musical comedy at the Duke of York's Theatre were 'young men and women who worked hard for their living at the desk or behind the counter' (Archer 1897, pp. 298–301).

BIBLIOGRAPHY

NINETEENTH-CENTURY NEWSPAPERS AND PERIODICALS

Articles from the following newspapers and periodicals are archived by the British Library and have been consulted at Gale Databases online at http://find.galegroup.com.

The Country Gentleman and Sporting Gazette
The Era
The Daily News
Fun
Funny Folks
The Graphic
Judy
Le Follet
Lloyds Weekly Newspaper
Moonshine
The Morning Post
The Pall Mall Gazette
Punch
Reynolds' Newspaper
The Sporting Times
The Standard
The Times
Young Folks Paper

© The Author(s) 2016   231
M. Goron, *Gilbert and Sullivan's 'Respectable Capers'*, Palgrave Studies in British Musical Theatre, DOI 10.1057/978-1-137-59478-5

Other Newspapers and Periodicals Consulted

All the Year Round
 The Daily Chronicle
 The Daily Express
 The Daily Telegraph
 The Fortnightly Review
 Fraser's Magazine
 The Idler
 The Illustrated London News
 The Illustrated Times
 The Million
 The Morning Advertiser
 The Musical Herald
 The Musical World
 The Observer
 St James's Gazette
 The Saturday Review
 The Theatre
 Topical Times
 Truth
 The Westminster Gazette
 The World
 The Young Woman

Manuscripts

D'Oyly Carte Papers, Theatre Museum, London. Abbreviated in annotations to DC/TM.

London County Council Metropolitan Archive (GLC/AR/BR/19/0047).

Quotations from W.S. Gilbert's Libretti Are Taken from

Bradley, I. (2001). *The complete annotated Savoy Operas.* Oxford: Oxford University Press.

PRIMARY SOURCES CITED OR REPRODUCED

Archer, W. (1886). *About the theatre.* London: T. Fisher Unwin.

Archer, W. (1897). *The theatrical 'World' of 1896.* London: Walter Scott.

Archer, W. (1904). *Real conversations.* London: Heinemann.

Bagehot, W. (1867). *The English constitution.* London: Chapman & Hall.

Bancroft, M., & Bancroft, S. (1909). *Recollections of sixty years.* London: John Murray.

Barrington, R. (1908). *Rutland Barrington, by himself.* London: Grant Richards.

Barrington, R. (1911). *More Rutland Barrington—By himself.* London: G. Richards.

Blaythwayte, R. (1898). *Does the theatre make for good? An interview with Mr. Clement Scott.* London: A.W. Hall.

Bond, J. (1930). *The life and reminiscences of Jessie Bond the Old Savoyard.* London: John Lane the Bodley Head.

Bond, J. (n.d.). *London Metropolitan Archive UK Civil Divorce Records, 1858–1911;* Held at Ancestry.co.uk [Online]. Accessed 3 March, 2014, from http://interactive.ancestry.co.uk/2465/40243_636897_2665-00000/28586?backurl=http per cent3a per cent2f per cent2fsearch.ancestry.co.uk per cent2fcgi-bin per cent2fsse.dll per cent3fgst per cent3d-6&ssrc=&backlabel=ReturnSearchResults#?imageId=40243_636897_2665-00012

Cellier, F., & Bridgeman, C. (1914). *Gilbert, Sullivan and D'Oyly Carte.* London: Pitman.

Dickens, C., Jr. (1888). *Dickens Dictionary of London.* London: Old House Books. reprinted 1993.

Filon, A. (1897). *The English Stage.* London: John Milne.

Fitzgerald, P. (1894). *The Savoy Operas and the Savoyards.* London: Chatto & Windus.

Gilbert, W., & Goldberg, I. (Eds.). (1931). *New and original extravaganzas.* Boston: John W. Luce & Co.

Greenwood, J. (1867). *Unsentimental journeys; or byways of the modern Babylon.* London: Ward, Lock and Tyler.

Grossmith, G. (1888). *A society clown: Reminiscences.* Bristol: J.W. Arrowsmith.

Grossmith, G., & Grossmith, W. (1896). *Diary of a nobody.* Ware: Wordsworth. reprinted 1994.

Hardy, T. M. (1910). *How to train children's voices.* London: J. Curwen.

Hartley, C. (1860). *The Gentleman's book of etiquette and manual of politeness.* Boston: G.W. Cottrell.

Hollingshead, J. (1877). Some theatres and their audiences. In C. Dickens (Ed.), *All the year round.* London: Chapman & Hall.

Hullah, J. (1842). *Wilhelm's method of teaching singing.* London: Kilkenny. reprinted 1983.

James, H. (1905). *English hours.* London: Heinemann.

Kaye, W. (1860). *The Cornhill Magazine, 2.*

Lamb, A. (Transl.). (1972). *Meine Erinnerungen,* excerpted in: 'At the Savoy Theatre'. *Gilbert and Sullivan Journal,* May, 417.

Lawrence, D. (Ed.). (1965). *Bernard Shaw: Collected letters, 1874–1897.* London: Reinhardt.

Lewes, G. (1875). *On actors and the art of acting.* New York: Greenwood. reprinted 1968.

Lytton, H. (1922). *The secrets of a Savoyard.* London: Jarrolds.

Mudie-Smith, C. (1903). *The religious life of London.* London: Hodder and Stoughton.

Passmore, W. (1900–13), reproduced (1996). *Sir Arthur Sullivan Sesquicentennial Commemorative issue 1842–1992* (Vol. 2) [Sound Recording] (Symposium).

Passmore, W. (1930). Some recollections of Savoy Days. *Gilbert and Sullivan Journal,* June, 1, 152.

Phipps, C. (1881). *Savoy theatre plans* [Art] (London County Council Metropolitan Archive (GLC/AR/BR/19/0047)).

Phipps, C. (2014). *The first musicals* [Online]. Accessed 3 March, 2014, from http://www.vam.ac.uk/content/articles/t/the-first-musicals/

Roberts, A. (1927). *Fifty years of spoof.* London: The Bodley Head.

Sands, J. (2008a). *Patience programme* [Online]. Accessed 24 June, 2013, from http://diamond.boisestate.edu/gas/patience/programmes/prog_1/pc_prog_1.html.

Sands, J. (2008b). *Virtual Museum* [Online]. Accessed 1 August, 2009, from http://math.boisestate.edu/GaS/museum/progs.html.

Sands, J. (2011a). *HMS Pinafore programme* [Online]. Accessed 25 June, 2013, from http://diamond.boisestate.edu/gas/pinafore/programmes/prog_1/pf_prog_1.html.

Sands, J. (2011b). *Merrie England programme* [Online]. Accessed 25 June, 2013, from http://diamond.boisestate.edu/gas/savoy/merrie_england/me_prog/me_prog.html.

Sands, J. (2011c). *Mikado Programme* [Online]. Accessed 25 June, 2013, from http://diamond.boisestate.edu/gas/mikado/programmes/prog_4/mk_prog4.html.

Sands, J. (2012). *Utopia, limited programme* [Online]. Accessed 25 June, 2013, from http://diamond.boisestate.edu/gas/utopia/programmes/prog_1/ul_prog_1.html.

Sands, J. (2014). *Thespis programme* [Online]. Accessed 12 March, 2014, from http://math.boisestate.edu/GaS/thespis/prog/prog_1.html.

Scott, C. (1875). A plea for the pit. *The Era Almanack.*

Smiles, S. (1859). *Self help.* London: John Routledge.

Smiles, S. (1880). *Duty.* London: John Murray.

Spence, E. F. (1910). *Our stage and its critics*. London: Methuen.

Taine, H. (1872). *Notes on England*. London: Thames and Hudson. reprinted. 1957.

Taylor, H. S. E. (1887). *An entirely irrational musical Parody in one act and a deed entitled Ruddy George or, Robin Redbreast*. Unknown: Stage Memories. reprinted 2012.

Temple, R. (1902), reproduced (1999). *The art of the Savoyard* [Sound Recording] (Pearl).

The Mikado. (1939). [Film] Directed by V. Shertzinger. Great Britain: Universal Pictures.

Thorne, G. (1897). *Jots*. Bristol: Arrowsmith.

Wagner, L. (1899). *How to get on the stage and how to succeed there*. London: Chatto & Windus.

Watson, A. E. (1918). A sporting and dramatic career. In H. Orel (Ed.), *Gilbert and Sullivan: Interviews and recollections*. Macmillan: Basingstoke. reprinted 1994.

SECONDARY SOURCES

Ainger, M. (2002). *Gilbert and Sullivan—A dual biography*. Oxford: Oxford University Press.

Allen, R. (1958). *The first night Gilbert and Sullivan*. London: Chappell.

Altick, R. D. (1973). *Victorian people and ideas*. New York: W.W. Norton.

Bailey, P. (1998). *Popular culture and performance in the Victorian City*. Cambridge: Cambridge University Press.

Baker, A. (2005a). *Moore (Lilian) Decima (1871–1964), actress. Oxford Dictionary of National Biography* [Online]. Accessed 24 February, 2014, from http://www.oxforddnb.com/index/62/101062730/

Baker, R. (2005a). *British Music Hall: An illustrated history*. London: Sutton.

Banks, J. (1954). *Prosperity and parenthood: Study of family planning among the Victorian Middle Classes*. London: Routledge & Kegan Paul.

Barker, K. (1985). Thirty years of struggle: Entertainment in provincial towns between 1840 and 1870. *Theatre Notebook, 39*(1), 25–9.

Barton Baker, H. (1904). *The history of the London Stage and its famous players (1576–1903)*. London: George Routledge and Sons.

Best, G. (1971). *Mid-Victorian Britain*. London: Weidenfeld & Nicolson.

Bockock, R. (1986). *Hegemony*. London: Tavistock.

Booth, M. (1980). *Prefaces to English nineteenth century theatre*. Manchester: Manchester University Press.

Booth, M. R. (1991). *Theatre in the Victorian Age*. Cambridge: Cambridge University Press.

Borsay, P. (2006). *A history of leisure*. London: Palgrave Macmillan.

Boyd, K., & Macwilliam, R. (2007). Rethinking the Victorians. In K. Boyd & R. McWilliam (Eds.), *The Victorian studies reader*. London: Routledge.

Bradley, I. (2005). *Oh Joy! Oh Rapture! The enduring phenomenon of Gilbert and Sullivan*. Oxford: Oxford University Press.

Bratton, J. (2003). *New readings in theatre history*. Cambridge: Cambridge University Press.

Bratton, J. (2009). Clement Scott, the Victorian Tribal Scribe. *Nineteenth Century Theatre and Film*.

Bratton, J. (2011). *The making of the West End Stage*. Cambridge: Cambridge University Press.

Briggs, A. (1988a). *Victorian things*. London: Batsford.

Briggs, A. (1988b). Victorian values. In: *Search of Victorian values*. Manchester: Manchester University Press.

Burke, P. (1992). *History and social theory*. Cambridge: Polity Press.

Cannadine, D. (1992). Gilbert and Sullivan: The making and un-making of a British 'Tradition'. In R. Porter (Ed.), *Myths of the English*. London: Polity.

Cannadine, D. (1998). *Class in Britain*. London: Yale University Press.

Carlson, M. (1989). *Places of performance*. New York: Cornell University Press.

Carlson, M. (2003). *The haunted stage*. Ann Arbor: University of Michigan Press.

Chapple, K. (1993). The Savoy theatre 1881. In K. T. J. Chapple (Ed.), *Reflected light—The story of the Savoy Theatre*. London: Dewynters.

Croll, A. (2007). Popular leisure and sport. In C. Williams (Ed.), *A companion to nineteenth century Britain*. Oxford: Blackwell.

Crossick, G. (1977). *The lower middle class in Britain 1870–1914*. London: Croom Helm.

Crowther, A. (2000). *Contradiction contradicted—The plays of W.S. Gilbert*. London: Associated University Presses.

Crowther, A. (2011). *Gilbert of Gilbert and Sullivan: His life and character*. Stroud: The History Press.

Curtin, M. (1994). *Propriety and position*. New York: Garland Publishing.

D'Cruze, S. (2004). The family. In C. Williams (Ed.), *A companion to nineteenth-century Britain*. Oxford: Blackwell.

Dark, S., & Grey, R. (1923). *W.S. Gilbert; His life and letters*. London: Methuen.

Daunton, M. (2000). Public life and politics. In: C. Mathew, ed. *The nineteenth century*. Oxford: Oxford University Press.

Davidoff, L., & Hall, C. (2002). *Family fortunes: Men and women of the English middle class, 1780–1850*. London: Routledge.

Davis, T. C. (1991a). *Actresses as working women—Their social identity in Victorian culture*. London: Routledge.

Davis, T. C. (1991b). The Savoy Chorus. *Theatre Notebook*, Vol. 44, no. 1

Davis, T. (2000). *The economics of the British Stage 1800–1914*. Cambridge: Cambridge University Press.

Davis, J. (2004). Actors and their repertoires. In J. Donohue (Ed.), *The Cambridge history of British theatre—Volume 2* (pp. 1660–1895). Cambridge: Cambridge University Press.

Davis, J., & Emeljanow, V. (2001). *Reflecting the audience: London theatregoing, 1840–1880.* Hatfield: University of Hertfordshire Press.

Dillard, P. (1991). *'How quaint the ways of paradox'—An annotated Gilbert and Sullivan bibliography.* Metuchen: The Scarecrow Press.

Dollimore, J., & Sinfield, A. (1985). *Political Shakespeare: New essays in cultural materialism* (1st ed.). Manchester: Manchester University Press.

Fischler, A. (1991). *Modified rapture: Comedy in W.S.Gilbert's Savoy Operas.* Charlottesville: University of Virginia Press.

Flanders, J. (2006). *Consuming passions: Leisure and pleasure in Victorian Britain.* London: HarperCollins.

Fortier, M. (2002). *Theory/Theatre.* Abingdon: Routledge.

Foster, G. (2000). *Troping the body.* Carbondale: Southern Illinois University Press.

Gardner, V. (2007). By herself: The actress and autobiography, 1755–1939. In M. Gale & J. Stokes (Eds.), *The Cambridge companion to the actress.* Cambridge: Cambridge University Press.

Goodman, A. (1988). *Gilbert and Sullivan's London.* London: Faber & Faber.

Goron, M. (2010). 'The D'Oyly Carte Boarding School'—Female respectability in the theatrical workplace 1877–1903. *New Theatre Quarterly volume xxvi, part, 3.*

Green, M. (1962). *Martyn Green's treasury of Gilbert and Sullivan.* London: Joseph.

Gunn, S. (1999). The public sphere, modernity and consumption: New perspectives on the history of the English middle class. In A. Kidd & D. Nicholls (Eds.), *Gender, civic culture and consumerism: Middle class identity in Britain* (pp. 1800–1940). Manchester: Manchester University Press.

Gunn, S. (2000). *The public culture of the Victorian middle class: Ritual and authority and the English Industrial City, 1840–1914.* Manchester: Manchester University Press.

Harari, Y. N. (2011). *Sapiens—A brief history of humankind.* London: Vintage.

Hayter, C. (1987). *Gilbert and Sullivan.* London: Macmillan.

Hewitt, M. (2008). Class and the classes. In C. Williams (Ed.), *A companion to nineteenth-century Britain.* Oxford: Blackwell.

Hibbert, C. (1976). *Gilbert and Sullivan and their Victorian World.* New York: American Heritage Publishing.

Himmelfarb, G. (1995). *The de-moralization of society. From Victorian virtues to modern values.* New York: Knopf.

Houghton, W. E. (1957). *The Victorian frame of mind, 1830–1870.* Newhaven and London: Yale University Press.

Howard, D. (1986). *London theatres and music halls*. London: Library Association Publishing.

Howarth, J. (2000). Gender, domesticity, and sexual politics. In C. Matthews (Ed.), *The nineteenth century*. Oxford: Oxford University Press.

Jackson, R. (1989). *Victorian theatre*. London: A & C Black.

Jackson, L. (2001). *Gallery of illustration* [Online]. Accessed 12 July, 2010, from http://www.victorianlondon.org/entertainment2/galleryofillustration.htm

Jacobs, A. (1992). *Arthur Sullivan—A Victorian musician*. Oxford: Oxford University Press.

James, L. (2006). *The middle-class: A history*. London: Little, Brown.

Jones, B. (1996, November). The Rutland Barrington memorial. *The Gilbert and Sullivan News, 11*(7).

Jones, B. (2011). *Helen Lenoir, Gilbert and Sullivan's partner*. London: Basingstoke Books.

Joseph, T. (1982). *George Grossmith*. Bristol: Bunthorne Books.

Joseph, T. (1994). *The D'Oyly Carte Opera Company 1875–1982*. Bristol: Bunthorne Books.

Joyce, P. (1994). *Democratic subjects: The self and the social in nineteenth-century England*. Cambridge: Cambridge University Press.

Kidd, A., & Nicholls, D. (1999). History, culture and the middle classes. In: *Gender, Civic Culture and Consumerism: Middle Class Identity in Britain 1800 – 1940*. Manchester: Manchester University Press.

Knapp, R. (2009). Tracing Gilbert and Sullivan's legacy in the American musical. In: *The Cambridge Companion to Gilbert and Sullivan* (pp. 207–15). Cambridge: Cambridge University Press.

Knowles, R. (2004). *Reading the material theatre*. Cambridge: Cambridge University Press.

Langford, M. (1980). *The story of photography*. London: Focal Press.

Langland, E. (1995). *Nobody's Angels: Middle class women and domestic ideology in Victorian culture*. New York: Cornell University Press.

Lee, J. (2010). *The Japan of pure invention*. Minneapolis: University of Minnesota Press.

Lloyd, F., & Wilson, R. (1984). *The official D'Oyly Carte picture history*. London: Weidenfeld & Nicholson.

MacPhail, R. (2011). *The Mikado (Film Extras)* [Interview] 2011.

Mander, J., & Mitchenson, J. (1976). *The lost theatres of London*. New English Library.

Mason, M. (1994). *The making of Victorian sexuality*. Oxford: Oxford University Press.

McConachie, B. (2007). Historicizing the relations of theatrical production. In J. Reinelt & J. Roach (Eds.), *Critical theory and performance*. Michigan: University of Michigan Press.

Mugglestone, L. (1990). Ladylike accents: Female pronunciation and perceptions of Prestige in nineteenth century England. *Notes and Queries, 231*.

O'Brien, K. H. F. (1974). The house beautiful: A reconstruction of Oscar Wilde's American Lecture'. *Victorian Studies, 17*(2).

Olwage, G. (2004). The class and colour of tone: An essay on the social history of Vocal Timbre'. *Ethnomusicology Forum, 13*(2).

Oost, R. B. (2009). *Gilbert and Sullivan: Class and the Savoy Tradition, 1875–1896*. Farnham: Ashgate.

Osterman, M. (2009). *George Eastman House. Notes on photographs: Wet collodian on glass negatives* [Online]. Accessed 25 February, 2014, from http://noteson-photographs.org/index.php?title=Wet_Collodion_On_Glass_Negative

Parker, P. (2008). Personal Email.

Perkin, H. (1969). *The origins of modern English society 1780–1880*. London: Routledge & Kegan Paul.

Perkin, H. (1989). *The rise of professional society: England since 1880*. London: Routledge.

Perkin, J. (1993). *Victorian Women*. London: John Murray.

Picard, L. (2005). *Victorian London. The life of a city 1840–1870*. London: Weidenfeld & Nicolson.

Pick, J. (1983). *The West End: Mismanagement and Snobbery*. Eastbourne: John Offord.

Platt, L. (2004). *Musical comedy on the West End Stage*. London: Palgrave Macmillan.

Postlewaite, T. (2007). George Edwardes and musical comedy. In T. C. Davis (Ed.), *The performing century*. Palgrave Macmillan: Basingstoke.

Postlewaite, T. (2009). *The Cambridge introduction to theatre historiography*. Cambridge: Cambridge University Press.

Potter, J. (1998). *Vocal authority—Singing style and ideology*. Cambridge: Cambridge University Press.

Powell, K. (1997). *Women and Victorian theatre*. Cambridge: Cambridge University Press.

Power, G. (2007). *Who Was Who—Online edition*. Oxford: Oxford University Press.

Prestige, C. (1971). D'Oyly Carte and the Pirates: The original New York productions of Gilbert and Sullivan. In: J. Helyar (Ed.), *Gilbert and Sullivan. Papers presented at the International Conference held at the University of Kansas in May 1970*. Lawrence: University of Kansas Libraries.

Price, R. (1977). Society, status and Jingoism, the social roots of lower middle class patriotism, 1870–1900. In G. Crossick (Ed.), *The lower middle class in Britain*. London: Croom Helm.

Rappaport, E. (2000). *Shopping for pleasure: Women in the making of London's West End*. Princeton: Princeton University Press.

Rhys Morus, I. (2008). The sciences. In C. Williams (Ed.), *A companion to nineteenth century Britain*. Oxford: Blackwell.

Rollins, C., & Witts, R. (1962). *The D'Oyly Carte Opera company in Gilbert and Sullivan Operas. A record of productions 1875 – 1961*. London: Michael Joseph.

Rowell, G. (1979). *The Victorian theatre 1792–1914* (2nd ed.). Cambridge: Cambridge University Press.

Russell, W. (1888). *Representative actors*. London: Frederick Warne & Co.

Russell, D. (2004). Popular entertainment, 1776–1895. In J. Donohue (Ed.), *The Cambridge history of British theatre—Volume 2: 1660 to 1895*. Cambridge: Cambridge University Press.

Sanderson, M. (1984). *A social history of the acting profession in England, 1880–1983*. London: The Athlone Press. From Irving to Olivier.

Schoch, R. W. (2003). *Victorian theatrical Burlesque*. Burlington: Ashgate.

Schoch, R. W. (2004). Theatre and mid-Victorian society. In J. Donohue (Ed.), *The Cambridge history of British theatre* (Vol. 2, pp. 1660–1895). Cambridge: Cambridge University Press.

Scott, D. (1988). Music, morality and rational amusement at the Victorian middle-class Soiree. In B. Zon (Ed.), *Music and performance culture in nineteenth century Britain*. Farnham: Ashgate.

Scott, J. (2006). *Social theory*. London: Sage.

Shchivelbusch, W. (1995). *Disenchanted night—The industrialisation of light in the nineteenth century*. Berkeley: University of California Press.

Smith, V. (2007). *Clean—A history of personal hygiene and purity*. Oxford: Oxford University Press.

Smither, H. (2000). *A history of the Oratorio: Vol. 4: The Oratorio in the nineteenth and twentieth centuries* (1st ed.). Chapel Hill: University of North Carolina Press.

Stedman, J. (1972). From dame to woman: W.S. Gilbert and theatrical transvestism. In M. Vicinus (Ed.), *Suffer and be still: Women in the Victorian Age*. Indiana: Indiana University Press.

Stedman, J. (1996). *W.S. Gilbert—A classic Victorian and his theatre*. Oxford: Oxford University Press.

Stone, D. (2001a). *Rutland Barrington* [Online]. Accessed 12 July, 2010, from http://math.boisestate.edu/GaS/whowaswho/index.htm

Stone, D. (2001b). *Who Was Who in the D'Oyly Carte Opera Company 1875–1982* [Online]. Accessed 12 July, 2010, from http://math.boisestate.edu/GaS/whowaswho/index.htm

Stone, L., & Stone, J. C. F. (1984). *An open elite? England 1540–1880*. New York: Oxford University Press New York.

Sweet, M. (2001). *Inventing the Victorians*. London: Faber & Faber.

Taylor, G. (1989). *Players and performance in the Victorian theatre*. Manchester: Manchester University Press.

Thompson, F. M. L. (1988). *The rise of respectable society*. London: Fontana.

Tosh, J. (1999). *A man's place. Masculinity and the middle-class home in late Victorian England.* New Haven and London: Yale University Press.

Wahrman, D. (1995). *Imagining the middle class: The political representation of class in Britain, c. 1770 – 1840.* Cambridge: Cambridge University Press.

Walters, M. (1998). A brief overview of the life of Rutland Barrington. *The Gilbert and Sullivan News, II, no.* 13.

Walters, M. (2000). A Parody of a Parody: Ruddy George or Robin Redbreast. *The Gilbert and Sullivan Journal,* Autumn/Winter.

Webb, J., Schirato, T., & Danaher, G. (2002). *Understanding Bourdieu.* London: Sage.

Weber, W. (1996). *The rise of musical classics in eighteenth-century England: A study in canon, ritual and ideology.* Oxford: Clarendon Press.

White, J. (2008). *London in the nineteenth century* (2nd ed.). London: Vintage.

Wiener, M. (1981). *English culture and the decline of the industrial spirit, 1850– 1980.* Cambridge: Cambridge University Press.

Williams, R. (1980). Base and superstructure in Marxist cultural theory. In R. Williams (Ed.), *Problems in materialism and culture.* London: Verso.

Williams, R. (1982). *The sociology of culture* (1st ed.). New York: Shocken.

Williams, C. (2011). *Gilbert and Sullivan: Gender, genre, parody.* New York: Columbia University Press.

Williamson, A. (1982). *Gilbert and Sullivan Opera.* London: Marion Boyars.

Wilmore, D. (2013, August 8) (DVD). 'Victorian Theatre'. In: *The magic of Gilbert and Sullivan.* 3 Day Symposium, Buxton.

Wilson, F. (1989). *An introduction to the Gilbert and Sullivan Operas.* New York: Pierpoint Morgan Library.

Wilson, A. (2003). *The Victorians.* London: Hutchinson.

Wolfson, J. (1999). *The art of the Savoyard—CD liner notes.* Wodhurst: Pearl.

Zakreski, P. (2006). *Representing female artistic labour: Refining work for the middle class woman.* Aldershot: Ashgate.

Index

© The Author(s) 2016
M. Goron, *Gilbert and Sullivan's 'Respectable Capers'*, Palgrave Studies in British Musical Theatre, DOI 10.1057/978-1-137-59478-5

Printed by Printforce, the Netherlands